COMPETITIVE INTELLIGENCE AND GLOBAL BUSINESS

COMPETITIVE INTELLIGENCE AND GLOBAL BUSINESS

Edited by
David L. Blenkhorn
and Craig S. Fleisher

PRAEGER

Westport, Connecticut
London

Library of Congress Cataloging-in-Publication Data

Competitive intelligence and global business/edited by David L. Blenkhorn and Craig S. Fleisher.
   p.   cm.
   Includes bibliographical references and index.
   ISBN 0–275–98140–1 (alk. paper)
   1.   Business intelligence.   2.   Competition.   3.   International business enterprises—Management.   4.   Strategic planning.   5.   Comparative management.   I.   Blenkhorn, David L.   II.   Fleisher, Craig S.
HD38.7.C6594   2005
658.4'72—dc22   2004018110

British Library Cataloguing in Publication Data is available.

Library of Congress Catalog Card Number: 2004018110
ISBN: 0-275-98140-1

First published in 2005

Praeger Publishers, 88 Post Road West, Westport, CT 06881
An imprint of Greenwood Publishing Group, Inc.
www.praeger.com

Printed in the United States of America

The paper used in this book complies with the Permanent Paper Standard issued by the National Information Standards Organization (Z39.48-1984).

10   9   8   7   6   5   4   3   2   1

Contents

Preface

This book represents our contribution to the literature that arises at the intersection of competitive intelligence (CI) and global business. To help us focus as we pulled together our thoughts on the topic, we asked ourselves the following questions. Our answers, also listed below, helped form the basis for this book.

Why edit a book about competitive intelligence (CI) and global business?

Globalization permeates almost every aspect of contemporary business. Barriers to international commerce and trade are being reduced through the efforts of the World Trade Organization (WTO), the European Union (EU), and other regional trade blocs that are also expanding. Work in general is taking on a global perspective, in part because of enhanced communication technologies. The digitalization of markets (e.g., electronic exchanges, the Internet) has changed both the way business operates and the way people think about competition. New economies and economic features, represented most starkly by the dot-com bubble of the late 1990s, have arisen; this has resulted in executives questioning the status quo and has often complemented a variety of industrial reconfigurations. These changes occurring around the globe to industries and the players within them require that decision-makers use CI tools and skillsets to develop an enhanced awareness of competitors and the competitive environment.

We edited this volume particularly for two groups of individuals: strategic managers operating in firms with multiple locations around the globe and CI practitioners. Strategic managers will benefit from the variety of helpful perspectives given by our experienced contributors on a wide range of topics associated with competing and managing CI in the global marketplace—especially since CI is often absent from the advanced education curricula and programs to which they were most likely exposed. CI practitioners will particularly benefit from our extensive focus on the global implications and impact of commerce on their practice and discipline—an area that has been underdeveloped in the CI scholarship.

Why is this book appropriate now?

The pace of business has increased considerably in the last half-dozen years (e.g., business moving at "Internet speed," organizations' ability to customize customer responses in real time). Global competition is a $365 \times 24 \times 7$ phenomenon. We have seen many recent examples where different parts of the world have adopted new technologies, new products, and so on before the huge U.S. consumer market that serves as the basis of much management and CI literature. This means that some of the assumptions that were formally taken for granted (i.e., causal path dependencies) don't work in the ways in which we formerly understood them. Previous sequences of events may not be repeated in the future (i.e., the past becomes less reliable as a predictor of the future).

There have been critical developments affecting the intersection of CI and global business. For example, some stakeholder groups (both business and non-business types) have had an increased interest to protect themselves from global events and trends. Non-business factors, such as the actions taken by global interest groups, have increasingly changed the level and nature of the competitive and non-competitive playing fields (e.g., advocating for the humane treatment of livestock, cutting of old growth forests, driving fuel-guzzling vehicles). CI practitioners and strategic planners should develop an increased awareness of these issues to ensure that organizational decision-makers are kept "ahead of the curve," which itself moves more rapidly than in the past.

How is our approach different from that of other global CI literature that is currently appearing? What is unique about this volume?

It is our opinion that no significant global CI book has been published since about 1993. The vast majority of recent CI literature has retained a country-centric approach, meaning that authors typically look at developments through their own acculturated and institutionalized lenses. We state this based not only on our own experience and research but also on the evidence we have gathered from practitioners and managers. For example, recent visits to several CI conferences held outside of the United States have given us ample opportunities to witness and hear European CI practitioners, as a vocal group, steadfastly claim that there are fundamental differences in how CI is approached and practiced in their marketplaces as opposed to how it is practiced in the United States.

We have made a conscious effort to recognize that approaches to CI will differ around the world from the accepted, mostly U.S. grounded, CI norms. This book's two editors have had extensive opportunities to interact with changing norms in CI and global business over the last few years by traveling to numerous countries and geographic regions to give seminars and courses, facilitate workshops, address industry groups, and advise companies, exposing them to a wide diversity of cultures and business practices. These experiences have given us perspective and allowed us to make meaningful comparisons while remaining cognizant of the differences that exist between the "accepted wisdom" of the field and the emerging wisdom that originates from new geographic sources.

What is our rationale for the book's four sections?

From our observations and experiences with CI in many countries of the world, we believe that the process of practicing CI in a one-country, domestic setting takes on a new level of complexity when it is practiced across multiple countries or when a global perspective is undertaken. The book's first section, "The Global CI Process," addresses some of these fundamental issues. We have found that many CI practitioners and organizational decision-makers have a country-centric view of the world and are not fully apprised of the "big picture" as it relates to their industry and their firm's global positioning. Section Two, "The Global CI Environment," covers key contextual issues that must be addressed when thinking globally. We have seen that for many reasons CI practitioners do not fully understand and appreciate the differences that exist when conducting business on a global scale. From a management perspective, operating the CI function within a multi-country firm presents many unique challenges that do not arise when operating from or within a single nation-state. A number of these unique differences are addressed in Section Three, "Global CI Management." Without resorting to case studies to make specific points, Section Four, "Country-, Industry-, and Process-Specific Studies in Global CI," addresses specific CI process-related issues. It also offers snapshots of CI within several specific countries to illustrate just how different practicing multi-country and global CI can be from having a one-country, domestic focus.

Now that we have finished this book, what would we have done differently?

We recognize that we could improve upon some aspects of this book if we were to tackle this subject matter in the future. For example, the vast majority of our contributors have researched their specific topic from a Canadian perspective. Authors from a variety of countries could write the same chapters, perhaps coming to differing conclusions. Our future efforts as well as the state of our scholarly understanding would be enhanced by having authors from multiple nation-states tackle these and other subjects, enriching the understandings developed in this volume by our contributors.

We acknowledge that there is often overlap and interchangeability in using a number of terms that arise throughout this volume; this applies in particular to the terms "multinational," "international," and "global". In academic practice, these terms have distinct definitions. Because this book is written to be accessible to both practitioners and academics, we have permitted our contributors to utilize the more popular, as opposed to academic, nomenclature. So as not to mislead our academic colleagues, in our first chapter we provide the academic distinctions among the different terms.

One key aim in this volume is to provide policy-level guidance for managers and practitioners. It has not been our intention to give step-by-step instructions of how to conduct CI in every country of the world. Although we think this is a laudable objective for authors and practitioners in our field, we believe there is an insufficient base of empirical research, or a lack of documentation of practice or scholarship, for such an achievement at this time. We would love to see our academic colleagues and CI practitioners actively address the already large and still growing agenda of research questions at the interface of CI and global business. The two of us expect to be more active researchers in this subject matter area in the years to come.

We expect to stimulate others to begin closing some of the knowledge gaps that we have explicitly and implicitly identified throughout this book's chapters. We also hope this book encourages practitioners to share their experiences and observations with researchers in the field. We anticipate the book will compel our readers to question some, if not a large number, of their current practices and understandings. Our aim is that this volume be viewed as a valuable contribution to the knowledge of competitive intelligence in global business. Whether we have achieved our aim is a decision left in the hands of our readers, as it should be.

David L. Blenkhorn
School of Business & Economics
Wilfrid Laurier University
75 University Avenue West
Waterloo, Ontario, N2L 3C5
Canada
telephone: 519-884-0710 x2467
fax: 519-884-0201
e-mail: dblenkhorn@wlu.ca

Craig S. Fleisher
Odette School of Business
University of Windsor
401 Sunset Avenue–508 OB
Windsor, Ontario, N9B 3P4
Canada
telephone: 519-253-3000 x3455
fax: 519-973-7073
e-mail: fleisher@uwindsor.ca

Acknowledgments

Producing an edited book requires the coordination of many people, and in this respect, we have been very fortunate in the makeup of our high-quality team. We gratefully acknowledge the contributions of our chapters' authors, for their work forms the essence of the book. We always enjoy working with our collaborating colleagues and believe that our interaction with them improves the published effort. Our book production team at Wilfrid Laurier University, consisting of Elsie Grogan, who handled the word-processing, and Laura Kittel, who assisted in editing, were invaluable in producing the final product. A special thank-you goes to Victor Knip, our long-time assistant, contributor, and sounding board for our projects. We also appreciate the support of Nick Philipson and his capable team at Praeger Publishing.

A gracious thank-you goes to our many students and colleagues at Wilfrid Laurier University's School of Business and Economics (Waterloo and Toronto campuses), the University of Windsor's Odette School of Business, Stellenbosch University's Centre for Knowledge Dynamics and Decision-Making, the Sydney Graduate School of Management (Australia), Graduate School of Business Leadership at the University of South Africa (UNISA), Helsinki School of Economics (Finland), the University of Sydney (Australia), Penn State University (USA), Waikato Management School (New Zealand), Manchester Metropolitan University and Leicester Business School (UK), and the Research/Intelligence Analyst Program at Mercyhurst College (USA).

We also wish to acknowledge and thank our colleagues and contacts at many organizations who have had input into our knowledge and understanding of global competitive intelligence. Among the most notable are the Academy of International Business (AIB), American Marketing Association (AMA), Academy of Management, CoEmergence Inc., Competitive Business and Analysis CC, Canadian Association of Security and Intelligence Studies (CASIS), the Conference Board, Frost & Sullivan, Intellier, International Association of Business Communicators (IABC), International Association of Business & Society (IABS), Issue Management Council, Journal of Competitive Intelligence and Management (JCIM), Marcus-Evans Conferences, the Mindshifts Group, Performance Measurement Association, PRISTOP, the Sherman-Kent Center, the Society of Competitive Intelligence Professionals (SCIP), South African Association of Competitive Intelligence Professionals (SAACIP), SCIP-Australia, various national intelligence agencies, and Novintel Inc.

We gratefully acknowledge the financial support provided by the Research Office at Wilfrid Laurier University, which provided us with a book preparation grant that greatly assisted us. The Odette Research Chair in Business in the University of Windsor's Odette School of Business provided additional funding assistance that was instrumental in helping us finish this effort.

Finally, we owe a debt of gratitude to our families and friends, all of whom were very understanding and supportive as we completed this project. We hope that this effort was a rewarding experience for those who were involved in its development as well as for those individuals who read its contents.

THE GLOBAL COMPETITIVE INTELLIGENCE PROCESS

1

The State of Our Understanding of Research and Practice in Competitive Intelligence and Global Business

David L. Blenkhorn and Craig S. Fleisher

The globalization of markets is forcing borders to become invisible as economic barriers disappear. Through efforts of the World Trade Organization (WTO), countries in Europe and North America have agreed to open markets and to coordinate macroeconomic policies. In fact, the Multilateral Agreement on Investment (MAI), which would give countries and foreign investors a Charter of Rights, was close to being accepted before a number of nationalists mounted a vigorous campaign to put it on hold. This thrust toward globalization raises a great number of challenges and opportunities for firms that want to succeed in the global marketplace. Accurate and timely competitive intelligence (CI) can mean for these firms the difference between making correct or incorrect global strategic decisions.

This is a book about CI and global business. Doing business in the new world "disorder" invariably includes a global element. The advent of vast global organizations competing for survival has brought the term "competitive intelligence" to the forefront of business operations. The recent explosion of e-business and its enabling technologies allows vast global electronic networks to level the business field for those companies aware of their competitors and of the competitive factors that will affect them now and into the future. Knowing who you are dealing with—particularly on the other side of the world—is a key challenge in global e-business. You may wonder, for example, what your potential suppliers, joint venture partners, or competitors are *really* like. One needs accurate, complete, and timely information before making key business decisions in a global context.

Conducting CI on a global scale involves several challenges:

- Being unaware of the critical elements in a foreign business environment and, as a result, not being cognizant of the critical questions to ask.
- Having difficulty obtaining the necessary in-country secondary and primary data, because you may not know the sources or the language(s).
- Lacking a thorough understanding of the relevant countries' norms and cultures, transforming raw data into information and actionable intelligence incorrectly and drawing the wrong conclusions. You must ask yourself just what the intelligence means in terms of the countries' norms and cultures.
- Identifying the principal problems and barriers encountered when conducting international CI data research.

Since Roukis, Conway, and Charnov (1990) assessed the global business landscape over a decade ago in their book *Global Corporate Intelligence: Opportunities, Technologies and Threats in the 1990s*, many changes have taken place in the world order of business. It is our objective in this book to address the latest changes and prescribe the future role of CI in global business.

A word about terminology is in order at the outset of the book. In both the academic and popular business press, there sometimes is confusion, overlap, and interchangeability in the use of words such as "domestic," "international," "global," and "multinational" as they relate to business. For the purposes of this book, we will use the following terminology.

Domestic business—a firm that restricts its efforts, including its business perspective, to within the borders of the country where it is based.

International business—a business that develops and performs its activities across national boundaries.

Global business—in the macro sense, a business viewing the whole world as one entity or market and seeking to overcome the individual approaches or single-country points of view; standardizing operations when there are cultural similarities and altering them when differing cultures warrant such action. The literature often uses "international" and "global" interchangeably.

Multinational business—a firm engaged in a variety of activities (e.g., sales, production, research and development) outside the borders of its home country; and running its business depending upon the choices available anywhere in the world.

Because this book is aimed at practitioners as well as academics, we have allowed our many contributors to utilize the more popular, as opposed to academic, nomenclature.

WHY AN APPRECIATION OF GLOBAL CI IS IMPORTANT

The reasons for establishing global CI are the same drivers that propel domestic intelligence operations, but differences in scope are present, different lenses are utilized, and different challenges emerge, such as these:

- *Sensitivity*. One must be sensitive to cultural, societal, regulatory, legal, and economic factors.
- *Frustration*. The challenges faced by global CI may seem insurmountable to a domestically focused CI operation, leaving many to ask why your company should bother with them at all.
- *Preparedness*. Experience has taught us that when it comes to cross-cultural trade, businesses in general are ill-prepared to deal with foreign cultures.
- *Unfamiliarity*. When looking internationally, firms have to compete on strange turf where everything is different: the customer, the institutional environment, trade barriers, the workforce, the "style" of doing business, and, perhaps the most important factor, the culture.
- *Resources Investment*. The global trend is one of investing in knowledge and people, which leads to the next section on intelligence-driven global markets.

GLOBAL MARKETS ARE INTELLIGENCE-DRIVEN

Now, more than ever, competitive advantage in global markets is intelligence driven. Competitive intelligence that targets foreign-based companies, whether state or privately owned businesses, joint ventures, or foreign subsidiaries, requires a thorough understanding of the local country's unique business culture and environment. Companies operating in foreign markets (or contemplating doing so) should be very interested in their competitors' and potential competitors' business strategies, cost structures, and other factors that may allow these competitors to challenge them in foreign and home markets.

Addressing CI in a global context, this book highlights those aspects of conducting CI nationally that differ or become more complex when the global dimension is added. Whether companies like it or not, globalization is here to stay. For firms to survive and prosper, a thorough understanding of the whole world is mandatory. CI can greatly facilitate this understanding.

GLOBAL CI ADDS COMPLEXITY AND A NEW DIMENSION TO THE DOMESTIC CI PROCESS

Conducting CI in a global context builds upon a solid domestic foundation, with mission-critical challenges arising in many of the CI process steps. The CI infrastructure is quite different when your firm is doing business in many countries, as opposed to operating in only one. The CI task complexity takes on a new meaning when you are dealing with different languages, cultures, ethics, and legal structures. Social and business norms and customs differ dramatically around the globe. Sources and reliability of data and information also differ greatly as business is conducted away from one's home country. The analysis and interpretation stage must be undertaken with a thorough understanding of how offshore business systems work.

DIFFERENCES IN MANAGING DOMESTIC VERSUS INTERNATIONAL/GLOBAL CI

According to Hill (2003), managing international or global businesses is different from managing domestic business organizations for a number of prominent reasons, including the following:

- All nation-states are different from one another.
- Managers of international and global business organizations face a larger number of problems and wider range of complexities than those faced by their counterparts in domestic organizations.
- Managers in international and global businesses must navigate a trickier and wider array of limits imposed by governmental intervention in the ever-changing international investment and trading systems.
- International transactions typically involve an array of different conversions, including conversions of languages, understandings, cultures, and currencies.

Like others before us (Prescott & Gibbons, 1993), we suggest as a premise for this chapter that the basic processes of CI are more similar than different for organizations in domestic and global contexts; however, we recognize that there are fundamental differences in how organizations of different origins compete as well as critical differences in the way the nature and structure of business competition unfolds in different settings. In other words, the differences in the CI systems of domestic and global competitors have more to do with the systems' contexts and inputs rather than the systems' processes and outputs. The process, methods, and techniques used in performing CI are generally the same regardless of where it is practiced; nevertheless, there are differences in the various nation-state and multinational environments within which it is applied and practiced. Besides the obvious differences (those that arise out of different languages, cultures, political systems, and social mores), ethical and legal standards affecting CI can differ from country to country and region to region. For example, unless it is authorized by a court order, intercepting a competitor's faxes or cell phone calls is viewed to be both illegal and unethical in the United States—a practice sometimes associated with CI that remains above the law in a variety of other countries.

There is a plethora of scholarship on international business, management, marketing, and strategy functions, and many concepts have been developed, tested, and validated in this field (see, for example, Hill [2003] or other textbooks in the area of international business). Nevertheless, scarcely any scholarship has been developed dealing specifically with the global dimensions of CI (Dishman, Fleisher, & Knip, 2003). There has been one major book-length treatise on global CI, an impressive effort edited by Prescott and Gibbons (1993), who identify seven themes of international CI:

- *Fragmented Global Intelligence Industry:* low entry barriers, few opportunities for scale economies, diverse products, constantly evolving customer needs across a range of CI-affiliated producer segments
- *Global Information Collection:* variations in CI types, timeliness, accuracy, and data-collection motives; ethical standards; language issues; and country-specific idiosyncrasies associated with CI
- *Challenges to Interpretation:* for example, sources, often culturally derived, that are easily subjected to misinterpretation
- *Ethics:* both in collection and protection, dealing with international codes of conduct
- *Multinational Management of CI Programs:* coordination and infrastructures
- *Role of Governments:* different types relative to private and public-sector CI
- *Learning:* challenges to organizations to improve their strategies and performance over time

There is some published anecdotal evidence of nation-state–based differences in CI practice. Firms in Japan, France, Germany, Sweden, and Israel openly acknowledge that business and competitive intelligence is a recognized part of their key decision-making processes (Kahaner, 1996). Despite the relative lack of empirical research in the field of global CI, some argue that firms domiciled in nation-states (e.g., Japan) and regions outside of the United States (e.g., Europe) tend to place a greater implicit if not explicit premium on the conduct of CI (Calof, 1997). This premium takes on any number of forms, such as these:

- A greater relative percentage of formalized CI teams in international firms than would be found in U.S. firms.
- The view that part of the normal cultural fabric of doing business in countries that are predicated on collectively oriented cultures and the establishment of social networks. This cultural phenomenon can be witnessed in Korean *chaebols*, Chinese *guanxi*, or Japanese *keiretsu*.
- The fact that CI is a common part of the important decision-making processes in marketing, R&D, and strategy, among other areas, in these nation-states.
- The regular budgeting of CI activities. These CI teams don't need to produce the kind of quantitative evidence of their return that seems to be needed in the United States.
- The higher degree of CI collaboration between government and private-sector entities.

KEY GLOBAL CI PRACTICE ISSUES

There are a number of critical issues that affect the way that a globally oriented company identifies the key intelligence topics (KITs) it needs to research in order to assess its competitive environment:

- *Global Competitive Trends.* Just where is the global marketplace headed in your specific industry or product or service category? Which firms will likely be the future trendsetters?
- *Customer or End-user Preferences and Trends.* Are there global shifts in customer or end-user desires and needs? If so, who and what are influencing these shifts and how is your competition managing these shifts? How do these shifts affect the way you should be doing business, now and in the future?
- *Technological Trends.* How will technology affect your industry and its customers? Are you at the leading edge of these new technologies and how to manage them? How will your current and potential future competitors handle these new technologies?

- *Diversification Opportunities.* What are the opportunities for global diversification? What is the global landscape like in these prime areas for diversification? What competitive opportunities and risks would you likely encounter in the near, medium, and long terms?

- *Internal Capabilities.* Does your firm possess the necessary resources (human, financial, relationships, etc.) to be successful in the global marketplace? If gaps exist, how can they be closed? How long will it take to become a sustainable global player?

- *Joint Ventures, Strategic Alliances, and Other Partnering Opportunities.* Given the realities of your organization, do these relationships make sense in your globalization efforts? If so, which type(s) of relationship(s) are in your best interests? How do you assess the compatibility of your firm with potential partners to ensure success?

- *General Nation-state and Regional Economic and Business Conditions.* How can you accurately assess the current and future political and business conditions in specific areas of the world? Which sources should be consulted to get accurate, unbiased information?

- *Regulatory Issues.* What are the laws and regulations in your global area(s) of focus? Are they about to change? How does the local legal system actually work? How does it compare to other areas of the world in which you operate and with which you are familiar?

- *Supplier Trends.* What is the nature of the supplier base in your focused global area(s)? Will this change in the future? Is there a global shift in your current supplier base? If so, what is the nature of this shift and how will it affect your operations?

- *Understanding Reasons for Past International Successes and Failures.* Why are the current winners in your industry successful globally? What have you learned from past failures in the global marketplace? The more that organizations are willing to increase their emphasis on historical and current data analysis, the more CI can contribute to organizational learning.

- *Performance.* Is there a global shift of power in your industry? Where are the current industry leaders located? Will this shift in the future? Does the global marketplace have different performance indicators than the domestic one?

THE CI OPERATION IN A GLOBAL COMPANY: STRUCTURE AND SYSTEMS

The orientation toward the CI function in a global company must take into account *structure*—the way the function is organized, and *systems*—

the tools used and operations performed by CI practitioners to achieve their objectives.

Structure

A basic dilemma faced by "globalizing" firms is that of a centralized versus decentralized CI structure. Centralized authority offers efficient decision-making that comes from executives in one location who are considering the global "big picture," yet those in the field in specific countries and regions know the realities of the local environment. Local managers are best equipped to make the decisions needed to meet the needs of local markets and abide by host government policies. Some key structure-related questions to be considered:

- In global and international firms, is CI best organized in a centralized or decentralized fashion?
- How can CI best support decisions about the nature of global strategic alliances to enter? For example, which potential alliance partners fit best with the firm's objectives, mission, and value system? Once the alliances have been contracted, in what ways can CI be useful in helping the firm reduce or minimize a partner's opportunism? Should different CI structures be developed to address the various stages of your firm's international development as it moves from being a domestic company, to an exporter, to one with international divisions, to a multinational, to a global firm?
- Is there a specific CI structure that should be used with multinational corporations (MNCs) making specific strategic choice decisions (e.g., firms using specific international, multi-domestic, global, or transnational strategies)?
- Is there a specific CI structure that should be used to help your organization make entry decisions such as which foreign markets to enter? When is it appropriate to enter these markets? What should be the optimum scale of entry and the nature of strategic commitment that is made?
- How can CI best help with choice of entry mode decisions in terms of utilizing exporting, licensing, franchising, joint ventures, or wholly owned subsidiaries?

Systems

CI systems include those hard (technical, hardware, programs, etc.) and soft (policies, culture, etc.) facets of the organization that enable CI work to be conducted. Some key systems-related CI questions to be considered:

- Can systems be developed that assist in the translation of information from several languages and multiple formats? Will information and communication systems allow for access to and fusion of intelligence from all sources around the globe?
- How can your company develop information systems that allow the company to capitalize in real time on the 24/7 flood of information that becomes available at their various global sites and to employees located in all time zones?
- Can your company identify regions or clusters of CI process excellence in which to assign specific CI tasks (e.g., data-gathering on technological developments from within a national cluster of excellence in the field)?
- Can your company develop policies and practices that will enable you to benefit from cultural advantages that can be gained from CI networks and practices in certain regions?
- Will specific software facilitate improved analysis of data coming from diverse international sources? Related to this is the need for private-sector CI groups to improve their access to, and collaboration with, national governments and government vendors that have the data they need.

CULTURAL BARRIERS CAN BE THE BIGGEST CHALLENGE IN CONDUCTING GLOBAL CI

Each country has its own culture, with several different cultures often present in one country or region. Each culture has unique idiosyncrasies, which are often missed, ignored, or misunderstood by outsiders. The importance of beliefs and traditions may explain the rationale for certain business decisions and behaviors. Habits and customs, if not understood by outsiders, may seem irrational when practiced in a business setting. Specific norms and practices must be understood for what they represent and are often context-specific. To accurately understand the importance and meaning of cultural background, actions, and cues, CI practitioners must obtain a comprehensive understanding of the culture within which they are researching. However, this is often very difficult to accomplish.

ETHICAL, LEGAL, AND REGULATORY CHALLENGES IN GLOBAL CI

The professional practice of CI places ethical and legal conduct at a high priority level. However, the term "ethics" has vastly differing meanings, and laws are often different in various countries and regions around the world. What is considered ethical in one country, region, or business culture may be quite unacceptable in another part of the world. Some ethical and legal issues must be addressed before conducting global CI:

- Will your offshore research team follow your accepted ethical standards?
- How are data and information collected in the targeted country or region?
- What are the accepted ethical norms in the targeted country or region?
- Just what is legal and illegal in the targeted countries?
- What are the legalities in gathering data and information in the targeted countries?

Just because something is legal does not mean that it is ethical. Being aware of ethical and legal differences will allow CI professionals to add more value to their organizations and will assist in avoiding problems in these areas before they occur. It is incumbent upon the CI professional to know the local rules.

GLOBAL CORPORATE COMPETITIVENESS AND CI

Far too often corporate leaders place too little value on the knowledge foundation on which global competitiveness will be built (Simkins, 1998). Corporate planners are inundated with so much international data and information that deciding which will have an impact on their strategic direction is very confusing and difficult. Three questions arise:

1. How do we organize the global information in a way that is meaningful to us?
2. How do we separate what is important from what is not?
3. How can we base strategic planning on this new knowledge?

Thinking globally comprises more than a set of skills; it is an orientation to the world, a mindset that allows the professional to see and intuitively understand things that others do not see, nor understand. This book aims to elucidate those concepts, techniques, and skills that will facilitate CI practitioners and corporate strategists in attaining this global mindset. With this mindset in place, you will more clearly understand and make better decisions in the global marketplace.

GLOBAL SCANNING TO TRIGGER UNCERTAINTY

In their book *Competitive Intelligence: Scanning the Global Environment*, Salmon and de Linares (1999) trace the growth in global competition, which they posit was triggered by the rapid rise in the 1980s of the "tiger" economies of Southeast Asia. This, coupled with radical shifts in the environment—an aging population in the West, population explosion elsewhere, rising concern for health and the environment, and great technological changes—has contributed to the recent globalization of business. This globalization makes it necessary for firms wishing to stay ahead of the curve and be successful to scan the global environment. Global scanning should not simply be viewed as a means to reduce uncertainty; it should also serve to trigger uncertainty for management. This uncertainty gives rise to a heightened importance of CI, ensuring that increased environmental scanning leads to the production of accurate intelligence, resulting in the making of better strategic global decisions.

E-BUSINESS, GLOBALIZATION, AND CI

With today's electronic networks, driven by the Internet and other forms of low-cost, efficient, worldwide communication, the world has truly become a global village. More and more companies have realized that exporting and its accompanying global mindset is, not something they "need to have," but, rather, a critical success factor. This has presented opportunities for CI professionals, especially those with international networks that can be accessed on demand as opportunities arise. These favorable relationships represent the upside of e-business for the CI professional; the downside is Netspionage, which is described next.

GLOBALIZATION HAS ATTENDANT THREATS

While globalization has brought many positive aspects to the world business order, serious downsides have emerged. While the revolution in communications technology has facilitated the interrelated new world order, security threats, outside threats to corporate intelligence data security, defense-related computer security, terrorist threats to corporations, financial warfare, and the increased risk of making incorrect strategic decisions if armed with unreliable corporate intelligence have become more prominent. An example is the global threat to information and CI. The advent of the Internet, global information infrastructure (GII), and national information infrastructures (NII) has led to the practice of "Netspionage" (network-enabled espionage) (Boni & Kovacich, 2000). The recent burgeoning worldwide interconnectivity has enabled Netspionage agents, fueled by brutal global competition, to utilize worldwide electronic networks to obtain information on competitors and competition, often without questioning the ethics or legality of their methods.

THE BOOK'S FRAMEWORK

This book's objective is to examine the role of CI in the context of global business. In doing so, we posit this question: Just what are the differences in CI when the dimension of globalization is added to the lens of the CI practitioner and the business strategist? The basic fundamentals of good CI practice still apply and form the foundation of CI practiced in a global context, and this book seeks to build upon these basics to raise CI awareness and practice to a new level.

Section One: The Global CI Process

This section examines how the components of the CI process take on an expanded complexity and dimension when globalization enters the equation. Following methods and practices that have a proven record of success in domestic CI may provide sub-optimal results or fail completely when tried in a global setting. The chapters in this section range from an explanation of KITs practiced in a global setting, to best practices in global CI, to a comparison of domestic and global CI programs.

Section Two: The Global CI Environment

This section examines the global CI environment from macro and micro points of view. The legal environments encountered in practicing global CI are addressed and guidelines are presented to assist practitioners in navigating potentially treacherous waters. The impact of the Internet in the facilitation of global CI practice is stressed, with guidelines given for its optimum role in CI.

Section Three: Global CI Management

The similarities and differences between domestic and global CI are highlighted in this section in an effort to address global CI management with a strategic model, as well as to discuss the issues of how to organize and where to locate the CI function within an organization. The section aims to bring insight into the complexity of viewing CI through global lenses. In addition, this entire section directs attention to the contrast in knowledge, skills, and abilities of international versus domestic CI practices.

Section Four: Country, Industry, and Process-Specific Studies in Global CI

This section commences by examining through case examples how top-performing companies practice global CI. Next, the CI practices in several countries are presented to illustrate how diverse the methods can be in achieving similar CI objectives in countries of very diverse size, cultures, geographic location, level of development, and business practices. The section also addresses how the rapid globalization of the world auto industry affects the process of how CI should be practiced. The section ends with a recap on the current state of CI for global business, projections going forward, and what research should be carried out to assist in mapping a future course for CI in a global setting.

The contents of this book, when synthesized, should enable the reader to develop a comprehensive international CI framework as a means of understanding and overcoming the many challenges and barriers in global business. Performing CI in a global context creates special challenges, but they are well worth conquering to maximize the potential benefits from conducting business globally.

REFERENCES

Boni, W.C., and G.L. Kovacich. (2000). *Netspionage: The Global Threat to Information*. Boston, MA: Butterworth-Heinemann.

Calof, J.L. (1997). "For King and Country . . . and Company." *Business Quarterly* 61(3): 32–39.

Dishman, P., C.S. Fleisher, and V. Knip. (2003). "A Chronological and Categorized Bibliography of Key Competitive Intelligence Scholarship." *Journal of Competitive Intelligence and Management* 1(1–3).

Hill, C.W.L. (2003). *International Business: Competing in the Global Marketplace*. 4th ed. New York: McGraw-Hill.

Kahaner, L. (1996). *Competitive Intelligence: From Black Ops to Boardrooms—How Businesses Gather, Analyze, and Use Information to Succeed in the Global Marketplace*. New York: Simon & Schuster.

Prescott, J.E., and P.T. Gibbons. [eds.] (1993). *Global Perspectives on Competitive Intelligence*. Alexandria, VA: Society of Competitive Intelligence Professionals.

Roukis, G.S., H. Conway, and B.H. Charnov. [eds.] (1990). *Global Corporate Intelligence: Opportunities, Technologies, and Threats in the 1990s*. Westport, CT: Quorum Books.

Salmon, R., and Y. de Linares. (1999). *Competitive Intelligence: Scanning the Global Environment*. Washington, DC: Brookings Books.

Simkins, R.A. (1998). "The Global Mind." *Competitive Intelligence Magazine* 1(2): 34–36.

2

Key Intelligence Topics (KITs) in Competitive Intelligence and Global Business

Meera Mody

Competitive intelligence (CI) is a formalized yet continuously evolving process by which CI professionals evaluate industry forces and competitor dynamics in the marketplace (Prescott & Gibbons, 1993). Micro-environmental forces—such as capabilities and behaviors of competitors, buyers, suppliers, potential new entrants, and substitute products or services providers—are evaluated to assist management in making correct strategic decisions that can maintain or create a sustainable competitive advantage. CI programs also assess macro-environmental trends—such as political developments, economic conditions, social trends, legal and regulatory changes, international market trends, and technological developments—that can have a direct or indirect impact on the competitive landscape.

In recent years, a new competitive landscape has emerged due to increased globalization and technological advances (Hitt, Keats & DeMarie, 1998). This new landscape is hyper-competitive with an increased focus on product and service innovation and customer satisfaction. Businesses are reinventing themselves with new business models to protect their existing markets and to expand into newly emerging global markets. CI plays an important role in navigating businesses through this volatile and ambiguous competitive landscape and exploiting the opportunities created by global markets. All organizations have access to information, but the one that transforms this information into actionable CI and links it to strategic decisions has the competitive advantage (Muller, 1999). The actionable intelligence provided by a CI program can make a valuable contribution to decisions regarding strategic planning, mergers and acquisitions, regulatory requirements for exporting to new markets, international market penetration, product launching, pricing, recruiting in new countries, cultural settings, strategic alliances for distribution channels, research and development (R&D) activities, and much more.

As the competitive landscape has grown larger and more complex, so has the role of CI programs in these global organizations. It can be a daunting task for a CI professional to meet all of these diverse CI needs without any direction or focus from senior management. Identifying and prioritizing an organization's critical CI needs and then focusing on delivering actionable intelligence to meet those needs is critical for both the success of the CI program and for the success of the organization (Herring, 1999). In 1999, Jan P. Herring introduced the concept of a Key Intelligence Topics (KITs) process for the identification of senior management's primary intelligence needs in his *Competitive Intelligence Review* article, "Key Intelligence Topics: A Process to Identify and Define Intelligence Needs."

This chapter outlines the KITs (also known as critical intelligence needs, CINs) assessment process and the key forces that influence the KITs identified by senior executives. Different types of KITs and the advantages of carrying out the formal KITs exercise are also discussed. Also included in this chapter is an analysis of data from primary and secondary research sources, as well as a breakdown of KITs pursued by global and North American organizations into three broad categories: strategic, early warning, and key player.

Analyzing the KITs of global companies will give a better understanding of the companies' changing CI needs. It will help CI professionals determine the types of CI activities that may be most beneficial as more and more domestic organizations expand into the global marketplace or compete against global forces in their domestic marketplace.

It is hypothesized that as markets become more global, the number of requests coming from senior executives for strategic KITs will grow. Advances in technology and automation of CI programs will put tactical CI at the fingertips of internal clients. The CI professional's role will evolve into providing more and more strategic CI to decision-makers with business development, market planning or research, product development, financial planning, R&D, and strategic planning responsibilities.

THE KITS PROCESS

The heart of the KITs process involves an interactive dialogue between CI professionals and key decision-makers of the organization. The purpose of the dialogue is to identify key strategic issues where intelligence can add value to strategic decision-making. The CI cycle starts with the identification of KITs by management, forming the basis for planning and direction-setting. This phase is followed by the creation of a knowledge base through an internal audit and information processing, gathering relevant intelligence, analyzing and producing actionable intelligence, and disseminating intelligence to management and other users. In essence, KITs become the filters through which information-gathering and analysis processes pass. Figure 2.1 depicts the key interactions of the CI department with other functions of the organization.

As is evident from Figure 2.1, KITs identification requires two-way communication between CI professionals and key users. Typically, the CI manager proactively seeks out principal decision-makers and helps them define their intelligence needs through a formal interview process. The interview protocol with open-ended and non-directive questions is used for consistency purposes (Francis & Herring, 1999). Better articulation of critical intelligence needs results in better CI outcomes. The first KITs interview is conducted during the planning stage of the CI program, and ongoing KITs interviews refine the user's needs and keep communication channels open. The main barrier to any KITs interview process is

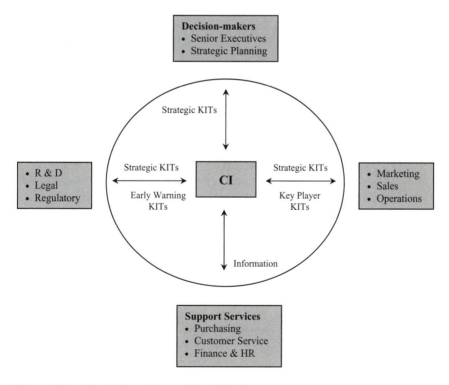

Figure 2.1   Key Interactions of the KITs Process.

miscommunication between the CI professional and the CI user. This may be due to any one of many reasons, such as lack of cooperation, lack of awareness about the benefits of CI, lack of credibility of the interviewee, or lack of clarity about CI needs. It is CI professionals' responsibility to establish open communication channels and facilitate the ongoing dialogue between the CI department and all other internal CI clients.

Herring first used the KITs interview method at Motorola during the 1980s; since then, many companies, such as Xerox, Nutrasweet, Texas Instruments, Merck, and Southwestern Bell, have used the KITs process as a first step in setting up new CI capabilities. In 1993, IBM used the KITs process in its pilot project to revise its CI functions (Behnke & Slayton, 1998).

KITS TYPES

KITs defined by CI clients are categorized according to different KITS types to better understand the needs of the clients and to plan out CI functions of the organization. Different CI academics have used various criteria to categorize KITs. Prescott (1989) segmented KITs into offensive, defensive, and informational types. Gilad's (1993) Cerberus model of CI function divided needs into three "lines": dedicated intelligence support for top management, tactical field support, and a passive monitoring system. Dugal (1998) divided clients' KITs into 10 basic CI "products." After interviewing 1,000 CI clients, Herring (1999) narrowed KITs down to three functional categories.

Strategic Decision and Action KITs

Strategic KITs feature CI contributing directly to key decisions regarding strategy formulation and implementation. Strategic KITs take many different forms, depending on the department that requests them. Some examples of strategic KITs are strategic investment decisions about alliances and acquisitions, strategy decisions about expansion in global markets, and strategic human resources issues about hiring and retaining key employees. As shown in Figure 2.1, senior management and strategic planning department KITs fall into this strategic category. An R&D department's requests about technological competitiveness and competitors' product development plans also fall into this category. Typical strategic KITs requested by the legal and regulatory department relate to competitors' efforts to acquire proprietary information and intellectual property. The strategic needs of marketing, sales, and distribution functions relate to CI in terms of the industry's response to new product rollouts. A CI program can make valuable contributions to production's decisions about expanding capacity with new processes and production facilities. Strategic KITs almost always result in actionable CI and are a tangible measure of the value of a CI department (Herring, 1999). Strategic KITs not only help business leaders in strategic decision-making but also aid in resource allocation and investment decisions.

Examples of strategic KITs pursued by global organizations include

- identification and profiling of international competitors, licensing partners, or acquisition targets
- assessment of the risk and opportunity of doing business in a foreign country
- formulation of product development strategies to improve competitive advantage
- identification, evaluation, selection, and relationship management of strategic alliance partners and distribution channel partners
- defining and analyzing cultural sensitivities for sales, marketing, and promotional campaigns in a foreign land

Early Warning KITs

Early warning KITs include threats arising from a competitor's initiatives, technological surprises, and government actions. Typically, R&D, legal, and regulatory departments identify these KITs during a needs assessment interview. Marketing departments, however, may benefit from the early warning of new product rollouts by competitors. A typical example of the use of early warning KITs is the strategy employed by pharmaceutical companies where the market is flooded with price incentives just prior to the launch of a new product by a competitor. Also, early warning of changes in the bargaining power of suppliers can add value to decisions the operations department of the organization may face. Not all early warning KITs address threats from the changing environment; some early warning KITs identify opportunities for the organization. Some early warning KITs result in actionable CI (Herring, 1999).

Examples of early warning KITs pursued by global organizations include

- tracking business, political, and economic developments as they unfold
- developing a so-called "radar screen," thereby enabling systematic competitive intelligence on key competitors and their takeover, merger, or acquisition activities
- knowing the prevailing business climate
- early warning of changes in international policy

Key Player KITs

Key player KITs emerge from rivalry among existing firms in an industry and the threat of new entrants and substitute products in the marketplace. A marketing department's request for intelligence about key competitor profiles falls into this category. Because a competitor profile generally does not translate into actionable CI, key player KITs are tactical in nature. Marketing and sales departments are the main users of key player KITs.

Examples of key player KITs pursued by global organizations include

- monitoring the sales, investments, and partnerships of competitors
- investigating suppliers and subcontractors
- constructing baseline profiles of competitor capabilities and intent
- providing ongoing competitive reviews and profiles regarding strategies, marketing, branding, R&D, operations, key personnel, and organizational structure of key competitors

Support functions, such as customer services, human resources, finance, and purchasing, as well as salespeople, are valuable sources of information for CI professionals because they are the front-line people who are in touch with all of the players of the marketplace. From a global perspective, people working in these functions and local salesforces can provide valuable insight into local cultural and societal differences that may have a profound effect on performing CI in foreign countries.

INTERRELATEDNESS OF KITS TYPES AND STRATEGY

The three KITs types are inter-related. In fact, early-warning KITs may evolve into strategic decision KITs, while strategic decision KITs may require the input of a key player KIT. None of the KITs operate in complete isolation from one another. KITs are driven by management's view of the organization's future strategy and the competitive environment in which it operates. Figure 2.2 captures the interrelatedness of the KITs types and the fit of the CI department within the organization's strategy and environment.

The strategy of the organization takes into account the opportunities and challenges in its competitive environment. During a KITs interview, the strategic planning department identifies the specific CI needs based on this perceived linkage or absence of linkage between the firm's strategy and the environment. CI seeks out early warning KITs and key player KITs through environmental scanning, some of which translate into strategic KITs and feed into actionable strategic CI, signaling a need to modify the existing competitive strategy. Francis and Herring (1999) analyzed KITs of

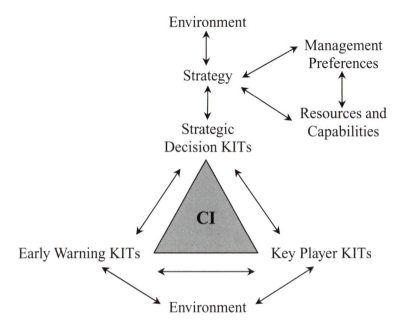

Figure 2.2 KITs and Strategy.

12 client companies and concluded that the distribution of key intelligence topics, as identified by executives, is the product of the organization's current and past experiences and reveals the company's "competitive psyche."

Changes in the environment, such as globalization of the industry, upset the link between the organization's competitive strategy and its capabilities. This leads to an increasing need for new sets of capabilities. Many organizations respond to changing needs by forming alliances with other firms (Nohria & Garcia-Pont, 1991). KITs identified during this phase of alliance formation are mainly strategic in nature.

BENEFITS OF THE KITS PROCESS

The benefits of the KITs process are many.

- The KITs process takes the guesswork out of the CI program and sets the agenda for the CI program. The KITs process ensures that the CI program is needs-driven (Fleisher, 2001).

- The closer a CI function is organized around demand, the higher are its chances of success (Gilad, 1993).

- The KITs process identifies resource constraints faced by the CI department in meeting all CI needs. KITs identification allows CI professionals to organize, prioritize, and allocate their scarce resources to the few key intelligence issues that meet senior executives' CI needs. The CI manager may even arrange to seek outside help if the KITs identified by management are beyond the CI program's existing reach.

- The KITs process forces management to take a critical look at their strategy and identify gaps or potential opportunities that may exist in the ever-changing marketplace.

- Analysis of KITs can reveal management's blind spots and help correct unfavorable situations.

- The outcome of actionable CI and its connection back to management's KITs evangelizes the importance of the CI program by linking CI to the bottom line of the organization.

- KITs interviews create open communication channels to support ongoing CI functions.

- The KITs process also helps build CI culture within the organization.

KITS OF GLOBAL AND DOMESTIC ORGANIZATIONS

The primary KITs pursued by global CI programs focus on foreign governments, foreign markets, and foreign competitors (Sheinin, 1996). Through literature research (Francis & Herring, 1999) and a personal communication via email with Mr. Francis (a recognized CI expert), KITs of six organizations with a global strategy and six organizations with a North American strategy were identified and categorized into three broad KITs types. The data obtained by Francis and Herring were further analyzed from global and domestic strategy perspectives.

Results of KITs Types Identified by Global and North American Organizations

The total number of KITs identified by the management of global and North American organizations ranged from 18 to 71. These KITs were divided into three categories, and the percentage of the total KITs that fall into the three categories was calculated. The mean percentages of six global organizations and six companies with North American strategy and ideal KITs distribution as described by Francis and Herring (1999) are shown in Table 2.1. Ideal KITs distribution was established by Francis and

Herring based on its appeal to the executive group, its "actionableness," and its added value to the organization.

As shown in Table 2.1, mean percentage KITs identified by global organizations fell into the ideal category distribution for all three categories. The mean percentage KITs identified by organizations with North American strategies was higher in the key player KITs category than the ideal distribution. In fact, five out of six companies with a North American strategy identified higher than 30% key player KITs. These findings about KITs identified by North American companies were attributed to a strong sales culture, a marketplace with many competitors, and the entrepreneurial culture of the organization (Francis & Herring, 1999).

High value for strategic KITs for global companies clearly indicates that the management of global organizations is more concerned about strategic KITs than key intelligence KITs. High value for early warning KITs for global organizations is probably indicative of the dynamic nature of the global marketplace.

Although early warning mean percentage KITs identified by organizations with North American strategies fall into the desirable range, three out of six organizations had early warning KITs below the desirable range. This was attributed to simple lack of knowledge and lack of appreciation for early warning CI among U.S. managers (Francis & Herring, 1999). Lack of interest in early warning KITs was also attributed to a lack of prior experience with surprises or to having had too many surprises in the past and feeling helpless as a result.

KITs Processes and KITs Types at Canadian Global Organizations

An electronic survey was conducted to understand the needs assessment processes carried out by the CI professionals of two Canadian global

Table 2.1
KITs Distribution and Strategy

Strategy	Mean Strategic KITs %	Mean Early Warning KITs %	Mean Key Player KITs %
Global	40	33	26
North American	37	25	38
Ideal KITs distribution range	>35	>20	<30

companies. The purpose of this survey was to understand the process as well as the KITs types identified by management. The standard questionnaire used for the survey is shown in Table 2.2.

Both Canadian organizations had done thorough CI needs assessment and audits before embarking on their new CI programs. CI needs assessment was carried out informally on an ongoing basis as well as formally every year, and it was used to refine and define CI needs. CI needs were both tactical and strategic in nature. CI needs assessment has helped CI professionals at these organizations deliver more focused CI, both in terms of content and dissemination.

Table 2.2
Needs Assessment Process Survey

Objectives	1. To understand the needs assessment process carried out by global organizations' competitive intelligence departments.
	2. To identify the key intelligence topics pursued by global Canadian organizations.
Questions	1. Did you or your colleagues perform a formal needs assessment exercise with your management and other users of CI before starting the CI program?
	2. How was the needs assessment process carried out? Was it a formal or an informal process?
	3. Was it carried out only at the beginning of the CI program or is it reevaluated periodically?
	4. What were the five key needs identified by your management?
	5. Did you organize needs in any categories like competitor analysis, early warning analysis, tactical, strategic, etc.?
	6. Are your key intelligence needs more tactical or strategic?
	7. How has a needs assessment process benefited your CI program?
	8. In hindsight, would you approach needs assessment any differently?
	9. Do you have a central CI department for each region, or does each business unit have its own CI department?

Examples of KITs identified by Canadian global companies include

- strategic alliance and potential partnership investigations
- foreign market trends and their influence on the industry
- product positioning, promotion, and pricing matrices for foreign markets
- new product development and technological breakthrough scanning
- monitoring underlying fundamental competitive, technologic, and regulatory trends

KEY INFLUENCES BEHIND KITS IDENTIFICATION

The competitive environment, management's perception of that environment, and the strategy of an organization dictate management's CI priorities. Several other factors that also play a role in management's identification of KITs are discussed next.

Global versus Domestic Organizations

Global companies are becoming more global; some domestic companies are growing globally, and other domestic companies are facing competition from the global organizations in their domestic competitive landscape. These companies can benefit from early warning KITs to find out if foreign competition is taking any initiative to enter their marketplace. Some domestic companies compete solely in domestic markets, but they may have foreign suppliers and may face issues with global raw material suppliers.

Competitive Environment

Michael Porter's Five Forces model (1979) describes the complexity and volatility of the competitive environment in which businesses operate. Unless entry barriers are set up, lucrative profits attract new entrants to the competitive landscape. Businesses with low profit margins look for efficiencies in the system and evolve into new business models or look for new opportunities in global markets. Businesses increasingly depend on strategic KITs for winning strategies and sustainable competitive advantage. A study by Deloitte Consulting found that 76% of companies in the telecommunications industry recognize that they need strategic CI programs (Marceau & Sawka, 1999).

Management's Perception

Sometimes the top management of leading companies becomes too complacent and oblivious to real threats in the marketplace due to an exaggerated perception of their company's market position. Hence, they may downplay their strategic marketing CI needs. Other times management may become preoccupied with competing against current competitors. Consequently, new entrants in the marketplace may take them by surprise. KITs identified by management are not always rational.

Tactical versus Strategic CI

Typically, market penetration strategy requires more tactical CI on existing competitors, whereas market expansion or growth strategy focused on new segments and geographic areas requires strategic CI. As well, CI requested by lower or middle management is tactical, while CI requested by senior management of an organization with external focus is strategic in nature (Turner-Shoemaker, 2001).

Offensive versus Defensive Strategy

Companies' profitability goals can range from maximization of shareholders' value (growth) to the maintenance of a positive cash flow (defensive strategy). Similarly, a company's strategy also includes market focus, such as customer group and geographic area (Broome, 2001). Global companies with a growth strategy engage in CI related to strategic actions and decision KITs, such as the acquisition of a target to gain entry into a foreign market, and strategic alliances for distribution channel choice. Conversely, with increased competition from global players, domestic companies engage in defensive CI, such as the description of current and potential key players.

New versus Well-Established CI Programs

Most newly established CI departments in North American organizations start out as an extension of strategic marketing research, with CI activities primarily focused on providing key player KITs. Key player KITs are easiest to obtain. Although key player CI very seldom results in actionable company initiatives, it serves many purposes for newly appointed CI professionals. During this introductory period, a resourceful CI professional develops a good grasp of the industry, sets up networks for information flow, creates a CI culture, and earns credibility as a resourceful and informed professional.

Innovative versus Maturing Products

Companies with products in their early product development stage monitor science and technology for a competitive advantage (Ashton, Johnson, & Stacey, 1994). Technology monitoring generally involves early warning KITs. In contrast, businesses with products in the maturing or declining product life cycle stage pursue more key player KITs.

FUTURE OF KITS IN THE GLOBAL MARKETPLACE

It is hypothesized that as markets become more global, senior executives will request more strategic KITs. This increasing demand for strategic KITs analysis will provide the impetus for more investment in CI resources and capabilities. Also, as the benefits of CI become more evident, KITs will grow from tactical to strategic in both domestic and global organizations.

Internet technology and sophisticated CI software applications are rapidly becoming available globally. Businesses will increasingly use these tools to develop winning strategies. Advances in information technology and automation of CI programs will put tactical CI at users' fingertips. CI professionals will find themselves providing more and more strategic CI to decision-makers with business development, market planning or market research, product development, financial planning, R&D, and strategic planning responsibilities. In fact, CI will become a state of mind, rather than an isolated process. The "new world" will feature CI embedded in strategy development, with a hub-and-spoke structure, and a deep commitment from senior management (Pepper, 1999).

REFERENCES

Ashton, W.B., A.K. Johnson, and G.S. Stacey. (1994). "Monitoring Science and Technology for Competitive Advantage." *Competitive Intelligence Review* 5(1): 5–16.

Behnke, L., and P. Slayton. (1998). "Shaping a Corporate Competitive Intelligence Function at IBM." *Competitive Intelligence Review* 9(2): 4–9.

Broome, P. (2001). "Making Competitive Intelligence Work for the Small Business," pp. 200–209 in C.S. Fleisher and D.L. Blenkhorn [eds.], *Managing Frontiers in Competitive Intelligence*. Westport, CT: Quorum Books.

Dugal, M. (1998). "CI Product Line: A Tool for Enhancing User Acceptance of CI." *Competitive Intelligence Review* 9(2): 17–25.

Fleisher, C.S. (2001). "An Introduction to the Management and Practice of Competitive Intelligence (CI)," pp. 3–18 in C.S. Fleisher and D.L. Blenkhorn [eds.], *Managing Frontiers in Competitive Intelligence*. Westport, CT: Quorum Books.

Francis, D.B., and J.P. Herring. (1999). "Key Intelligence Topics: A Window on the Corporate Competitive Psyche." *Competitive Intelligence Review* 10(4): 10–19.

Gilad, B. (1993). "A Self-Examining Test for the Corporate Intelligence Professional: Where Are You on the Chart?" pp. 205–212 in J.E. Prescott and P.T. Gibbons [eds.], *Global Perspectives on Competitive Intelligence*. Alexandria, VA: Society of Competitive Intelligence Professionals.

Herring J.P. (1999). "Key Intelligence Topics: A Process to Identify and Define Intelligence Needs." *Competitive Intelligence Review* 10(2): 4–14.

Hitt, M.A., B.W. Keats, and S.M. DeMarie. (1998). "Navigating in the New Competitive Landscape: Building Strategic Flexibility and Competitive Advantage in the twenty-first Century." *Academy of Management Executive* 12(4): 22–42.

Marceau, S., and K. Sawka. (1999). "Developing a World-Class CI Program in Telecoms." *Competitive Intelligence Review* 10(4): 30–40.

Muller M-L. (1999). "South Africa: An Emerging CI Player." *Competitive Intelligence Review* 10(4): 74–78.

Nohria, N., and C. Garcia-Pont. (1991). "Global Strategic Linkages and Industry Structure." *Strategic Management Journal* 12(summer): 105–124.

Pepper, J.E. (1999). "Competitive Intelligence at Procter & Gamble." *Competitive Intelligence Review* 10(4): 4–9.

Porter, M.E. (1979). "How Competitive Forces Shape Strategy." *Harvard Business Review* 57(2): 137–145.

Prescott, J.E. (1989). "Competitive Intelligence: Its Role and Function within Organizations," pp. 1–13 in J.E. Prescott [ed.], *Advances in Competitive Intelligence*. Alexandria, VA: Society of Competitive Intelligence Professionals.

Prescott, J.E., and P.T. Gibbons. (1993). "Global Competitive Intelligence: An Overview," pp. 1–27 in J.E. Prescott and P.T. Gibbons [eds.], *Global Perspectives on Competitive Intelligence*. Alexandria, VA: Society of Competitive Intelligence Professionals.

Sheinin, C.E. (1996). "Assessing Global Competition," *Competitive Intelligence Review* 7(3): 86–88.

Turner-Shoemaker, V. (2001). "Using a Marketing Framework to Communicate Competitive Intelligence Results," pp. 100–109 in C.S. Fleisher and D.L. Blenkhorn [eds.], *Managing Frontiers in Competitive Intelligence*. Westport, CT: Quorum Books.

3

In Search of Best Practices in Global Competitive Intelligence

Kirsten Rowatt

In the modern global economy, competitive intelligence (CI) is recognized as a primary tool in achieving sustainable competitive advantage. Organizations must not only keep abreast of the dynamic characteristics of this new business landscape, they must also learn how to adapt systems, structures, and cultures to maximize internal capabilities. Best practice organizations commonly implement and integrate a strong global CI function as a critical step in this process.

This chapter presents a model to explain the process by which best practice organizations can maximize the benefit of global CI. To begin, an overview of the nature of globalization and its historical context is described. Next, a summary of the dynamic features of today's business environment is offered. From this, three unique domains of global CI are identified. The relevant critical success factors of each domain are explained in detail. These factors are highlighted as they pertain to the development of a strong global CI function.

The Triad framework is then introduced to demonstrate the importance of the integration of global CI with the three core elements of technology, human capital, and culture. The Triad framework provides a basis upon which organizations can advocate the development of an integrated global CI function. A brief review of organizational changes at Procter and Gamble provides a competitive business application of the framework and is followed by a succinct presentation of its challenges and limitations.

THE AGE OF GLOBALIZATION

The nature of doing business has radically evolved over the past century, marked by three pivotal disruptions that have characterized and propelled economic forces. The first disruption, occurring at the turn of the twentieth century, led nations into the industrial revolution in which automation and mass production characterized business practices. The second disruption, commonly referred to as the "technological revolution" (Roukis, Conway, & Charnov, 1990), had the effect of forwarding information management technologies and strategies. The last and most pervasive disruption has provided an opportunity for global connectedness in proportions previously unseen. This new age of knowledge management, referred to as the "intelligence age" (Tyson, 1988), is characterized by two complementary trends:

1. Technological advances that connect world information systems
2. The emergence of a global economy

The new global economy is based on a myriad of complex business and information relationships. In this new business landscape, organizations that develop competency in managing the challenges of a diverse, expansive, and dynamic business environment outside the boundaries of conventional microeconomic theory will be successful (Roukis, Conway, & Charnov, 1990).

A New Global Economy

A primary contributor to the advent of the new global economy has been the successive introduction of Internet-based innovations. External to the organization, increased information availability is

- enlarging market size
- encouraging industry consolidation
- decreasing patent effectiveness
- collapsing time and geographical boundaries

Internal to the organization, increased information availability is

- improving product and service customization and responsiveness
- shortening time-to-market
- shrinking product life cycles

- fostering rapid product innovation,
- facilitating in-depth customer relationship management techniques
- growing CI opportunities

The dissolution of political, economic, and trade barriers has blurred industry boundaries and intensified the generation of transnational relationships and cross-border synergies (Hitt, Keats, & DeMarie, 1988). Successful multinational corporations will foster a globally minded culture focused on balancing internal and external domestic and global concerns through highly coordinated and collaborative processes and technologies.

Modern Competitive Advantage

The pervasive impact of technological advances and the global economy sows the seeds of change that continually frame modern competitive scenarios. Achieving information competence is now an order qualifier. Domination of future markets and sustainable competitive advantage depend upon the development of information-sharing and learning cultures that value innovation and encourage strategic flexibility (Hitt, Keats, & DeMarie, 1988). The increased uncertainty, ambiguity, and complexity of the new competitive landscape requires a very responsive external focus that balances a long-term vision with short-term objectives while continually remaining flexible to change.

Critical Success Factors for Global CI

With the emerging global economy positioned for sustainable growth through 2015 (Talkington, 2001), CI's role within multinational companies will intensify. Similar to their domestic counterparts, global CI practitioners must focus on timely and comprehensive collection, management, analysis, and dissemination protocols. As organizational cultures develop learning- and technology-enabled formats, the most valuable global CI will still be derived from internal sources (Boshyk, 2001). In order to keep pace with the dynamic nature of the global environment, CI will need to become a 24/7 venture as company leaders demand more frequent reporting to support accurate, strategy-related decisions.

Critical success factors for global CI operations can be divided into three domains, as depicted in Figure 3.1. The larger block arrows indicate the existence of prerequisite relationships between each domain. The single-lined arrows denote the interactive and complementary natures of the three domains. In the face of dynamic and complex global challenges, synergy arises when all domains are activated and supported simultaneously, providing a strong foundation upon which sustainable competitive

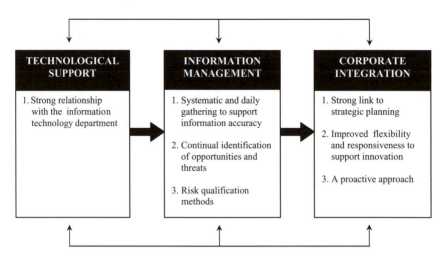

Figure 3.1 Representation of global CI critical success factors, within three interrelated domains.

advantage can be achieved. The key success factors associated with each domain and their relevance to global CI are detailed in the individual descriptions of each domain.

Technological Support

Effective and integrative application of information technology (IT) is a key requirement for global success. IT improves collaboration and coordination of knowledge-sharing and intelligence efforts. Only companies capable of building a strong knowledge base will survive the customization and innovation challenges of a global economy (Kadayam, 2002). Aimed at harnessing the knowledge and intelligence of all employees, knowledge management instruments must provide extensive data about customers, competitors, suppliers, strategic alliances, and future opportunities and threats. Extensive collaboration between the IT and CI functions will guarantee alignment of organizational and technological requirements.

Traditional knowledge management routines are now being replaced by Mobilization of Collective Intelligence (MCI) strategies (Boshyk, 2001). This leading-edge practice is based on three core components: individual, organizational, and external intelligence. This approach offers a broad, future-oriented, dynamic, integrative, and innovative approach to data collection and management. Strong collaboration between CI and IT personnel will ensure that the proper technological base exists to support and maximize the benefits of the MCI approach.

The IT department also functions as a data quality gatekeeper, improving the relevance and user-friendly nature of global CI. Ultimately, the IT department, through its inter-, intra-, and extranet capabilities, serves as the channel for all intellectual and knowledge capital. A strong working relationship offers maximum benefits to both IT and CI functions.

Information Management

Information accuracy and timeliness gain importance in a global economy. To provide benefit and keep pace with dynamic industry forces, CI operations must be committed to systematic, daily, around-the-clock surveillance and data collection.

Proficiency at the data-gathering level will promote competence in the early identification of opportunities and threats. This is a key success factor in the development of sustainable, strategic competitive advantage. As organizations cultivate more inter-firm partnerships, in-depth intra-organizational understanding and industry and competitor awareness will maximize benefits and minimize risks associated with such ventures.

A method for qualifying the risk associated with strategic decision scenarios is critical in the analysis and reporting of global CI. As the complexity and quantity of strategic options increase, so will the demand for effective evaluation of their inherent strengths and weaknesses.

Corporate Integration

The dynamic nature of the intelligence age is hastening the acceptance of perpetual strategy (Tyson, 1988) as a premise for gaining sustainable competitive advantage. This approach requires continuous reengineering and constant monitoring of internal and external environments, including stakeholder actions and options. The development of perpetual strategy must be linked directly to strategic management processes through CI information management, analysis, and reporting operations.

Global CI processes and systems must remain flexible in their approach, adapting new methodologies and tactics as each unique situation demands. Cross-functional integration and decentralization of the global CI function are critical to building in the responsiveness required by the increased innovation and competitiveness of the global landscape. The amount and speed of information gathered are too great to be handled by the CI department alone (Hall, 2001). Reliance on unsystematic, unsophisticated techniques and information sources *must* end if a firm is to be successful in practicing global CI. Strong inter-functional relationships must be developed, supported, and sustained to properly diffuse the CI mandate throughout the organization.

To provide maximum benefit, global CI operations must adopt a more proactive approach to intelligence dissemination. Early warning intelligence derived through a strong information management process will allow CI departments to drive the adoption of new organizational concepts, processes, structures, products, technologies, and strategies. Such an approach will help gain the support of management—a fundamental requirement for the effective development and maintenance of new corporate priorities.

A FRAMEWORK FOR SUCCESS

Hitt, Keats, and DeMarie (1998) have noted that "successful globalization strategies will ultimately depend upon the advantages created by the intersection of technology, human capital, and culture." Global CI lies at the heart of this initiative, both driving and being driven by these three internal dimensions. Organizations pursuing best practice strategies in global CI must learn how to leverage these functionalities to best support the development of these three core dimensions.

In the Tripod framework shown in Figure 3.2, the global CI function is represented by the core inner triangle, connecting the three core dimensions of technology, human capital, and culture. Best practice organizations will establish CI structures, systems, and processes such that the function itself becomes "boundaryless"—embedded in routine organizational practices.

The development of an interconnected series of cross-functional relationships and processes related to technology, human capital, and cultural capabilities is portrayed through the solid wedges emanating from each apex of the inner triangle. The wedge-like shape denotes the bi-directional linkage between each dimension and the CI function. As the strength and number of these interrelationships increase, so does the pervasiveness of global CI practices within the organization. The ultimate goal for successful transnational corporations is to enlarge the size of the inner triangle to the extent that it merges directly and completely with each element of the tripod, creating a flexible, responsive, sustainable, and inimitable competitive advantage.

The three tripod domains (technology, human capital, and culture) should not be developed independently of one another. The interconnectedness of these three domains is depicted by the thinly lined, bi-directional arrows linking each element. Success in one dimension can directly or indirectly affect success in another, as illustrated in the following summaries.

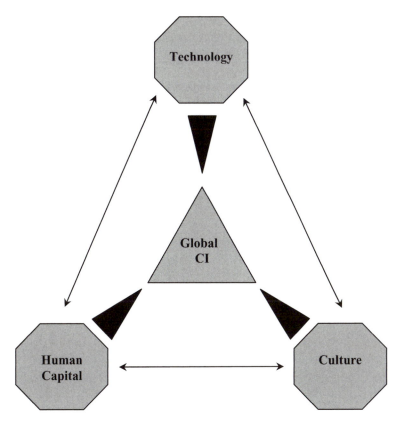

Figure 3.2 Tripod framework for establishing best practices in global CI.

Human Capital

Developing and sustaining a new form of leadership capable of under-standing cultural and market diversity will be fundamental to success in the new global economy. Referred to as strategic leadership (Talkington, 2001), cutting-edge and globally minded business leaders possess the fol-lowing characteristics (Simpkins, 1998):

- Intellectual and social curiosity
- Desire for acclimatization without assimilation
- Creative ability to seek and deconstruct veiled patterns
- Ability to adapt to unexpected developments and situations
- Strong intuition and awareness of their own cultural orientation

Individuals with these traits have the ability to identify and capitalize on existing opportunities and threats. CI practitioners must be aware of these pertinent characteristics and must commit to incorporating such individuals in their internal and external networking endeavors. Recruiting practices within the firm as well as within the CI function should encourage the hiring of these unique business leaders.

Adhering to integrative and proactive CI processes will further engage and motivate globally minded business leaders and will allow the organization to benefit from the synergies that arise when key individuals are involved in and committed to strategic visioning processes. Since organizational leaders are the fundamental drivers of culture (Simon, 1999), it is important for CI practitioners to utilize and advocate on behalf of globally minded business leaders.

Culture

To be successful in the intelligence age, companies must become knowledge-oriented learning organizations committed to information-sharing and diversity. Key factors of a knowledge-sharing culture are

- promotion of cost-effective exploitation of internal resources (Fraser, Marcella, & Middleton, 2000)
- encouragement of individual motivation and company innovation
- fostering of an atmosphere of trust

All these factors are prerequisites for the exploitation of competitive synergies. Affiliation with globally minded and internationally comprised executive leadership teams will assist in the formation of the appropriate internal environment.

In adapting to a changing global environment, organizations face many challenges and barriers stemming from internal sources. A strong interconnectedness between CI and the development of culture will help minimize potential barriers. Proactive promotion of global efforts and results will improve the value attributed to information and the identification and understanding of the threats and opportunities facing the organization.

Effective propagation and integration of CI enhances organizational learning by affecting the core dimensions in the following ways (Pole, Madsen, & Dishman, 2000):

- Questioning the status quo
- Decreasing complacency
- Challenging assumptions

- Minimizing corporate arrogance
- Increasing patterns of collaboration

Similarly, a strong connect to organizational culture allows improved marketing of CI outcomes and facilitates organizational change. Change efforts intertwine with organizational learning and intelligence networks. Together these accountabilities provide the proper forum for idea exchange, timely recognition and pursuit of potential synergies, and identification of opportunities and threats. A strong global CI function provides immeasurable value to the development of a learning culture.

Technology

Competition in today's global economy is built on an extensive knowledge foundation that promotes the technical and social aspects of information and knowledge sharing. Logical and effective systems and procedures that incorporate the most recent and most relevant technological innovations are required. Systems and procedures must be developed to adjust information-sharing rules and to encourage the active participation of all key stakeholders. The use of quality integrative technology can promote a knowledge-sharing culture and encourage the development of a learning organization.

Given that any strategic plan is only as good as the information upon which it is based (Montgomery & Weinberg, 1998), it is through collaboration with the global CI function that these synergies can be achieved as expertise on corporate needs and technological capabilities is exchanged.

COMPETITIVE BUSINESS APPLICATION

Many organizations, such as Dow Chemical Company, IBM, Motorola, Xerox, and American Express, are making advances in best practices of global CI (American Productivity and Quality Center, 1998).

Procter and Gamble (P&G), a U.S.-based consumer products company, offers approximately 250 distinct brand options in over 130 countries worldwide. Its global operations employ 106,000 individuals in over 80 countries. P&G's mission "to make life better" (Miller, 1999) for its nearly 5 billion consumers is supported by a focus on six core values.

- People
- Leadership
- Integrity
- Trust

- Ownership
- A passion for winning

Respect for the individual and mutual interdependence are the main principles to which P&G prescribes. Innovation through strategic focus is viewed as the cornerstone of the business.

Over the past five years, P&G has positioned itself as a forerunner in CI by undergoing a pivotal internal change process. The evolution has included, but not been restricted to, the following seven key stages (Miller, 1999):

1. Installation and implementation of *AskMe* knowledge-sharing software
2. Establishment of Innovation Net, an employee collaboration portal
3. Introduction of cross-functional teams
4. Reframing of interdepartmental and CI links
5. Support of diversity and a learning culture
6. Instatement of a Knowledge Council
7. Initiation of top-down support and visibility

Analysis of these stages alongside the components of the Triad framework clearly demonstrates why P&G is viewed as a global CI best practices organization. The company has recognized that the key to sustainable competitive advantage through innovation requires an intense and timely internal and external focus. All the modifications undertaken have advanced the company's ability to remain competitively responsive and proactive. This has allowed it to remain a strong competitive force within the boundaries of its industry. The company has altered its internal structures, processes, philosophies, and values to improve the ability of all employees to intensify their involvement and performance in all stages of strategic planning and implementation. In doing so, P&G has created a learning organization and culture that harnesses and maximizes the potential of all its employees and improves the firm's responsiveness to external opportunity and threats.

The Triad framework can be analyzed from two distinct perspectives. From the first perspective, changes to the three outer dimensions of technology, human capital, and culture result in changes to the inner global CI function. From the second perspective, alterations to global CI processes affect the three outer dimensions of technology, human capital, and culture.

Changes to Outer Dimensions Affect Inner Global CI Function

The introduction of knowledge-sharing and portal collaboration technologies has supported the development of a learning culture and allowed P&G to leverage the knowledge of each and every employee. Continued focus on technology, human capital, and culture has led P&G to develop a Knowledge Council that focuses on discovering new methods of accessing, utilizing, and implementing knowledge and knowledge management techniques. This corporate-wide best practice has ensured that the company remains at the forefront of technological and method-oriented innovations.

Top management support of a sharing culture and an acceptance and respect for diversity of individuals are core philosophies promoted throughout P&G. Now established as a learning organization, P&G offers all employees training and development in strategic planning. This effort helps to maximize company synergies, innovation strategies, and results. The institution of cross-functional teams has also supported the impact of this initiative by providing a procedural context in which information sharing can be maximized.

The change initiatives undergone at P&G have clearly targeted the elements of technology, human capital, and culture. They have also introduced company values, structures, and processes that reinforce and support the continued development of each of the key dimensions of technology, human capital, and culture, as represented in the Tripod framework. This inward wave of change supports all the key success factors within the three domains required for the development of a strong global CI function: technological support, information management, and corporate integration. In doing so, P&G has established a solid base into which a solid global CI function can be integrated.

Changes to Inner Global CI Function Affect Outer Dimensions

This immense change to the inner function has moved corporate global CI away from its report-focused beginnings toward an integrated platform in which structures and processes are inexplicably linked to a new culture that supports information sharing and strategic planning. In effect, the company has reframed the linkages between its global CI function and all other internal units. The introduction of approximately 30 cross-functional teams has helped support this initiative.

Decentralization of the global CI function has been initiated in order to improve collaboration and early identification of external threats and opportunities. Strong internal collaboration has been made possible through the development of key connections with the IT department. This has provided universal access to a company intranet, upon which relevant and timely information is shared on a continual basis.

This outward-moving change has allowed P&G to leverage its global CI function to assist in the development of its organizational change process and to support the integration of its technological, human capital, and cultural capabilities. In doing so, P&G now focuses not only on competitor strengths and weaknesses but also on new strategic business and market opportunities.

BENEFITS AND LIMITATIONS

The process of integrating CI within an organization such that it becomes a new way of thinking rather than a unique set of individual operations and processes can be challenging. The FIICH model for CI knowledge management processes (American Productivity and Quality Center, 1998) can provide direction to companies focused on pursuing best practices in global CI. This model is best used in conjunction with the above principles. The FIICH model consists of the five stages:

- Focus
- Implementation
- Institutionalization
- Change
- Honing

The FIICH model both reinforces the strategies and principles of the Triad framework and provides a procedure by which global CI functions can remain responsive and relevant.

It must be noted that production of actionable CI is an order qualifier for best practices in global CI. Success in global CI will not be achieved unless the organization has already committed to leveraging its information for action through a seven-stage focus: dynamism, decentralization, IT support, strategic linkages, customer analysis, comprehensive and timely analysis, and cultural integration (American Productivity and Quality Center, 1997).

Development of strong CI knowledge and infrastructure, as well as top management support, is the key to leveraging knowledge and instituting organizational change. Individual companies must ensure that they possess adequate technological resources and personnel expertise to carry forward all phases of corporate integration. In such a rapidly changing technological environment, this will be a difficult challenge. Without the full visual support of senior management, insurmountable barriers will manifest in counterproductive attitudes and resource unavailability.

This type of all-encompassing corporate systemic change and integration process requires an enormous time commitment. Companies seeking instantaneous results will be easily discouraged. Only those organizations committed to a long-term vision will stand to reap the benefits achievable under the globally focused, integrated, responsive system and culture.

Human capital will provide key advantage in the global economy. It is imperative that transnational companies both develop a culturally diverse workforce and learn how to use cultural differences to their advantage. Failing to do so will jeopardize all aspects of the integration process.

Even with the right people in place, multinational organizations must first value strategic processes and position their global CI units to assist them in both setting and achieving corporate objectives. A lack of strategic focus sets a formidable barrier to success in a global economy.

CONCLUSION

The new business landscape of the intelligence age is punctuated by continual disruption and change. Awareness of the three domains of global CI—technological support, information management, and corporate integration—and their related critical success factors is a must for organizations committed to achieving sustainable competitive advantage into the future. A complete understanding of the Triad framework offers great advantage to organizations pursuing competitive advantage in today's global economy. Exploration of the three domains of technology, human capital, and culture, and their relevant key success factors, can provide best practice organizations with a preliminary understanding of the base requirements for effective global CI. The Triad framework identifies the three core dimensions through which essential structural and procedural integrations must be made. It also reinforces the position and importance of an integrated global CI function. P&G is emerging as a leader in the field of CI. Through its global CI initiatives, it has asserted itself as a best practice organization against which others must compete.

REFERENCES

American Productivity and Quality Center. (1997). *Competitive and Business Intelligence: Leveraging Information for Action.* Consortium Benchmarking Study Best Practice Report. Houston, TX: American Productivity and Quality Center.

American Productivity and Quality Center. (1998). *Managing Competitive Intelligence Knowledge in a Global Economy.* Consortium Benchmarking Study Best Practice Report. Houston, TX: American Productivity and Quality Center.

Boshyk, Y. (2001). "Beyond Knowledge Management: How Companies Mobilize Experience." *Financial Post* (May 29): M10.

Fraser, V., R. Marcella, and I. Middleton. (2000). "Employee Perceptions of Knowledge Sharing: Employment Threat or Synergy for the Greater Good." *Competitive Intelligence Review* 11(2): 39–52.

Hall, C. (2001). "The Intelligent Puzzle." *Competitive Intelligence Review* 12(4): 3–14.

Hitt, M.A., B.W. Keats, and S.M. DeMarie. (1998). "Navigating in the New Competitive Landscape: Building Strategic Flexibility and Competitive Advantage in the Twenty-first Century." *The Academy of Management Executive* 12(4): 22–42.

Kadayam, S. (2002). "The New Business Intelligence." *KM World* 11(1): S6–S7.

Miller, S.H. (1999). "CI of 'Singular Importance' Says Procter and Gamble's Chairman." *Competitive Intelligence Magazine* 2(3): 5–7.

Montgomery, D.B., and C.B. Weinberg. (1998). "Toward Strategic Intelligence Systems." *Marketing Management* 6(4): 44–52.

Pole, J.G., E. Madsen, and P. Dishman. (2000). "Competitive Intelligence as a Construct for Organizational Change." *Competitive Intelligence Review* 11(4): 25–31.

Roukis, G.S., H. Conway, and B.H. Charnov. [eds.] (1990). *Global Corporate Intelligence: Opportunities, Technologies, and Threats in the 1990's*. Westport, CT: Quorum Books.

Simon, N.J. (1999). "The Effects of Organizational Culture on the CI Process." *Competitive Intelligence Review* 10(1): 62–70.

Simpkins, R.A. (1998). "The Global Mind." Competitive *Intelligence Magazine* 1(2): 34–36.

Talkington, A. (2001). "Global Leadership: What Chemical Industry CEO's Think about Managing the Global Enterprise." *Chemical Market Reporter* 260(3): 34.

Tyson, K.W.M. (1988). "Perpetual Strategy: A Twenty-first Century Essential." *Strategy & Leadership* 26(1): 14–18.

4

Moving from a Domestic to a Global Competitive Intelligence Perspective: Learning from World-Class Benchmark Firms

Jeff MacDonald and David L. Blenkhorn

Companies that are expanding internationally take care not to assume that their successful domestic competitive intelligence (CI) programs will serve their global requirements. Due to the many different external variables that exist in foreign countries, international CI (ICI) programs are more complex than domestic programs. Some of the more important differences are listed in Table 4.1. Research (Ganesh, Miree, & Prescott, 2003) shows that the basics of CI are practiced around the world, but little is known about the factors that influence country-specific operations. Also, multinational firms show a lack of knowledge about coordinating CI practice globally. Stanat and Seydel (2002) point out key areas to observe when conducting CI in the expanding European Union (EU), and these areas can be extrapolated to apply to global CI. This chapter attempts to fill this void in knowledge about moving from domestic-focused CI to a global focus by examining the differences between domestic and international CI programs and offering methods and strategies through which companies can successfully execute their advancement into global CI. The objective is to demonstrate ICI complexities and the areas upon which domestic companies should focus when looking to expand their operations to global marketplaces. Failure to recognize the additional pitfalls that ICI presents in the design and implementation of ICI programs can easily result in the failure of the intelligence program. In contrast, the ability to build plans to address or avoid complex ICI pitfalls will result in more successful programs that harvest actionable information and lead to greater international success. This chapter will assess how best practice companies develop CI infrastructures to leverage

Table 4.1
Global CI Complexity

Key factors that vary among countries and complicate global competitive intelligence (ICI) in comparison to domestic competitive intelligence (DCI) include

- Macro-economic variability
- Regulatory variability
- Political variability
- Language and linguistic context interpretation variability
- Consumer preference variability
- Consumer wealth variability
- Business ethics variability
- Employee loyalty variability
- Internal company culture variability

- Physical infrastructure variability
- Communication infrastructure variability
- Technology variability
- Intensity of competition variability
- Raw and human resource variability
- Inter-cultural and inter-country regional histories
- Varying norms of cultural interaction

knowledge, regardless of where in the world it was produced. Further, this chapter will build upon the existing best practice literature to provide a framework for companies contemplating conducting CI on a global basis.

LEARNING FROM WORLD CLASS BENCHMARK FIRMS

Over the years, the American Productivity and Quality Center has conducted benchmarking studies identifying processes that leading-edge companies use in their CI programs. One of their studies (Prescott, Herring, & Panfely, 1998) identified seven key findings of successful CI programs, and they serve as a good starting point to examine the complexities of an international versus a domestic CI program. A follow-up study applied their findings to firms conducting CI in a global context (American Productivity and Quality Center, 1998).

The following sections explain the basic American Productivity and Quality Center's seven-step research framework enhanced by the added complexity of the global dimension.

Evolving, yet Stable, CI Infrastructure

The American Productivity and Quality Center (1998) study found that successful companies had the following four essential components of an effective CI infrastructure.

1. Experienced personnel who successfully developed CI programs in several different business units
2. Staged development of CI networks

3. Dispersed CI champions at all levels of the organization
4. Entrenched CI cultures held by all employees

These essential components hold true both domestically and on the international stage, although international execution is more difficult for the reasons cited in Table 4.1. Domestic companies may have individuals with both company and industry experience at a domestic level, but they may not possess international experience. Those individuals possessing the full suite of desired experience are difficult to find or develop. Successfully entrenching company culture and developing remote CI champions when entering new countries is a large hurdle to overcome.

Decentralized Coordinated Networks

Decentralized CI networks are crucial to ensuring that local information is picked up close to the source and acted upon quickly. Coordinating information networks over larger geographies and countries is key for a multinational company to compete effectively on a global basis. A company expanding internationally must first focus on establishing local networks (employee, supplier, distribution, media, regulatory, governmental, financial information pipelines, etc.) within a new country to ensure survival against direct competition in the new market. Learning how local networks function in foreign countries can be a daunting task for a company entering foreign territory. Differences in business practices, corporate ethics, information incentives, and competition laws must be understood prior to entering a new country or geographic region. The ability to hire local staff who understand the business culture of the entering company and also are well versed in the target country's business practices will certainly help speed the setup of local CI networks.

Once local networks are well established and are functioning, the company must work at coordinating its local and central networks to harvest information that will pick up on international trends, opportunities, threats, and so on, and advance its global competitiveness.

Responsive Information Technology (IT) System Operating as a Learning Tool

A domestic company entering a new country either as a start-up or through acquisition will have IT challenges, including difficulties with its CI systems. The new country may have different IT infrastructures (access, band-width, operating languages, etc.), different employee IT literacy, and, if entering by acquisition, the new company will most likely not have systems that are directly compatible with the existing domestic system.

Beyond the software and hardware issues, employees in the new country may speak languages different from the primary language used in the parent company. In order to design IT systems that can be used as international learning tools, certain standards of communication must be developed and utilized by all who use the systems. In addition, the system that is created must be responsive enough to meet the varying information requirements in different countries, which are based on local business needs. The coordination of systems will take time to complete, and the most important immediate need will be the capability of local systems and processes to meet local needs, followed by their integration into the company's global systems. Entering companies must avoid the pitfall of believing that their existing systems will meet all the business requirements in a new country. Keeping an open mind and learning how to adapt systems to meet unique local requirements are essential for international success.

Linkages

The American Productivity and Quality Center (1998) study identified that successful companies are proficient at linking the strategic planning process with the tactical components within the organization and establishing a circular feedback loop focusing on continual improvement between the two. A company that has done this well domestically will have several additional factors to consider in operationalizing strategic goals in foreign countries. Operating tactics may have to be quite different in each foreign country in order to reach common strategic goals. For example, if growth of market share is a strategic goal for the company, the tactical approach may be basement pricing in a country with intense competition for the product, while in another country with a highly affluent population, the strategy may be above-average pricing designed to convey a quality image. Effective local competitive and market intelligence systems that assimilate into company-wide systems allow multinational companies to succeed in reaching their strategic goals by using different tactical approaches in different countries. Continual monitoring of success and circular feedback between local operations and central strategy-makers will improve upon existing linkages.

Customer-Feedback-Implementation Linkage

Similar to the linkages described above, local operators in different countries will have varied—and often dissimilar—CI requirements to assess and implement local tactical options. International companies must be even more sensitive to these local operators' requirements than domestic companies to ensure that the central CI staff is meeting the needs of local operators. Differences in business environments, languages, local competitors, and regulations all have the potential to create misunderstandings between central and local employees. Dedicated attention to understanding local CI requests, bilateral participation in the creation and implementation of processes, and follow-up on the effectiveness of processes will create better systems and, most important, will serve as a learning tool to better understand international business practices and cultures.

Hypothesis-Driven Recommendations

The American Productivity and Quality Center (1998) study found that successful companies had CI operations that were able to make recommendations through hypothesis-testing and were able to infer greater meaning from the recommendations resulting from the hypothesis-testing by custom-formatting the recommendations for different audiences. Through consistent demonstration of their capabilities, successful CI departments build essential credibility.

This success factor becomes more complicated when moving from domestic to international operations. An international company must learn how to best format presentations and information for managers in different countries who speak different languages and have different customs and business cultures. To build credibility takes time when employees in a foreign country are skeptical of the parent company, especially following an acquisition.

Institutionalizing Intelligence Cultures

Developing CI in the company culture to the degree that every employee understands that contributing to CI is an essential part of his or her job is probably the most difficult CI success factor to instill within an organization. In addition to understanding their CI role, employees must know how to share CI information within the firm (thereby creating a learning organization). Both domestic and international companies move toward this culture by utilizing senior management champions, marketing CI capabilities to all employees, and offering incentive activities. International firms will have to involve senior management at a local level, break down cross-border suspicions, encourage trust, and utilize an array of incentive programs effective in different countries. Consistent reinforcement of CI in the company culture that is backed up by the demonstration of tangible results will pay dividends over time.

OVERCOMING INTERNATIONAL OBSTACLES

The seven key findings of the American Productivity and Quality Center (1998) study hold true for both domestic and international CI programs. Additional obstacles and pitfalls exist on several levels (refer to Chapter 1 for an elaboration of these obstacles and pitfalls) and must be overcome in making the leap from a DCI program to a successful ICI program. Figure 4.1 summarizes some of the considerations required for a successful international CI program in the context of the Diamond-E framework.

The focal point of Figure 4.1 is the *Strategy* box, which highlights a key objective of CI—to provide actionable intelligence that enables management to make better strategic decisions. Because the global dimension affects many key decisions in today's corporate environment, it is critical that any CI input to these decisions transcends a domestic-level perspective and reaches an international one. Key inputs into the strategic decisions are multiple influencing factors, which are categorized in Figure 4.1 as *Management Preferences, Organization, Resources,* and *Environment.*

Management Preferences at the head office of a multinational company with a global perspective are often at odds with individual country managers, who sometimes fail to see the "big picture." This can affect both the liaison with and the directions to the CI people. The CI function must clearly understand and carefully manage any conflicting objectives from these two groups to ensure that any actionable intelligence provides optimal value to the organization as a whole, while at the same time securing the buy-in of any affected country managers.

The *Organization* itself can present conflicting signals to the successful implementation of global CI. In a multinational company, often the resources of the head office and multiple in-country locations differ greatly. Typically, the parent company or head office location garners the prime resources and expertise, and in-country operations often fare much less well. This can affect both the quality and expediency of CI operations, especially in a disbursed or decentralized CI organization.

Resources are always an issue in global CI and are much more far-reaching than financial resources. In many in-country disbursed locations around the globe, it is necessary to develop local resources and capabilities. Reliable sources of data/information and contacts, often taken for granted in the home country, may be non-existent or very difficult to obtain in remote locations. The key challenge to the centralized CI operation is to integrate all the parent company and head office and local in-country resources into a CI system benefiting the organization as a whole, as well as each in-country user.

The *Environment* in which global CI is conducted is multifaceted and complex; many of its components are often trivialized or completely

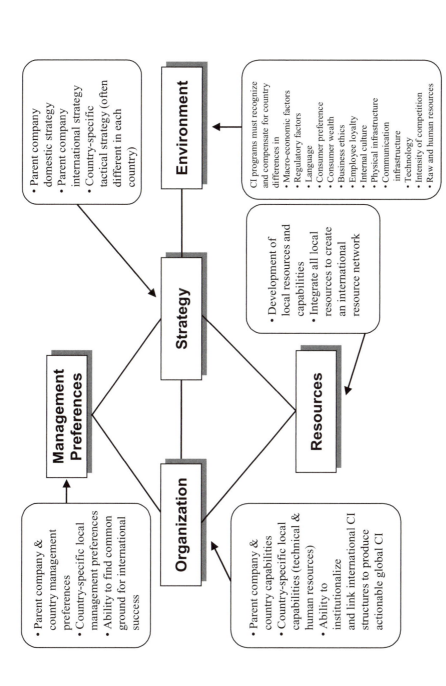

Figure 4.1 International CI: Multiple Influencing Factors (*Source:* adapted from Crossan, Fry & Killing [2002]).

misunderstood by the CI practitioner looking through a domestic CI lens. Figure 4.1 lists the key environmental factors of which the global CI function must be cognizant. These multiple influencing factors are elaborated upon in depth in many of the other chapters in this book.

THE TRANSFORMATION FROM DOMESTIC TO GLOBAL CI

Expanding horizons from practicing domestic CI to global CI is not a natural evolution, although the uninitiated may so believe. In her article "Seven Steps to Global CI," Robertson (1998) states:

> The reasons for establishing international competitive intelligence are the same drivers that propel domestic intelligence operations. Assessing competitors and potential suppliers, new market opportunities, and other changes in the market become vital for successful product launches and marketing initiatives when these are internationally constructed. The challenges posed by international CI can seem insurmountable to a domestically focused CI organization, but don't be dissuaded.

The American Productivity and Quality Center benchmarking study entitled *Managing Competitive Intelligence Knowledge in a Global Economy* (American Productivity and Quality Center, 1998) used the FIICH (Focus, Implement, Institutionalize, Change, Hone) model to describe how best-in-class companies organize their ICI programs. Using the FIICH template, this chapter proposes a step approach for companies to use when making the jump from a DCI to an ICI program. The steps are illustrated in Figure 4.2.

Step 1: Focus the CI Knowledge Management Efforts

A company should begin designing an ICI program with the end results in mind, which, to be effective, should include as a minimum the following elements.

- Improved market knowledge
- Improved cross-functional relationships within the overall organization
- Greater confidence in making strategic plans at both the international and the local levels
- Improved product quality versus the competition
- Improved risk identification and risk minimization (Gilad, 2003)

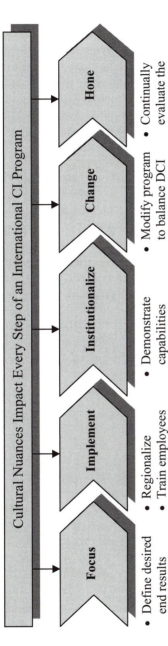

Cultural Nuances Impact Every Step of an International CI Program

Focus
- Define desired end results
- Involve senior management
- Define immediate requirements
- Resource gap analysis
- Learn local cultural nuances
- Set operating ethics
- Plan sequential stages

Implement
- Regionalize
- Train employees
- Fulfill local intelligence needs
- Challenge all information
- Utilize local employees and resources
- Standardize practices

Institutionalize
- Demonstrate capabilities
- Market CI
- Develop CI initiatives
- Involve business partners
- Begin to establish links to international CI requirements

Change
- Modify program to balance DCI and ICI requirements
- Drive international CI program integration

Hone
- Continually evaluate the focus and whether program is fulfilling its mandate
- Modify program or focus as required

Figure 4.2 Developing an International Competitive Intelligence Program.

- Improved opportunity identification
- Improved international competitiveness
- Continuous process improvement

Ensuring senior management support of and participation in ICI program development is vital right from the beginning. The company should define how it will go about obtaining the desired results in stages and what resource gaps need to be bridged at each stage. Given that a comprehensive DCI program can take three to five years to implement, a company can expect that a good deal of time will be required to develop and implement an effective ICI program (Society of Management Accountants of Canada, 1996). A company should define what information is critical in the short, medium, and long term. Local intelligence requirements are of first priority to ensure local survival. The largest resource or knowledge gap in a foreign country will be a lack of cultural knowledge. A company will have to invest in a deep understanding and a broad general knowledge of the new country before it can develop specialized actionable intelligence (Werther, 1997). Further, the company will have to ensure that it understands local customs, communication intricacies, business ethics, regulations, and government relations. The company will have to decide upon how it will operate within the new context, set business and ethical standards, and convey that information to all its employees.

Step 2: Implement CI Knowledge Creation

In the initial implementation phase, the company should develop the organizational culture to establish and utilize CI knowledge. Training of employees, providing tools, and reinforcing the importance of CI in a persistent and rewarding manner will help develop the required culture. Reliance on local employees familiar with the norms and culture of the new country will help build local CI data quickly while avoiding the roadblocks a foreign employee may encounter. Primary sources of local data will come from local papers, local governmental census data, local consultants, and local suppliers. No matter how reliable the local data may appear, it is important that a company new to a region challenge all information until it is comfortable with the integrity of the source. With an eye to the future, the company should ensure as much as possible that it is standardizing its CI practices and tools with those that it had domestically so that future integration will be facilitated. SAP (www.sap.com), a leading international software producer, provides a good example of a company with extensive experience at standardizing information technology source text for future integration into broader systems.

Step 3: Institutionalize

Now that the company has set up networks to gather and analyze CI data in the new country, it is important to incorporate the practices into daily activities. Senior management should continue to communicate the importance of the CI functions to all employees, stressing that CI is a part of everyone's job. The company should begin to demonstrate to its employees the tangible results of the CI analysis being conducted and begin to market the CI capabilities or product line to local management. This is the time to begin broadening the CI net and developing relationships with suppliers and business partners in sharing information. In addition, the company should begin to establish links between its new regional CI programs, and its existing home country or international CI programs.

Step 4: Change

At this stage, the company should have a fairly well established and effective CI network operating in the new country. In order to realize the end goals set out in the original focus, the company must now drive full integration of its international CI programs; it should also begin to harvest global trends while continuing to meet each country's intelligence requirements. It is the synergy of the combined programs that will ultimately help develop and sustain international competitive advantage. The benefits of establishing standardized processes and systems at the beginning of program development are realized at the integration stage.

Step 5: Hone

As the ICI program matures, it is important to revisit the effectiveness of the program focus and the ability to deliver intelligence in support of this focus. Changes in global economies, competitor profiles, resources, and suppliers, among many other factors, can alter the effectiveness of the program. Continual improvement of the program is mandatory to ensure that the intelligence generated is effective and is always a best practice.

CONCLUSION

Moving from an established domestic CI program into the world of international CI can be a difficult process. Many cultural and resource obstacles will have to be overcome through a focused plan of staged integration involving heavy investment in employee training, participatory buy-in, and standardized tools. Based on the successful CI practice of world-class benchmark firms, this chapter has set out a methodology which firms can follow as they transition from domestic to globally focused CI. The resulting integrated international CI program will certainly be an internal competency that will provide competitive advantage over those competitors without a similar program. The management phrase "think globally, act locally" rings true both for today's globally focused world of business in general and for competitive intelligence in particular.

REFERENCES

American Productivity and Quality Center. (1998). *Managing Competitive Intelligence Knowledge in a Global Economy.* Houston, TX: American Productivity and Quality Center.

Crossan, M.M., J.N. Fry, and J.P. Killing. (2002). *Strategic Analysis and Action.* 5th ed. Toronto, ON: Prentice-Hall Canada Inc.

Ganesh, U., C.E. Miree, and J.E. Prescott. (2003). "Competitive Intelligence Field Research: Moving the Field Forward by Setting a Research Agenda." *Journal of Competitive Intelligence and Management* 1(1): 1–12.

Gilad, B. (2003). "The Next Step in the Evolution of Competitive Intelligence." *Academy Of Competitive Intelligence.* http://www.academyci.com/Resource Center/articles.html.

Prescott, J.E., J.P. Herring, and P. Panfely. (1998). "Leveraging Information for Action: A Look into the Competitive and Business Intelligence Consortium Benchmarking Study." *Competitive Intelligence Review* 9(1): 4–12.

Robertson, M.F. (1998). "Seven Steps to Global CI." *Competitive Intelligence Magazine* 1(2): 29–33.

Society of Management Accountants of Canada. (1996). *Developing Comprehensive Competitive Intelligence.* Management Accounting Guideline 39. Hamilton, ON: Society of Management Accountants of Canada.

Stanat, R., and J. Seydel. (2002). "Conducting Business Intelligence Gathering in Europe: Seven Key Areas." *Competitive Intelligence Magazine* 5(6): 34–37.

Werther, G.F.A. (1997). "Doing Business in the New World Disorder." *Competitive Intelligence Review* 8(4): 2–18.

5

Process Differences in Performing Global versus Domestic Competitive Intelligence Data Collection

Tracy Annett

"Why do successful companies fail? They fail because they no longer know how to read market signals" (Gilad, 1994). Managers today will agree that information is the basis for being able to decipher and read these market signals. Information is even more crucial in the global business environment that exists today, "where entirely new parameters and environments are encountered" (Czinkota, 1991). Therefore, the focus of this chapter is to identify the key differences that exist in performing global versus domestic competitive intelligence (CI) information or data collection. The objectives of this chapter are to address the following:

- Where does data collection fit into the CI process?
- Should global data collection be addressed differently from its domestic counterpart?
- What (if any) are the differences between global versus domestic data collection?
- What are the implications to the CI professional who is responsible for global CI?

This chapter will not provide a directory of the various sources of available global information. However, it is hoped that in answering the cited questions, the CI professional will better understand important steps in global data collection that will maximize effectiveness and provide insight on the necessary information to acquire.

THE IMPORTANCE OF THE DATA COLLECTION PHASE

Why focus on the data collection component of the CI process? The collection stage plays a key part in the quality, relevancy, and timeliness of the CI. There is a common saying in the CI profession that "garbage in equals garbage out." Therefore, it is important for the CI professional to avoid costly pitfalls when conducting CI. Examples of pitfalls include utilizing only easy-to-find resources, collecting too much data (resulting in data overload), or spending 80% of time and resources on the collection stage and leaving only 20% of time and resources for analysis.

The following list provides examples of what a formalized CI program, when implemented correctly, can help a company do (Kahaner, 1996):

- Anticipate changes in the workplace
- Anticipate actions of competitors
- Discover new or potential competitors or suppliers
- Learn from the successes or failures of others
- Increase the quality of acquisition targets and also the success of acquisitions
- Learn about new technologies, products, and processes that may impact the business
- Learn about political, legislative, or regulatory changes that may impact the business
- Assess new market opportunities

It is evident from the literature that due to the rapid pace of technological change, which has fueled the increasing pace of business and has made available vast amounts of information, companies need to have formalized CI programs now more than ever. In addition to rapid advancements in technology, the dynamic business environment has seen an increase in global competition, more aggressive competition from new and existing competitors, and rapid political changes (Kahaner, 1996). Managers also recognize that CI is the foundation for a competitive advantage (Prescott & Gibbons, 1993) and has the potential to minimize risk (Miller, 2000).

THE GLOBAL BUSINESS ENVIRONMENT AND CI

Why is there a need to look at international information collection? The previous section discussed the intense global business environment that exists today. To be successful in this global business environment, firms need to improve their foreign trade performance (Calof, 1997). This presents many challenges to the company that is immediately faced with language, cultural, and information barriers. In order to improve foreign trade performance, a company needs to have market information (Calof, 1997); to be able to conduct global business successfully, it needs an understanding of the critical elements of business practices (e.g., the decision environment) (Hoetker, 1996). This type of information may not be obvious in an unfamiliar business environment because there are special challenges that arise when conducting global CI, including the following (Hoetker, 1996):

- Without a good understanding of the critical elements of the foreign business environment, it is difficult to formulate the questions that need to be answered. These questions are the foundation for the data collection component of the CI process.
- It is more difficult to acquire data without knowledge of useful sources and an understanding of the language.
- Without an understanding of the cultural norms, it is difficult to interpret the data.

Therefore, the CI professional needs to be aware that special challenges exist for global CI data collection. From this awareness arises the question, "What are the differences between global data collection and domestic data collection, and how significant are they?"

Global versus Domestic Data Collection

Jonathan Calof, of the University of Ottawa, Canada, has prepared a discussion paper containing the results of a study that examines what information is most important to Canadian exporters and what sources of information are most important. The study, which was done by the Canadian government, also identifies the differences in the data collection process needs for more intensive exporters versus less intensive exporters (Calof, 1997). Over 200 Canadian exporters with varying degrees of export experience participated in this study. The survey format was similar to that of a domestic study completed in the United States by Prescott and Bhardwaj in 1995 (Calof, 1997). Calof compared the results of the two surveys to assess the differences between them. A summary of the findings is presented in Table 5.1.

He found that differences do exist between global and domestic data collection needs. The most important global information needs include identifying recommended agents, customer profiles, competitors, decision-makers, and decision criteria, as well as understanding the

Table 5.1
Differences between Domestic and Global CI

	Domestic	Global
Information Needs	• Industry trends • Identify potential competitors	• Identify recommended agents and customer profiles • Profile major competitors • Identify decision-makers and decision criteria • Determine administrative structure
Additional Data Needs for Intense Exporter	• N/A	• Advanced knowledge of tenders • Contact information for contract administers • Greater emphasis on local intelligence (competitors, customer profiles, and management practices)
Valuable Information Sources	• Computer databases and published sources	• Use of overseas personal contacts and foreign clients • Government agencies (e.g., embassies) • Trade fairs used to gather market intelligence • Commission a study to help develop market entry strategies
Other Differences	• Aware of competitors • Better understanding of customers and decision-making structure • Advantage of being immersed in culture	• Barriers (e.g., geographical, language, and cultural) may inhibit developing relationships required to gain market and customer knowledge

Source: Adapted from Calof (1997).

administrative structure (Calof, 1997). Domestic information needs focus on industry trends and on the identification of potential competitors, since information is already understood about the decision-makers and criteria (Calof, 1997). Differences also exist in terms of the most valuable sources of information. Based on the survey results, the most valuable information sources for global data collection include the use of personal contacts overseas, foreign clients, and government agencies (e.g., embassies) (Calof, 1997). Trade fairs are used to collect global market intelligence, and more intense exporters often commission studies to help in the development of market entry strategies (Calof, 1997). The most valuable information sources identified for domestic data collection include computer databases and published sources.

In addition to presenting the findings of the 1997 Calof study, this chapter looks at the findings of a literature review that identifies additional dimensions that distinguish the process of global CI data collection from its domestic counterpart. These dimensions—technology, information structure, and the decision environment—are discussed next.

Technology

Technological differences need to be considered when conducting global data collection. For example, key tools for collecting domestic data include telephones and computers. However, the status of "technologies for the production, storage, movement, analysis, and timing of information vary dramatically across countries" (Prescott & Gibbons, 1993). A case in point is that one of these technologies, Internet databases, has been established in North America for companies to inquire about online government tenders, but similar databases have not been established in other countries (Calof, 1997).

Information Structure

It is also important to gain an understanding of the information structure of the country in which the data collection is being performed, since the structure varies from one country to the next. It is important to realize that differences exist in published global information availability and reliability (Calof, 1997). "Countries vary in the types, timeliness, accuracy, and motives for data collection" (Prescott & Gibbons, 1993). For example, some countries have tight control on information, while others have no established data collection processes (Calof, 1997). The CI professional will need to find the most accurate and reliable sources of information. This requirement will raise several issues: Do the banks hold the most valuable information? Can newspapers be relied upon for unbiased information or is there strong government control? Is information found on the Internet reliable? In addition, other sources of information include government publications, trade associations, and informal information flows that exist at conferences and in study groups (Hoetker, 1996). Calof (1997) recommends that using caution when dealing with local data sources and contacting information intermediaries (e.g., embassies, chambers of commerce, staff located in foreign markets, suppliers or customers) is a good starting point to confirm the validity of data sources. As well, information intermediaries can provide an understanding of how information flows (Hoetker, 1996) and can shed light on the barriers and rituals of information collection in the country in which they are dealing. This is very important because the ethical standards for data collection practices also vary from country to country (Prescott & Gibbons, 1993).

Decision Environment

Country-specific information influences global competitive intelligence initiatives. It is necessary for the CI professional to understand how informational differences can act as competitive stimulants or constraints and, ultimately, how these differences affect the decision environment (Sheinin, 1996). According to Sheinin (1996), the differing decision environments in which companies operate is dependent on five forms of intelligence criteria: sociological, educational, economic, political, and geographic. Sociological intelligence encompasses cultural values and assesses attitudes related both to success and to authority and cooperation. Education intelligence is the process of evaluating educational standards by determining level, capacity, trainability, skills, transferability, and technology adaptability in the foreign country. Economic intelligence involves evaluating economic policies and standards. Political intelligence encompasses a review of the political environment in which the company must operate. Geographic intelligence includes an evaluation of the geographic criteria that relates to competition. It is necessary to evaluate these forms of intelligence to determine the environment the company operates in and its relation to business competition and position. A summary of the intelligence criteria and factors affecting the decision environment is presented in Table 5.2. The CI professional must answer these questions in order to evaluate the success or failure of business potential, specifically the courses of action required to enter and compete within foreign markets (Robertson, 1998).

Summary of Differences between Global and Domestic CI Data Collection

In summary, differences do exist between global and domestic data collection. The CI professional needs to be aware of these differences and challenges in order to avoid the costly mistake of assuming that what is important for domestic data collection also applies to its global counterpart. The following section offers the CI professional guidelines for performing effective global data collection.

GLOBAL DATA COLLECTION GUIDELINES FOR THE CI PRACTITIONER

What steps should CI professionals take to achieve effective global data collection in the pursuit of global competitiveness? Based on a literature review, this chapter presents guidelines composed of the following steps for the CI professional:

Table 5.2
Summary of Intelligence Criteria that Affect the Decision Environment

Intelligence Criteria	Factors Affecting Decision Environment
Sociological	• Does the culture view achievement and work as goals? • What is the view of wealth and material gain in that particular country's culture and business practices? • Are people willing to take on a reasonable degree of risk? • Do people embrace change or are they adverse to change? • Does the society adhere to communism or socialism? • What is the general attitude toward managers? • Are people able to advance in the workforce? • What is the relationship between unions and management?
Educational	• What is the general literary level? • Is specialized vocational or technical training available? • Is secondary and post-secondary education available? • Does management development training exist? • What is the general attitude toward education? • How well does education match the requirements of the workforce?
Economic	Factors affecting economic policy: • Does the country have an expansive or restrictive competitive environment? • Does the country favor domestic business? • Does the country accept foreign competition? • Do profit margins justify investment costs and associated risk? Factors affecting economic standards: • What is the basis of the economic system (e.g., private or public)? • Does market freedom exist (e.g., is there competition or restrictions)? • Is there monetary stability? • What is the extent of government controls (e.g., pricing, production, policies)? • What are the required labor policies? • What is the level of management quality? • Does the company adhere to global competitive market concepts (e.g., TQM)?
Political	• What are the laws, customs, and ethics that regulate competition? • What is the defense and national security policy? • Does the foreign policy affect foreign alliances and trade? • Does political stability exist? • What is the political organization within that particular country?
Geographic	• Identify target markets and understand demographics. • What are the different language and dialect locations? • How does climate and seasonality affect when products are produced and shipped? • What types of transportation and distribution networks are available? • Are adequate raw materials available? • What are the cost and nature of power or energy sources available?

Source: Adapted from Sheinin (1996).

- Conduct an internal audit.
- Get involved in the CI process early and define the CI project.
- Overcome cultural and language barriers.
- Create an intelligence map to focus research and sources.
- Complete a benchmark study against other companies with effective global CI units.

Each of the five steps is further discussed in the following sections.

Internal Audit

It is recommended that CI professionals conduct an internal audit to better understand the global intelligence resources already in existence within their company (Fuld, 1995). This audit will provide an inventory of company experts and resources that have not already been catalogued in the internal library (Fuld, 1995). As well, this process will highlight any gaps within internal knowledge and sources prior to engaging external sources (Robertson, 1998). The process can be kept simple by auditing one department or regional office at a time. During the audit process, the information can be compiled into a database management program or data warehouse so that all employees will have access (Fuld, 1995). A benefit of the audit is that the process promotes communication and centralization of information. This is an important step to dissolving any potential boundaries and global data silos that may exist within the company (Liautaud, 2001). The CI professional may also take this opportunity to communicate the value of the CI department to managers as a means of gaining buy-in from employees and senior management.

Early Involvement

In order for the CI professional to gain a sense of the reasons underlying the request for CI and to identify the proper questions to ask when conducting global data collection, it is necessary that he or she become involved in the CI process as early as possible (Hoetker, 1996). In the findings presented by Czinkota (1991), information needs differed depending on the stage of market research required—a finding that reiterates the importance of a CI professional's early involvement. When a company is in the preliminary market-screening stage, it is more beneficial to collect general information, rather than specific information, about the physical, political, economic, and cultural environment (Czinkota, 1991). In contrast, when a company is analyzing the market potential and market access information, more detailed information (trade limitations, tariff levels, legal restrictions, local production, and consumption, etc.) is necessary (Czinkota, 1991).

Early involvement is not enough to ensure a successful CI project. During the project definition phase, the CI professional needs to "ensure that all parties involved know and understand the nature of the assignment, the expertise required to develop the information, and the analytical processes used to generate the competitive intelligence" (Elizondo & Glitman, 2002). There are two important decisions the CI professional must make in completing global CI:

- What needs to be done?
- Which way to go?

To make the first decision, the CI professional must clearly define the project and understand the business objective, the intelligence users' needs, how the CI will be used, and the CI components essential to making the decision (Elizondo & Glitman, 2002). To determine which way to go, the following questions must be answered by the CI professionals during project definition (Elizondo & Glitman, 2002).

- Can you deliver the project using only internal resources?
- Do you have to subcontract portions to specialists?
- If subcontracting, do you use domestic specialists or specialists from the target market?
- If you use target market specialists, how do you identify qualified candidates, ensure quality control, and establish ethical standards?

In summary, it is critical that the CI professional get involved in the CI process early and clearly define the CI project objectives by collaborating with intelligence users. This is necessary for the CI professional to understand internal capabilities and needs prior to commencing the CI project, which can ultimately save both time and money over the course of the project (Elizondo & Glitman, 2002).

Overcome Cultural and Language Barriers

Once the CI professional has defined the intelligence needs, the next step is to understand the cultural context that affects the competitive environment. A good starting point is to answer the questions for each of the intelligence criteria presented in Table 5.2 (sociological, educational, economic, political, and geographic). An understanding of the cultural differences and social norms, and how both of these factors impact the competitive environment, will affect how well the CI professional gathers, analyzes, and applies the acquired intelligence (Fuld, 1995). This is a critical step, and the following example illustrates the importance of understanding cultural differences and social norms.

In North America it is acceptable to conduct primary research over the telephone via cold calling—an information-gathering methodology that is considered reasonably unobtrusive (Elizondo & Glitman, 2003). However, this tool is less effective in countries that place a high value on personal contact. In Japan, for example, "a person who answers a cold call will be very polite, uneasy and reluctant to talk about business matters" (Elizondo & Glitman, 2003). This example raises the issue of obtaining guidance in dealing with the multitude of different languages around the globe. Fuld (1995) offers several recommendations to overcome language barriers:

- Use your competitors' weak spots by applying the rule, "Wherever money is exchanged, so is information."
- Utilize local universities.
- Use your own employees who may speak another language or who have lived abroad.
- Use ethnic clubs.
- Use translation services.

These recommendations may offer a starting point when confronted with a foreign language in the data collection process.

It may be discovered that the most cost-effective and time-effective means to overcome cultural, language, and other barriers to performing CI is to use a specialist located within the target market. A local specialist may be able to advise the CI professional on social norms, may be familiar with the language skills needed to conduct secondary research, and will have local knowledge (Elizondo & Glitman, 2003). When hiring a local specialist (under subcontract or partnering), some factors to consider in selecting the best candidate include (Elizondo & Glitman, 2002):

- Staff availability and expertise
- Language skills
- Country expertise
- Equipment
- Confidentiality
- Reputation
- Ethics

It is also necessary to define the scope of the CI project and to budget for a local specialist in order to avoid poor communication of CI results or CI materials that will not be valuable to the intelligence user (Elizondo & Glitman, 2002).

Create an Intelligence Map

Fuld (1995) defines an intelligence map as "a country's information picture, a navigation chart for reaching your research destination. It uses the laws of the Ripple Effect and Intelligence Antennas to help shape your international research approach" (Fuld, 1995). Fuld defines the Ripple Effect law as "Information is most available at its source and becomes less available the farther it travels away from that source" (Fuld, 1995). The Intelligence Antennas law asserts that "each country or region has a set of intelligence antennas that act as information magnets and are superior in picking up and absorbing information in that country or region" (Fuld, 1995). Examples of intelligence antennas include government, regulations, technology, banks, and associations, and they vary from country to country (Fuld, 1995). To create an intelligence map, select and then list the best sources of intelligence antennas in order of importance and usability (Fuld, 1995). The intelligence map is a good starting point for the CI practitioner's data-gathering strategy. It should be noted that the development of a new intelligence map for a particular country could be a lengthy process. It may take the CI professional a long time to source out the most reliable data-intelligence antennas in each country and to develop the relationships necessary to acquire useful information.

Benchmark Analysis

The CI practitioner can complete a benchmark analysis to determine what other companies are doing well in terms of making rapid changes to compete in the global environment. Once the components that enable these companies to do well have been established, specific to global CI, the CI professional can make recommendations to management regarding those activities that should be adopted by their own company. Why should a CI practitioner whose company competes in the global business environment pay attention to other companies and foreign competitors? North American companies may have experienced lost market share to strong foreign competitors. For example, recall how the Japanese have taken away market share over the years in the automobile and electronics industries. The Japanese have picked America's brains by borrowing or buying technology and then selling it back to the United States in the form of finished products; they have also sent many of their engineers and students to study at American universities (Moffat, 1991). For many years there were too many barriers for U.S. companies to collect information on Japanese technology. These barriers included the lack of technology available to outsiders or for sale, as well as slow and expensive translation processes. These barriers are by no means insurmountable, however. Eastman Kodak is one example of how U.S. companies are overcoming global barriers, collecting ideas on new technologies before they appear in the United States, and developing relationships with Japanese universities, companies, and government agencies (Moffat, 1991). In the early 1990s, Eastman Kodak built a $70 million research center in Yokohama, Japan. The next step involved recruiting top scientists, funding research at universities, and providing scholarships to Japanese university students. Eastman Kodak reported that establishing a presence in Japan has opened up opportunities to develop relationships and gain access to technological information (Moffat, 1991). Eastman Kodak is a good example of how competitive information was acquired in the country of origin, which is always the best form of information.

CONCLUSION

Differences do exist between domestic and global data collection. Therefore, a CI professional cannot assume that the same processes that are effective for domestic data collection will be as effective for collecting global CI. These differences exist in the global environment due to unique barriers, including not knowing the information structure and decision environment, ignorance of relevant and reliable sources, limited access to sources, geographic barriers, and language and cultural barriers (Hoetker, 1996). Based on a literature review, this chapter has presented five guidelines for the CI professional to follow to establish an effective global data collection system. The guidelines include completing an internal global intelligence audit, getting involved in the CI process early in order to identify CI needs, overcoming cultural and language barriers, creating an intelligence map, and completing a benchmark study against other companies that have been successful in implementing global CI units. A CI professional may be required to invest much time and many resources to build a reliable global resources base. However, this process can help businesses achieve benefits in the long term. They will make better global business decisions, complete a successful global market entry, increase speed to market, and maintain a global competitive advantage.

REFERENCES

Calof, J. (1997). "So You Want to Go International? What Information Do You Need and Where Will You Get It?" *Working Paper 97-51* (December). Ottawa, ON: University of Ottawa.

Czinkota, M.R. (1991). "International Information Needs for U.S. Competitiveness." *Business Horizons* 34(6): 86–91.

Elizondo, N., and E. Glitman. (2002). "Cross-Border CI: Laying the Groundwork." *Competitive Intelligence Magazine* 5(6): 43–44.

Elizondo, N., and E. Glitman. (2003). "Modifying the Tool Set for Collection and Analysis." *Competitive Intelligence Magazine* 6(1): 42–43.

Fuld, L.M. (1995). *The New Competitor Intelligence: The Complete Resource for Finding, Analyzing, and Using Information about Your Competitors*. New York: John Wiley and Sons.

Gilad, B. (1994). *Business Blindspots: Replacing Your Company's Entrenched and Outdated Myths, Beliefs, and Assumptions with the Realities of Today's Markets*. Chicago, IL: Probus Publishing Company.

Hoetker, G. (1996). "Taking the Competitive Intelligence Effort Overseas: Four Special Challenges." *Competitive Intelligence Review* 7(2): 3–10.

Kahaner, L.K. (1996). *Competitive Intelligence: From Black Ops to Boardrooms—How Businesses Gather, Analyze, and Use Information to Succeed in the Global Marketplace*. New York: Simon & Schuster.

Liautaud, B. (2001). *E-Business Intelligence: Turning Information into Knowledge into Profit*. New York: McGraw-Hill.

Miller, J. [ed.] (2000). *Millennium Intelligence: Understanding and Conducting Competitive Intelligence in the Digital Age*. Medford, NJ: CyberAge Books.

Moffat, S. (1991). "Picking Japan's Research Brains." *Fortune* 123(6): 84–96.

Prescott, J.E., and P.T. Gibbons. (1993). "Global Competitive Intelligence: An Overview," pp. 1–27 in J.E. Prescott and P.T. Gibbons [eds.], *Global Perspectives on Competitive Intelligence*. Alexandria, VA: Society of Competitive Intelligence Practitioners.

Robertson, M.F. (1998). "Seven Step to Global CI." *Competitive Intelligence Magazine* 1(2): 29–33.

Sheinin, C.E. (1996). "Global CI: Assessing Global Competition." *Competitive Intelligence Review* 7(3): 86–88.

THE GLOBAL COMPETITIVE INTELLIGENCE ENVIRONMENT

6

Key Laws Governing the Practice of Competitive Intelligence in Global Business

Michelle Sandilands

Competitive intelligence (CI) practitioners working in the increasingly global business environment must be aware of all laws and regulations governing the practice of their profession. As businesses expand internationally, all corporate practices need to be verified to ensure they are operating lawfully within each new country. This is also true of a company's CI practices. For example, a legal means of collecting information about a competitor in Canada may be considered unlawful in Japan. In addition, a company should adjust its level of information security depending on the amount of protection offered within each country. If a country's laws are too lax, a company will have to improve its internal security to maintain a consistent level of defense.

Although most countries use the principle of trade secrets as the legal basis to protect a company's information, the application and enforcement of these laws varies significantly. This chapter explores the concept of trade secrets and its application in national and international laws and treaties. These laws are compared and contrasted by region, and the implications for CI practitioners working within these regions are discussed. Finally, this chapter provides a discussion regarding the future trend toward economic espionage and the introduction of more stringent laws.

BASIC LEGAL PRINCIPLE: TRADE SECRETS

CI is the legal and ethical collection and analysis of public information. CI practitioners working globally need to be aware of and understand all pertinent international laws and policies. Practitioners may be subject to the laws of the nation in which they are practicing, whether or not the act is physically committed in that nation. It is possible that someone gathering information in another country while residing in the United States will be subject to the jurisdiction of that other country (Ehrlich, 1998). The *territorial principle* states that a nation can exercise jurisdiction over a crime beyond its territory if it can show legitimate interest in the event or party.

Trade secret protection laws are the predominant means of controlling the practice of CI. A "trade secret" refers to any information that is not commonly known in the relevant industry and is used by a business to gain a competitive advantage. To qualify as a trade secret, the information must be proven to be secret, identifiable, and not easily determined (Magri, 1997). A trade secret can be an organizational structure, a design or formula, financial information, or customer list.

There are three primary legal theories that are used by legal regimes to protect trade secrets: contractual obligation, fiduciary relation, and misappropriation theories (Torres, 2001). Contractual obligation is the duty not to divulge or use trade secrets when a contract is in place that includes secrecy or a confidentiality commitment. Employment contracts, licensing agreements, and consultant contracts typically include this type of clause. The fiduciary relation theory suggests that, in some relations, there is an implied duty of secrecy. Therefore, confidentiality can be expected in some situations without an implicit secrecy agreement. The misappropriation theory states that trade secrets should not be obtained through improper means. Although reverse engineering is an acceptable means of obtaining a trade secret, theft is not. Therefore, while collecting information for synthesis into intelligence, CI practitioners have to ensure that they are not breaching any contractual or fiduciary obligations and that the information is being collected legally. Otherwise they could be held criminally or civilly liable.

NATIONAL LAWS

This section outlines the trade secret laws that influence the CI profession in four trading regions: North America, Europe, Asia, and Latin America. These four regions were selected because the countries within these regions have similar economic development, trade within the region, and impose similar trading restrictions and regulations.

North America

Trade secrets in the United States have traditionally been regulated by the common law of individual states. The state laws are all adaptations of the 1979 Uniform Trade Secrets Act.[1] To qualify as a trade secret, the information has to be distinguishable from general knowledge, a secret (or information that is not well known), of some value reflected in competitive advantage, and protected by the holder's reasonable measures to maintain secrecy. The legal protection comes in recognizing the misappropriation of a trade secret as an illegal act. Under state law, only civil claims can be brought against offenders. However, misappropriation of a trade secret also falls under the following federal statutes. The Economic Espionage Act[2] (USC, sections 1831–1839), the mail and wire fraud statutes[3] (18 USC, sections 1341 and 1343), and the Racketeer Influenced and Corrupt Organizations Act[4] (18 USC, sections 1961–1968). Under these statutes, misappropriation of a trade secret becomes a criminal charge (Ehrlich, 1998). The Economic Espionage Act (EEA), passed in 1996, makes stealing or obtaining trade secrets by fraud a federal crime. The EEA also contains an extraterritoriality clause, which extends the application of the act to U.S. citizens while abroad and non-citizens while on U.S. soil or abroad (Horowitz, 1999). In summary, the United States uses the misappropriation theory to protect trade secrets. Violations can result in civil and criminal charges. Criminal charges can be brought against anyone, regardless of U.S. citizenship and the location of the offense.

In Canada, breach of confidence is the main protection available for trade secrets. The requirements for taking action for breach of confidence are that the information was confidential, it was communicated in confidence, and it was misused by the party to whom it was communicated (Torres, 2001). Fundamentally, Canada uses the fiduciary relation theory to regulate the misuse of confidential information.

Europe

In general, the European countries offer a high level of protection for trade secrets. England, Germany, and France are reluctant to consider trade secrets as property, so protection comes in the form of breach of confidence (fiduciary theory) and contract law. England's trade secret protection is based on the breach of confidence concept, very similar to Canada's position. It states that there is a confidence relation between the rightful holder of a secret and the receiver of the confidential information. Germany, in Section 1 of the German Act Against Unfair Competition,[5] holds responsible for damages a person commits a dishonest act while conducting business or for the purpose of competition (Torres, 2001). France protects factory or manufacturing secrets and commercial secrets through tort of unfair competition and contract law. European patents are obtained and regulated very differently than in Canada or the United States. In fact, quicker and superior protection is offered with the European trade secret laws and subsequently provides an attractive alternative to patents.

Asia

Historically, the intellectual property system in Japan operated contrary to that of the United States by circulating intellectual property throughout the industry. Due largely to increased trade and shifts in employment patterns, Japan has amended its Law of Unfair Competition[6] to protect any manufacturing process, marketing practice, or other useful technical or business information (Magri, 1997). This Japanese law prohibits six unfair acts of obtaining, disseminating, or using the trade secrets, making it similar to trade protection laws in Western nations. However, the Japanese law offers no protection during litigation, since all court proceedings are open to the public. There is also limited third-party liability if a third party receives misappropriated information without being aware of the illegal means used to obtain it. This third party may continue to use the information, even after being made aware of the misappropriation (Magri, 1997). Patenting processes and rights in Japan are considered expensive, lengthy, and ineffective, creating an incentive to protect valuable information as a trade secret instead of applying for patent protection.

Instead of protecting trade secrets, some Asian governments require that the trade secret be divulged. In China, in order to enter into a license agreement that contains trade secret information, the information has to receive government approval. If the approval is not granted or expires, the trade secret information can be made public. Although Indian law has since been modified, in 1977 Coca-Cola had to abandon their operations in India to protect their trade secrets. At that time, India required a transfer of technology from any foreign companies operating in India to its Indian shareholders. Coca-Cola was forced to leave the country to protect its trade secrets (Magri, 1997).

A cultural consideration for trade secret protection in Asia is their view of the law versus that of most Western countries. Asian countries view the law as a flexible body of rules that are subject to change by a governing organization (Tsuruoka, 2002), whereas most Western nations view it as a rigid set of regulations that are applied consistently. Most legal actions in Asia are decided on a case-by-case basis. In addition, Asians tend to be non-litigious people and will settle many disputes without involving the legal system. Disputes are often settled informally and usually involve some sort of monetary compensation. These factors should be considered when interpreting the law and its enforcement in Asia.

Latin America

The Latin American region has traditionally protected trade secrets under competition and labor laws. Trade secrets are protected under competition law only if they are released or appropriated through dishonest business practices (Torres, 2001). Labor laws, using the fiduciary relation theory, state that an employee should show loyalty to an employer by not using or disseminating confidential information. Since 1990, Argentina and Chile have made amendments to their national legislation and Mexico has made changes to establish a framework for economic integration under the North American Free Trade Agreement (NAFTA).

In 1996, the Argentinean legislature passed an act to protect undisclosed information. It gives protection to commercially valuable secret information, given that the rightful holder of that information took reasonable measures to keep it secret (Torres, 2001). In Brazil, unfair competition is regarded as any person who "discloses, exploits or uses, without previous consent, confidential knowledge, information, or data which may be used in industry, commerce, or service rendering, unless the object of protection is in the public domain or it is obvious to a skilled person" (Torres, 2001).

Mexico has quickly evolved from a country lacking any intellectual property protection to one that is starting to develop a world-class system (Serrano, 1998). In Mexico, an industrial secret is defined as "any confidential information with industrial application, which gives a competitive or economic advantage to a physical or moral person over their competitors, as long as the holder of such information adopted the sufficient means or systems to preserve its confidentiality and restricted access" (Torres, 2001). Enforcement is the responsibility of administrative groups like the Mexican Institute of Industrial Property (IMPI), which creates several disadvantages (Serrano, 1998). For example, a conflict of interest may arise in cases where the IMPI acts as both a party and judge. In addition, obtaining damages or attorney's fees is impossible in an IMPI procedure and a separate proceeding before a trial court has to be initiated.

REGIONAL AND INTERNATIONAL TREATIES

Regional and international treaties attempt to address the issue of trade secret protection and unfair competition, but none are harmonized and many provide only minimal frameworks. International treaties such as World Intellectual Property Organization (WIPO) and Agreement on Trade-Related Aspects of Intellectual Property Rights (TRIPS) merely provide minimum legal standards for intellectual property protection and rely on member countries to enforce them. Regional treaties—NAFTA, EU (European Union), and Mercosur (customs union involving Argentina,

Brazil, Paraguay, and Uruguay, commonly called Mercosur, an abbreviation of the Latin American phrase for Southern Common Market: *Mercado Común del Sur*)—were developed to protect trade secrets while encouraging free trade and competition. However, the protection of intellectual property rights will restrict competition and is therefore in direct conflict with the essence of these treaties.

Paris Convention

The WIPO is a specialized agency of the United Nations that deals with international treaties for the protection of intellectual property. There are 178 member nations, and one of the treaties supported by the WIPO is the Paris Convention for the Protection of Industrial Property.[7] The convention was enacted to discourage unfair competition, as outlined in the following article:

Article 10[bis]
[Unfair Competition]

    (1) The countries of the Union are bound to assure to nationals of such countries effective protection against unfair competition.
    (2) Any act of competition contrary to honest practices in industrial or commercial matters constitutes an act of unfair competition.

As a member of WIPO, a country must abide by this article. However, the convention lacks enforcement provisions and consequently cannot be governed legally.

Trade-Related Aspects of Intellectual Property Rights (TRIPS)

The World Trade Organization (WTO) is the only global international organization that deals with the rules of trade among nations. All decisions are made through negotiations among the 144 member countries. In 1986, the Agreement on Trade-Related Aspects of Intellectual Property Rights (TRIPS)[8] was developed at the Uruguay Round of the General Agreement on Tariffs and Trade (GATT). The agreement sets forth provisions for protection of undisclosed information in Section 7.

Section 7: Protection of Undisclosed Information
Article 39 (2)

Natural and legal persons shall have the possibility of preventing information lawfully within their control from being disclosed to, acquired by, or used by others without their consent in a manner contrary to honest commercial practices so long as such information:

(a) is secret in the sense that it is not, as a body or in the precise configuration and assembly the circles that normally deal with the kind of information in question;

(b) has commercial value because it is secret; and

(c) has been subject to reasonable steps under the circumstances, by the person lawfully in control of the information, to keep it secret.

The TRIPS agreement requires each member country to set up a national enforcement system to protect intellectual property as addressed in Section 7. Other important characteristics of the agreement are a dispute settlement mechanism and a council in charge of monitoring domestic compliance.

North American Free Trade Agreement (NAFTA)

The NAFTA[9] also has provisions for ensuring trade secret protection among Canada, the United States, and Mexico. The agreement sets forth provisions for trade secret protection in Article 1711:

Article 1711: Trade Secrets

Each party shall provide the legal means for any person to prevent trade secrets from being disclosed to, acquired by, or used by others without the consent of the person lawfully in control of the information in a manner contrary to honest commercial practices, in so far as:

(a) the information is secret in the sense that it is not, as a body or in the precise configuration and assembly of its components, generally known among or readily accessible to persons that normally deal with the kind of information in question;

(b) the information has actual or potential commercial value because it is secret; and

(c) the person lawfully in control of the information has taken reasonable steps under the circumstances to keep it secret.

Article 1711 of the NAFTA is almost identical to the TRIPS agreement, with the exception of the definition of commercial value. The NAFTA agreement also protects information that has future or potential commercial value, as well as information that has existing value.

European Union (EU)

The EU does not have any specific legal provisions for trade secret protection. National laws are generally applied to resolve trade secret disputes. However, EU policy was created to ensure free trade and competition among the member countries, which conflicts with the idea of trade secret protection. The exercise of industrial or commercial property rights restricts competition, since the purpose is to give the owners some protection against competition by giving them monopoly rights for a period of time as a reward for their creative endeavor (Torres, 2001). Since conflict exists with trade secret protection in the EU, continued regional protection is in question.

Mercosur (Mercado Común del Sur)

Mercosur is an integrated economic region including Brazil, Argentina, Paraguay, and Uruguay as member countries. Very little success has been reached in developing intellectual property protection agreements, since Mercosur also faces the problem of conflict between industrial property protection and the policy of free competition (Torres, 2001).

IMPLICATIONS FOR CI

Laws regulating CI are all based on the principle of trade secret protection. Although all nations apply different laws and enforcement techniques, the principle of protecting trade secrets is consistent. Various international treaties have been developed to try to standardize intellectual property protection and provide guidelines for minimum legal standards across the globe. This standardization will encourage global investment, trade, and information-sharing.

North America and Europe have mature economies and developed legal systems. Asia and Latin America, however, are developing economies and are only just beginning to update and improve their competition and intellectual property laws. They are making the changes to encourage investment in their countries and promote trade with developed countries. Although Asia and Latin America are improving their laws, they lack strength and consistency in their legal systems with regard to enforcement. This leaves companies uncertain as to whether or not their trade secrets will be protected, and it makes these countries risky for investment and trade.

Implications of these international laws and regulations on global CI practitioners can be summarized as follows:

- Always be careful collecting information that can be construed as a trade secret, unless it is proven to be public information.
- Avoid coercing employees or ex-employees, since some countries make it unlawful to disseminate confidential information even without it being stated explicitly in an employment contract.
- Be careful of third-party liability, which some countries will enforce.

- Understand the laws, enforcement, and trial systems fully before beginning to practice in another country.

The implications of these laws for a company or for CI practitioners setting up an information security program can be summarized as follows:

- Always make trade secrets confidential and take all necessary means to prevent disclosure.
- Prepare complete employee contracts to ensure that confidential information cannot be divulged lawfully.
- Understand the foreign laws and court systems fully to make choices between pursuing legal retribution and preventing disclosure of intellectual property.
- Understand all legal implications fully before entering a new country, for example, limited third-party liability.

FUTURE TRENDS: ECONOMIC ESPIONAGE

An emerging topic in the field of CI is economic espionage. It is defined as "illegal, clandestine, coercive, or deceptive activity engaged in or facilitated by a foreign government designed to gain unauthorized access to economic intelligence, such as proprietary information or technology, for economic advantage" (Canadian Security Intelligence Service, 2000). Conversely, industrial espionage refers to the clandestine collection of information by companies and individuals against their competitors (Porteous, 1994). During a U.S. Chamber of Commerce symposium on February 9, 1999, Thomas Donahue (Chamber president) estimated losses of US$2 billion per month due to economic espionage (Canadian Security Intelligence Service, 2000).

The termination of the Cold War ended much of the global political and military espionage, and countries are now turning their intelligence units to economic use. An increasing number of countries, including the United Kingdom, United States, Australia, South Africa, and Russia, have made public declarations stating that they are using their intelligence organizations to conduct economic espionage and to protect against the economic espionage efforts of other nations (Kelly, 1999). Government intelligence is being used to provide counterintelligence support and economic intelligence to government decision-makers; monitor trade agreements; collect information on unfair practices; monitor "special activities" designed to influence events, behavior, or policy formulation in foreign lands; and pursue commercial information and technologies for favored commercial groups (Porteous, 1995, 1993). An example of such economic espionage is provided by a 1994 case in which a Japanese public television film crew visited dozens of U.S. biotechnology companies while filming a documentary on the industry. Although one affected company, Amgen, was alerted to the possibility that it was a cover for intelligence collection, it allowed the film crew to continue with hopes that it would improve Amgen's chances of breaking into the Japanese market. The crew filmed every document it could find (Pasternak & Witkin, 1996).

When President Clinton declared that the federal government would help the "Big Three" auto companies in an effort to improve American automotive technology, it was believed that the Central Intelligence Agency (CIA) would be instrumental in collecting intelligence. Although the Canadian Security Intelligence Service (CSIS) has made no official statement regarding its role in economic intelligence, there does appear to be an increased interest in the economic and commercial world.

Information that is commonly targeted through economic espionage includes product designs, marketing plans, bid proposals, pricing structures, and customer lists. Common methods of gaining this information are through planting a mole in the corporation to extract secrets, hiring individuals away from companies at salaries four to five times higher than their current salaries, and obtaining information from disgruntled employees and ex-employees setting up consulting firms (Cilluffo, 1998).

While economic espionage is a threat to national security, it is not necessarily illegal. It came as a shock to many in Britain to learn that a firm admitting to a three-year operation of surveillance, searching trash and briefcases, and planting a mole at their competitor's head office had done nothing illegal under current British law (Porteous, 1994). France passed a new law in 1994 to expand the definition of spying from the military and political spheres to include industrial operations as well. It purportedly also makes the collection of some open-source information illegal. Many illegal collection methods can be hidden in legitimate activities, making them more difficult to discover. Also, the line between industrial and economic espionage is often blurred because it is difficult to prove state sponsorship (Cilluffo, 1998).

Companies feel a reluctance to report known incidents of economic espionage because of a fear of adversely affecting stock prices and consumer confidence. In addition, employees may lose their jobs, copycats may be inadvertently invited by revealing weaknesses, and competitors may take advantage of negative publicity. In fact, 42% of all surveyed corporations have never reported a suspected incident of economic espionage (Pasternak & Witkin, 1996).

Economic espionage is booming because few penalties exist for those who are caught. Rarely do economic spies spend time in jail, nor are countries that encourage such activities often penalized. This trend will compel countries and international organizations to introduce stricter laws in an effort to quell the pursuit of economic gains through espionage. In the

United States, for example, the Economic Espionage Act was introduced so that the courts can now criminally charge anyone, irrespective of citizenship or location, of a fraudulent act. However, only international agreements that include an enforcement agency will be able to penalize violators and thus reduce government involvement.

CONCLUSION

Laws and regulations governing international practitioners of CI are all based on the concept of the protection of trade secrets. Global investment has been the driving force for many of the international changes because companies are reluctant to invest in a country if intellectual property can be easily exposed. Although international treaties have set minimum legal standards, it is still left to the individual countries to implement the laws and develop methods of enforcement. It remains to be seen if some individual countries are capable of fulfilling their international responsibilities by providing meaningful and effective enforcement mechanisms. Different cultural values and a country's stage of technological development can undermine the international goal of trade secret protection (Torres, 2001). CI practitioners and companies interested in pursuing opportunities in foreign countries need to completely understand the legal systems of those countries to ensure their CI efforts are legal. Equally important for CI practitioners is the need to protect their intellectual property when operating in countries with varying standards of protection. The trend of economic espionage should alert companies to the potential for highly sophisticated espionage operations within their walls. Increased international protection and enforcement, however, is expected in the future.

NOTES

1. The Uniform Trade Secrets Act of the U.S. Code is available at the website of the University of Pennsylvania Law School, http://www.law.upenn.edu/bll/ulc/fnact99/1980s/utsa85.htm.

2. The Economic Espionage Act of the U.S. Code is available at the website of the Society of Competitive Intelligence Professionals (SCIP), http://www.scip.org/Library/8(3)eea.pdf, or in the SCIP journal, *Competitive Intelligence Review* 1997, 8(3): 4–6.

3. The mail fraud and wire fraud statutes of the U.S. Code are available at the website of the U.S. Federal Department of Justice, http://www.usdoj.gov/usao/eousa/foia_reading_room/usam/title9/43mcrm.htm.

4. The Racketeer Influenced and Corrupt Organizations Act of the U.S. Code is available at the FindLaw website, http://caselaw.lp.findlaw.com/casecode/uscodes/18/parts/i/chapters/96/toc.html.

5. The German Act against Unfair Competition is available at the website of German patent law firm v. Bezold and Sozien, http://www.ip-firm.de/uwg_e.pdf.

6. An overview of the Japanese Law of Unfair Competition is available at the website of U.S. patent lawyers Myers Bigel, http://www.myersbigel.com/ts_articles/trade_secret3.htm.

7. The Paris Convention for the Protection of Intellectual Property is available at the website of the WIPO, http://www.wipo.int/clea/docs/en/wo/wo020en.htm.

8. Agreement on Trade-Related Aspects of Intellectual Property Rights is available at the website of the WTO, http://www.wto.org/english/docs_e/legal_e/27-trips.pdf.

9. The provisions regarding protection of intellectual property under the North American Free Trade Agreement are available at the website of the NAFTA Secretariat, http://www.nafta-sec-alena.org/english/nafta/chap-172.htm.

REFERENCES

Canadian Security Intelligence Service. (2000). "Economic Security." http://www.csis-scrs.gc.ca/eng/operat/es2_e.html.

Cilluffo, F.J. (1998). *Economic & Industrial Espionage.* Remarks to the World Economic Forum, Annual Meeting (January 31). http://www.csis.org/tnt/ao980131.html.

Ehrlich, C.P. (1998). "A Brief CI Compliance Manual." *Competitive Intelligence Review* 9(1): 28–37.

Horowitz, R. (1999). *Competitive Intelligence and the Economic Espionage Act: A Policy Analysis Adopted by the Society of Competitive Intelligence Professionals (SCIP) Board of Directors.* Alexandria, VA: Society of Competitive Intelligence Professionals.

Kelly, W.M. [chairman] (1999). "Economic Espionage," in *1999 Report of the Special Senate Committee on Security and Intelligence.* Ottawa, ON: Senate of the Government of Canada. http://www.csis-scrs.gc.ca/eng/operat/es2_e.html.

Magri, K.A. (1997). *International of Trade Secrets Law.* http://www.myersbigel.com/ts_articles/trade_secret3.htm.

Pasternak, D., and G. Witkin. (1996). "Industrial Espionage Threat, Japan and Others." *U.S. News and World Report* (May 6): http://vikingphoenix.com/politics/Election2000/Issues2000/NationalSecurity/frindesp.htm.

Porteous, S. (1993). "Economic Espionage." *Commentary: A Canadian Security Intelligence Service Publication* 32(May): http://www.csis-scrs.gc.ca/eng/comment/com32_e.html.

Porteous, S. (1994). "Economic Espionage (II)." *Commentary: A Canadian Security Intelligence Service Publication* 46(July): http://www.csis-scrs.gc.ca/eng/comment/com46_e.html.

Porteous, S. (1995). "Economic/Commercial Interests and Intelligence Services." *Commentary: A Canadian Security Intelligence Service Publication* 59(July): http://www.csis-scrs.gc.ca/eng/comment/com59_e.html.

Serrano, A.P. (1998). "Overview of Intellectual Property Enforcement in Mexico." Tucson, AZ: National Law Center for Inter-American Free Trade. http://www.natlaw.com/pubs/spmxip13.htm.

Torres, P.A.P. (2001). "Overview of International Trade Secret Protection." Tucson, AZ: National Law Center for Inter-American Free Trade. (February 15): http://natlaw.com/pubs/spmxip14.htm.

Tsuruoka, D. (2002). "Asian Perceptions of What Is Legal and Is Not Legal in Economic Intelligence Collection." Presentation Given at 2002 InfowarCon Conference on Cyber-Terrorism, Homeland Defense and Non Conventional Warfare. Norwalk, CT: Reed Exhibitions.

7

Global Competitive Intelligence in Top-Performing Companies

Rahim Kassam

The global economy has become the battleground for business competition, a game in which players struggle against each other to achieve profitable and sustainable advantages within the marketplace. Because there is no one final outcome, companies are consistently jockeying for position and trying to secure truly sustainable competitive advantage. Companies that have found a successful formula for playing "the game" have incorporated competitive intelligence (CI) programs into the formulation and implementation of their strategies.

This chapter explores how leading multinational companies have incorporated global CI into their strategic planning processes and how, in doing so, they have become successful in maintaining a sustainable competitive advantage over the competition. In particular, the focus will be on three multinational companies—3M, the Ford Motor Company, and Xerox. Specifically, the business strategies and practices of these three top global performers will be evaluated in order to ascertain the impact and value of global CI in the marketplace.

As defined by Prescott (1989), a CI program is "a formalized process by which a management team assesses the evolution of its industry, and the capabilities and behaviour of current and potential competitors in order to assist in maintaining or developing a competitive advantage." Prescott (1989) also notes that the role of a CI program can be addressed by answering the following five questions:

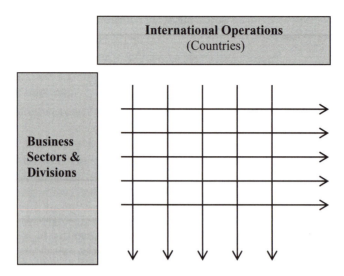

Figure 7.1 Organizational Structure of 3M Worldwide (*Source:* adapted from Gundling [2000]).

structured in such a way that each region and its major subsidiaries intersect with and are balanced by 3M's more than 40 business divisions, each of which has its own reporting lines (Gundling, 2000). Following a multi-level reporting matrix structure prevents the company from adopting a product or regional focus and instead encourages management as a whole to attend to the needs of consumers both on a local level and worldwide.

The development of global teams is yet another formal mechanism that has provided international employees the opportunity to work with U.S. counterparts in order "to bring a more intense focus, better cooperation, accelerated pace, and systematic follow-through to company efforts in markets where there are major growth opportunities" (Gundling, 2000). Mentoring programs allow workers from diverse specialties to share insight and innovative ideas with fellow associates situated in different parts of the world. Additionally, Corporate Enterprise Development is a 3M program used to identify and monitor new opportunities with significant export potential. New opportunities are identified by "tracking startup companies in relevant markets and technologies, allowing 3M to develop early business relationships while keeping abreast of new trends" (Gundling, 2000).

A key informal mechanism used to support innovation is friendship. The network of global contacts (or friends) built up through overseas travels, in combination with a low turnover of employees at 3M, has proved to be invaluable. This information network provides 3M with a competitive services" (Henderson, 2000). The Lead User Process is based on the realization that many products have their origins not in manufacturing companies such as 3M, but in the minds and workplaces of "everyday" people (Henderson, 2000). It is these lead users that are ahead of the market trends, and they should be consulted on ideas and plans for possibly innovative and effective products. The Lead User Process is about singling out lead users, learning from them, and creating solutions to address their needs. It will be only a matter of time before lead user needs become the needs of the consumer. Through the Lead User Process, the goal of 3M is to capture first-mover advantage by seeking out highly technical customer intelligence in order to satisfy a need that may act as a solution to a problem for the rest of the general market.

Eight 3M divisions to date have taken advantage of the Lead User Process for the purposes of innovation. Moreover, numerous other divisions will soon come on board. Although it is not a top-down, enforced approach to product development, the Lead User Process has been popularized by top company leaders and has generated positive feedback throughout this successful organization (Henderson, 2000).

3M's Pacing Plus Program

Management has also played an important role in the development of the unique culture at 3M. A number of processes have been developed to help maintain the company's competitive advantage in the industry. In particular, the Pacing Plus Program aids top management in establishing priority systems. With so many different products and services being offered by 3M, a process had to be developed that was effective at determining the most promising opportunities, as opposed to attempting to develop every possible idea that was presented. Promising projects that make it to the next level at 3M are defined as those that (Gundling, 2000)

- change the basis of competition in new or existing markets
- offer larger sales and profit potential, with attractive returns on investment
- receive priority access to 3M resources
- operate in an accelerated timeframe
- employ the best available product commercialization processes

In order for a product to proceed to the next level, intelligence must be gathered to determine what competitors are currently doing in the global market, what they are planning for the future, and whether the product in question could provide an advantage over the competition. If a new product could not be utilized to leverage the company into a more advantageous advantage that few corporations can match. "Trust, openness, mut commitment to a common enterprise—these are intangible but incredil valuable supports for innovative activity" (Gundling, 2000). Figure 7.2 flects the equal value that 3M ascribes to the formal and informal mecl nisms that have contributed to their strong innovation ethic.

A Culture That Promotes Information-Sharing

There are a number of other reasons why 3M has excelled in the area (global CI. One of the primary reasons is that the company has develope a culture that supports an information-sharing environment. "My exper ence is that the more we try to institutionalize CI, the less we seem to ac complish," notes David Drew (as quoted in Baatz, 1994), vice president o information technology for 3M. Drew also contends that "in intelligence it is more important to have the right people in the organization analyzing information than it is to have a system organizing information" (as quotec in Baatz, 1994).

To lower the costs and extra workload of keeping websites up to date in a host of languages, 3M Europe developed Webmaster, a web publishing application that allows 3M employees to put country-specific information into databases in their local languages (Gundling, 2000). These databases act as information pools, where employees can draw upon real-time data to generate web pages as customers post their inquiries and share corporate information and research created in different languages.

Gathering Intelligence from "Lead Users"

3M's innovative culture encourages employees to develop the Lead User Process. Intended to redefine the company's marketing strategy, this process offers a "systematic way for 3M's 55 divisions to identify new opportunities and quickly capitalize on them with appropriate strategies, products, and

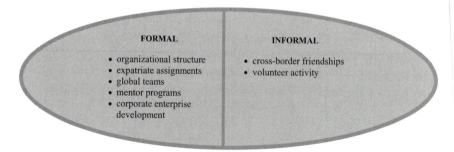

Figure 7.2 Formal and Informal Mechanisms Used to Support Global Innovation at 3M (*Source:* adapted from Gundling [2000]).

position, there would be no need for 3M to invest additional resources into a potentially lost cause.

GLOBAL CI AT THE FORD MOTOR COMPANY

In no other industry has competition among rivals been so intense on a global level as it has been in the automotive industry. Due to the cyclical nature of the business, rapidly changing technologies, and higher expectations of customers, automakers are forced to constantly monitor this volatile environment. Practices such as reverse engineering have been employed by Ford in the past to fully comprehend the design and possible cost structure of their competitors' cars (Prescott, 1989). Companies like Ford and Daimler Chrysler have in the past merged with other foreign automakers, seeking to become the dominant global leader in the automotive industry. The potential for mutual leverage of each party's research and development expertise, as well as the potential for merger partners to gain global reach and access to each other's customer and supplier base, are two of the primary advantages of international mergers.

Weathering the Japanese Storm

During the 1980s, Japanese automakers were stealing the show in the North American automobile market. Their lean production systems enabled them to produce cars that were more appealing to the North American market. Their product was also of superior quality and at a significantly lower price than that of their domestic rivals. This new production system was changing the competitive rules of the automotive industry, and Ford was aware that it had to change in order to survive. The retaliatory strategy involved exploiting Ford's superior competitive advantage of its foreign operations and integrating those operations on a global basis in order to reduce production costs and improve overall competitiveness (Studer-Noguez, 2002).

With Global Integration Comes Global Knowledge

With the transformation of Ford's organizational structure from a regional and functional structure to a matrix management system based on product lines, Ford implemented a corporate intranet that provided its workforce access to many of the company's resources such as product design, production management tools, and strategic information assets (Cronin, 1999). This information portal enabled its global user-base of approximately 200,000 to access more than 300,000 web pages from over 1,000 geographical locations. By providing employees with easier access to news clippings, stock prices, and other corporate data, Ford's aim was to boost productivity levels. Users could input personal web pages that could link to cost-saving business services such as electronic-paycheck presentation and text paging (Gladwin, 2001). In addition, internal websites for tracking design, production, quality control, and delivery were implemented for every model of car and truck.

Even though the human element of analysis is the most important part of CI, information technology plays a vital role in collecting and organizing data for a CI practitioner. When performing intelligence analysis for a multinational corporation, the importance of information technology is magnified. "Technology allows companies to do now what only countries could do previously" (Anthes, 1998). With over 80% of required information available in the public domain or from within the organization, Ford's corporate intranet allows its workforce to use the technology to post new information regarding their global competitors and any new developments anytime, anywhere. The information portal also acts as a tool for the CI practitioner to harness, organize, and index all information collected concerning the competition. Because top management and CI practitioners have real-time access to the information, this allows them to react more quickly to any new or emerging developments concerning their adversaries.

Global CI in Action: Hermosillo Assembly Plant, Mexico

Ford's investment in the Hermosillo assembly plant was the result of a joint venture with Mazda and was a competitive response to the joint venture between GM and Toyota at the NUMMI plant in California (Studer-Noguez, 2002). This American-Japanese partnership in Mexico is a case in point of CI at its best and clearly illustrates the successful transfer of technology in a cross-cultural environment.

Ford-Mazda conducted an extensive competitive analysis of all possible global options before ultimately selecting Hermosillo as the plant site. One principal reason was the geographic proximity of Hermosillo to the U.S. market. In addition, Mexico offered reduced transportation costs and lower wages, which in turn served to improve profitability margins. Weak labor unions in Mexico also contributed to the attractiveness of the region. Ford-Mazda also received substantial government incentives to locate in the country. Furthermore, due to growing political concerns regarding increased imports from Asia, the plant was not located there.

The Hermosillo Assembly Plant project has been considered a success in terms of product quality and manufacturing productivity. Consequently, Ford-Mazda was the first company of the Big Three to realize its Mexican operations. CI was utilized in disseminating the Japanese automotive manufacturing processes—the lean production system—and operationalized this information into the Mexican plant. Additionally, the plant was linked to Detroit's Lincoln-Mercury division and Mazda's plant in Japan, thus becoming fully integrated with the decision-making centers in Japan and the United States. The information received from global partners enabled Ford-Mazda to produce higher-quality cars that in turn proved to be a desirable commodity to consumers (Bannister, Muller, & Rehder, 1996).

GLOBAL CI AT XEROX: LEADING THE COMEBACK

The name Xerox has become synonymous with photocopiers and a multitude of other document-processing equipment. Even though the company has experienced many challenges, this global company is still considered one of the dominant leaders and innovators in the electronics industry. After the market share of Xerox was cut in half from 1976 to 1982 and the company was blindsided by one of its major competitors (Canon), CI played a dominant role in the company's resurgence.

Q: Who does CI within Xerox? A: The Lab

The CI activities at Xerox are split into global, national, and local levels that work in conjunction with each other. On a global basis, CI is conducted within the Xerox Business Divisions. These areas are concerned with developing products and services for a specific customer segment (Vezmar, 1996). The divisions seek out information that could possibly affect the long-term or strategic plans of Xerox. On a national level, the U.S. Customer Operations staff compiles and uses CI. On a local basis, Xerox has implemented 37 Customer Business Units across the country (Vezmar, 1996). These units are mandated with the task to search and interpret local data supplied by individual marketing managers, who are able to understand and explain the pricing strategies of other competitors and distributors in the industry.

Xerox also implemented a Competitive Evaluation Lab that is currently used to learn about research, and analyze market trends and competitors' products. Engineers perform reverse engineering applications to competitor products in order to determine the technology behind them and also to get an idea of the competitors' cost structures. Their goal is to identify and "understand every part, every feature, every strength, and every weakness, point for point" (Vezmar, 1996).

The Power of the People within Xerox

In order to take advantage of the wealth of knowledge that is available to the CI staff at Xerox, the company has developed a Competitive Hotline for their global sales force to telephone in competitive information. With the hotline accessible around the world, Xerox headquarters can be informed from anywhere in the world about developments regarding issues such as the location and identification of competitors worldwide, the industries they are in, and what applications they have. The power of human networks around the globe to share CI knowledge is a competitive advantage every company should possess. Monitoring competitive environments can become quite hindersome if a company is not well connected to its employees. The slightest piece of information can in some cases have an unquestionable impact on a multinational company. In addition, many CI representatives at Xerox have been able to nurture relationships with key Xerox people (American Productivity and Quality Center, 1998). By nurturing relationships with key members of the company, one can promote the cause and need of CI within the organization and also make it easier for people to approach one another and disclose information.

The Xerox Hotline has been successful in identifying new strategic actions required in order to remain competitive in the industry. An example of this occurred when a service representative received information about a competitor planning to offer service on Xerox products for the first time. This information was passed on to Xerox's CI group, who in fact verified this information with three additional clues—one being an advertisement in the classifieds for people with Xerox product experience (Naylor, 2000). This knowledge allowed Xerox to implement a counter-strategy to combat the announcement of the competitor's new service strategy.

Not only does Xerox receive information from its employees, the company also relies on its strong customer base for product improvements and possible new strategic direction. Xerox surveys approximately 5 million establishments around the United States—all current or potential customers— "and asks them what they value, what they do or don't like about our current competitors, and what they see as our strengths and weaknesses" (Vezmar, 1996). These data are transferred into a database that is accessible by sales representatives around the country. Armed with current and precise customer information, Xerox's marketing managers are able to develop strategies, and their sales representatives are able to anticipate customers needs.

Benchmarking to Rebound

After being blindsided in the early 1970s by its Japanese competitors, Xerox implemented a benchmarking strategy as part of its CI operation. The Japanese products were being introduced to the market in half the time, with one-quarter the design changes and one-third the expense. From 1976 to 1982, Xerox's market share and earnings had decreased by half. In order to get the company back on track, then-CEO David Kearns went to Fuji Xerox, a Japanese affiliate, to learn about its success. He bench-marked the Japanese quality processes, and upon his return to the United States he launched Xerox's own quality strategy, which helped the company regain market share and lead the industry once again. Clearly, competitive benchmarking still plays an active part in the success of Xerox.

THE SEVEN STEPS TO GLOBAL CI IN ACTION

All three multinational companies examined in this chapter have implemented the seven principles Robertson (1998) has deemed are required to successfully pursue global CI. For example, 3M assessed its current resources by identifying lead users within each of its company divisions to act as a knowledge base. These specialists are consulted for predicting future industry trends, allowing 3M to capture first-mover advantage in their respective markets. The Ford Motor Company has redesigned its corporate structure from a functional to a matrix management system. This non-hierarchical structure, supplemented by a wealth of information made accessible to employees via the corporate intranet, will enable Ford to become more responsive than its traditional hierarchical competitors and thereby maintain its dominant position in the automotive marketplace (Shaker & Gembicki, 1999). Finally, Xerox has assigned project leaders on a national and regional basis. This assignment allows for a single point of contact within the conglomerate and better coordination and sharing of information (Robertson, 1998).

OBSTACLES TO PERFORMING GLOBAL CI

When practitioners conduct global CI, they must be aware of cultural, societal, regulatory, legal, and economic factors that could be present in the data. Corporate and regional cultures influence the entire process of business intelligence. In order for CI analysts to gather, analyze, and plan strategy effectively, they must consider the competitor's cultural environment. It is important that the analysts assess the components that create the competitor's competitive advantage—domestically or globally—by becoming familiar with the cultures within the surrounding target company (Fuld, 1995). These factors can easily be overlooked during data collection or lost in the translation of data when the processes of business objectives are the focus. Fuld identified the following as the key components of cultural intelligence: national culture, location of the facility, overall economic climate, national government's culture, industry's culture, and company's corporate culture (Robertson, 1998). The ease with which intelligence is gathered, analyzed, and applied is dependent on its effect on global advantage, as well as on how well each of these cultural differences is understood. Conversely, if one is unfamiliar with the culture of a region or a company, signals sent out by overseas competitors or customers could possibly be misunderstood or misinterpreted (Fuld, 1995).

The presentation of results to decision-makers is another area of concern for a CI practitioner conducting global CI. Presentations need to be specifically tailored to the target audiences, whether domestic or foreign. Translating text presented into other languages could possibly become a concern if industry buzz words, company-specific terminology, or other non-translatable terms are used (Robertson, 1998). Therefore, a CI practitioner must be mindful not to translate information into anything that may inadvertently influence decisions of management when presenting to domestic or foreign audiences.

When performing global CI, it is also vital that while we continue to monitor what is going on in the global environment, we should not forget "what is happening in our own backyard." That is, it is important not to become so absorbed with what is happening outside one's organization that doing so detracts from focusing attention on what is happening internally within the organization. It is not always a deceitful competitor or an erratic customer that can cause harm to a company. There are multitudes of mundane ways a company can lose money that do not relate to the grand strategy. For example, while a company may be struggling with competitors to gain extra market share, a significant labor strike could inflict far greater damage on profits than the amount the "share war" might capture. A major strike by the United Auto Workers (UAW) against General Motors that cost the company over US$1 billion in profits in 1998 clearly illustrates why the primary focus must remain within the organization (Studer-Noguez, 2002).

Another problem that may arise is the leakage of information via departing employees, particularly with top management. With information being readily available in today's information-sharing environment, it is important to consider some form of security on certain proprietary information within the company. In most cases when employees leave, this issue is short lived and is treated as a risk of being in business. However, there may be some instances where it could become a major issue—usually when the damage is judged to be severe and the methods of passing on information can be proven to be illegal. The case of José Ignacio López (as well as a group of colleagues) leaving General Motors in 1993 to join Volkswagen is a prime example. This group of individuals was armed with enough information for General Motors to initiate a legal case against Volkswagen. General Motors ended up winning the case in 1997, gaining a US$1.1 billion settlement from Volkswagen. The legal team for General Motors claimed that the company had been victimized by international piracy and had been subject to unfair competition practices, citing the

Racketeer Influenced Corrupt Organization (RICO) Act in an attempt to protect intellectual property rights (Studer-Noguez, 2002).

CONCLUSION: BENEFITS TO PERFORMING GLOBAL CI

Through an evaluation of leading multinational companies—3M, the Ford Motor Company, and Xerox—this chapter has illustrated that there are numerous benefits to be derived from performing global CI. All three of these companies are considered global leaders in their industries, and each has incorporated CI into its strategic business planning and practices.

Today's global economy has become too competitive and fast paced for any company not to monitor its competition. Had Xerox not undertaken the benchmarking project with their Japanese partner Fuji, Xerox may not be in operation today. Xerox realized their corporate strategy had to be altered and undertook a benchmarking study on Japanese production methods. In addition, 3M's global network of partners and subsidiaries has enabled this company to keep its title as the "most innovative company" and allowed it to pull ahead of the competition. Ford has also been able to gain important intelligence information from its Japanese partner, Mazda; consequently, it saved US$2–3 billion in design costs when developing the Ford Focus—about-one-third to one-half the cost of its previous global car (Studer-Noguez, 2002). Without a company keeping an eye on the global arena, there is little evidence to show that it will successfully survive "the game." In the words of Frederick the Great, it is "pardonable to be defeated but never to be surprised."

REFERENCES

American Productivity and Quality Center. (1998). *Managing Competitive Intelligence Knowledge in a Global Economy*. Houston, TX: American Productivity and Quality Center.

Anthes, G.H. (1998). "Competitive Intelligence: IT Is Helping Companies Dig Up Vital Information on Their Archenemies." *Computerworld*. July 6. http://www.computerworld.com/news/1998/story/0,11280,31674,00.html.

Baatz, E.B. (1994). "The Quest for Corporate Smarts." *CIO* 7(21): 48–54.

Bannister, G.J., H.J. Muller, and R.R. Rehder. (1996). "Ford-Mazda's Hermosillo Assembly Plant: A Quality Benchmark Cross-Cultural Alliance." *Competitive Intelligence Review* 7(2): 11–19.

Cronin, M.J. (1999). "Nine Ways to Win on the Web—The Corporate Intranet: Ford Motor." *Fortune* 139(10): 115.

Fuld, L.M. (1995). *The New Competitor Intelligence: The Complete Resource for Finding, Analyzing, and Using Information about Your Competitors*. New York: John Wiley and Sons.

Gilad, B. (1998). "A Letter to a CEO, or What You Can Learn from the Corporate Chiefs at Microsoft, MTV, and the Hottest Tech Company Around." *Competitive Intelligence Magazine* 1(1): 11–15.

Gladwin, L.C. (2001). "Ford Launches Massive Corporate Portal." *Computerworld.* June 15. http://www.computerworld.com/softwaretopics/software/story/0,10801,61399,00.html.

Gundling, E. (2000). *The 3M Way to Innovation: Balancing People and Profit.* Tokyo, Japan: Kodansha International.

Henderson, C. (2000). "Finding, Examining Lead Users Push 3M to Leading Edge of Innovation." http://www.refresher.com/!leadusers.

Miller, S. (1998). "CI for Smaller, Faster World." *Competitive Intelligence Magazine* 1(2): 3–4.

Naylor, E. (2000). "Capturing Competitive Intelligence from Your Sales Force." *Competitive Intelligence Magazine* 3(1): 24–28.

Prescott, J.E. (1989). *Advances in Competitive Intelligence.* Alexandria, VA: Society of Competitive Intelligence Professionals.

Robertson, M.F. (1998). "Seven Steps to Global CI." *Competitive Intelligence Magazine* 1(2): 29–33.

Shaker, S.M., and M.P. Gembicki. (1999). "Competitive Intelligence: A Futurist's Perspective." *Competitive Intelligence Magazine* 2(1): 24–27.

Sheinin, C.E. (1996). "Global CI: Assessing Global Competition." *Competitive Intelligence Review* 7(3): 86–88.

Studer-Noguez, I. (2002). *Ford and the Global Strategies of Multinationals: The North American Industry.* London: Routledge.

Vezmar, J.M. (1996). "Competitive Intelligence at Xerox." *Competitive Intelligence Review* 7(3): 15–19.

8

Competitive Intelligence in Asia: The View Through Different Lenses

Babette Bensoussan

Despite standard management processes and activities, performing competitive intelligence (CI) in the West is not the same as performing it in the East. CI in Asia is typically hampered by the following factors (Fleisher, 2002):

- Data are difficult to obtain and their accuracy is more questionable than that found in the West.
- Governments play a disproportionate role in economic matters, and corporate decision-making is motivated by more than pure economic factors.
- Many local businesses are run by entrepreneurs operating within networks of other entrepreneurs, restricting the level of publicly available information and creating high entry barriers that can be difficult to penetrate.
- Markets are often polarized between the small urban elites and industrial markets and the larger cache of urban and rural low-income consumers.

This chapter will address some of the issues that CI practitioners in the West face when performing CI in the East and will predominantly review China and Japan, two key Asian markets that are in many ways at opposite ends of the CI spectrum in Asia.

CI CHALLENGES IN ASIA

Over the past decade there has been a massive shift in the global economies and manufacturing capacity of Asia. This has had some major implications for decision-making, among them these:

- More rigorous analysis is now required to support investment decisions in Asia.
- There is need for depth and quality of information services in Asia.
- A large proportion of important information is still not widely available, despite "information overload."
- Any available information still needs to be interpreted with a knowledge of background motives and cultural norms.

Conducting CI in Asia is not as easy or as straightforward as many would think. Asia is not one uniform market but, rather, a sum of many different and varied markets—such as Brunei, Cambodia, China, India, Indonesia, Japan, Korea, Laos, Malaysia, Myanmar, Pakistan, Philippines, Singapore, Thailand, Taiwan, Vietnam—and different cultures necessitate different approaches and methods to undertaking CI.

There are many business, religious, ideological, and cultural differences across Asia that are not as evident or as prevalent in the West. This means that the models of doing business and the collection of intelligence information present unique challenges across Asia.

In following the Intelligence Flowchart (see Figure 8.1), four areas in the process will be heavily influenced by the differences among various Asian markets. The four areas of the flowchart that need to be reviewed in light of each market's particulars are the planning, collection, analysis, and the "so what?" test.

Issues that need to be addressed in order to ensure the success of a CI project in the Southeast Asian region include information resources (or lack thereof), transparency, local reporting and regulations, cultural biases, government influence, the need for local human intelligence, and reliance on networks and connections. It is critical that CI professionals not assume that Western processes and attitudes will be just as relevant in Asia. For example, one of the key underpinning differences in Asia is the central role of government in business—and one regime may not necessarily maintain the same standards as the next. The role of government, at both the federal and local levels, cannot be underestimated. One needs to clearly understand ownership and key stakeholder relationships. For example, in certain countries, local governments may pay domestic staff for information on foreigners' activities or may look

and typically run "family firms." These are conglomerates—often group-ings of sometimes hundreds of much smaller companies—that are inter-linked across regions through cross-shareholdings, cross-directorships, and inter-family connections such as marriage (East Asia Analytical Unit, Australian Department of Foreign Affairs, 1995). Table 8.1 attests to this disproportionate ownership of Southeast Asian economies by the ethnic Chinese.

Common characteristics of the modus operandi (East Asia Analytical Unit, Australian Department of Foreign Affairs, 1995) of the Chinese include

- highly centralized decision-making
- low-margin and high-volume products to penetrate markets
- tight inventory control, resulting in low capital investment and high stock turnover
- lower transaction costs through a preference for doing business with ethnic Chinese networks
- internal financing where possible
- tendency to undervalue (and, where possible, to internalize the costs of) services and other intangibles, such as legal advice and research and development (R&D)

These characteristics are not individually unique to ethnic Chinese-controlled businesses, but they provide a cultural framework that defines the paucity of information available for CI today.

The single largest flow of foreign direct investment by these ethnic Chi-nese is directed to China. Since entering the World Trade Organization (WTO), China faces increased competitive pressure and new stimulus for the growth of standard management practices—not just from its own

Table 8.1
Ethnic Chinese Population and Market Share of Market Capital

	Share of Population	Market Share
Thailand	14%	81%
Singapore	78%	81%
Philippines	2%	55%
Malaysia	30%	69%
Indonesia	3.5%	73%

Source: Adapted from Asia-Pacific Editorial Consultants (2000).

Western-trained businesspeople but also from those ethnic Chinese investing in China. Here too in China, there are some unique underlying issues—some quite different from business operations outside of China run by Chinese.

The first one of these underlying issues is the Chinese government's concern with the mediocre performance of state-owned enterprises. In the past, state-owned enterprises did not compete against each other for markets or customers and Western management practices were therefore unknown. Second, the establishment of modern enterprise systems and the new independence of enterprise decisions has propelled local firms (under pressure from foreign firms) to perform better. Third, China has recently experienced an intensified entry of a new class of private and collective firms, a trend that is still flourishing.

In light of the overall need to be more competitive, and for effective CI in China, certain issues are predominant in the Chinese marketplace (Fleisher, 2002):

- Determining what information is needed and where it can be obtained is difficult.
- National information service systems are related to scientific, technical, and economic information systems, which provide support for government policy-making, planning, R&D, and technology transfer.
- Information has been sourced predominantly from competitors' product marketing and advertising data.
- Comparisons have been based on logic and quantitative analysis.
- Good relations with government and public officials at multiple levels were (and still are) important for commercial success.
- Many commercial decisions are based on political, not economic, criteria.

Today Chinese managers are learning to use modern information technologies and scientific methods to collect, select, analyze, and synthesize relevant information. Intelligence methods include technology monitoring, early warning systems, market investigation, competitor analysis, and strategy formulation to fill the need for maximizing opportunities in this growing market.

In addition, China has passed several laws and regulations to protect intellectual property and to address fairness in competition. Other laws are anticipated, which will facilitate market competition and provide some guidelines for CI professionals as well.

So while things are improving, albeit slowly, they are still not at par with Western information systems. Western CI practitioners need to be aware of these discrepancies when taking their planning and collection into account. Good information in China is still based on *who* you know.

CI practitioners need to be mindful of a number of pitfalls in gathering and analyzing information in China (Wang, 2002). While certain information may be easy to obtain through phone calls or face-to-face meetings, other types of information may be more difficult to obtain; for example, interviewees with a technical background may often be hostile to the interview process. To be successful at information-gathering in hostile environments, one must develop an understanding of the traditional Chinese style of business communication. Such communication tends to be relatively open in Western cultures, where questions are asked with the expectation that direct answers will be given in response. In traditional Chinese culture, however, questions are not answered directly. To a Westerner, this can be very frustrating indeed.

When analyzing public information in China, there are three key areas to keep in mind:

- *Underestimation* Government statistics are always understated, especially concerning the bottom-up approach for specific industries. Statistics collection is still based on the old system under the state-planned economy, and some private investment and activity is omitted.
- *Overestimation* This is typical in forecasting activities. It is often done for propaganda purposes and should be fairly easy to identify. Market intelligence companies tend to overestimate the market share of large enterprises.
- *Intentional Misleading* Typically, this amounts to an exaggeration of reality.

As a result of this weakness in information, analysis and strategy interpretation is also difficult. This can be evidenced by the following:

- *Wrong Decision-Making.* Repeat investment or duplication due to rapidly changing market conditions and poor information.
- *Kamikaze Marketing.* Lack of local professionalism and understanding of marketing tactics. For example, to a marketing manager in the West it may be clear that a company is "committing suicide" as a result of its strategies. Such activities, however, are repeated to such an extent that the analyst doubts the real purpose of the exercise.
- *Competition for Market Dominance.* Despite holding 60% of the market share, a local microwave manufacturer still promotes hard and competes on price. This is based on the perceived threat from emerging

foreign competitors and the desire to continually raise the barrier to entry.

In summary, a CI professional needs to understand three specific elements in the Chinese market:

- *Business Ownership.* Business ownership will determine whether a company has access to sources of funds, its degree of flexibility in choosing material sources, and its ability to respond to market needs. Ownership will also determine qualification for government most-favored policies, including taxation.
- *The Government's Involvement in a Certain Industry.* Government control assumes the form of many shapes in China, including funding, taxation, and management fees from state-owned enterprises. In addition, there are a number of industries still controlled by the government, including telecommunications; air, railroad, and ocean transportation; high technology; and military equipment manufacturing. Long-term relationships, a heritage from the former central planning system, also play an important and influential role.
- *Business Location.* As specific economic regions or economic development zones grow in China, it is becoming evident that local governments are extending "favored policy" offers to attract foreign investment. Location plays a role because business and living expenses vary widely in different counties, cities, and provinces and affects varying product cost structures and business strategies. Some locales and jurisdictions may have a strong emphasis on protectionism for local companies.

To be effective, Western CI professionals must understand China's unique business culture, the extensive role of government in a free market system that influences the competitiveness of China-based companies, company responses to market needs, and China's political, socioeconomic, and cultural realities. As previously mentioned, the CI practitioner needs to identify which external influencing factors affect these companies' integrated activities, and these factors are often unique to China and the ethnic Chinese.

THE JAPANESE

From an opposite perspective within Asia, the Japanese culture sees group conformity, consensus, and group success as major drivers. Generally speaking, the Japanese love information. The word *"Joho"* in Japanese has a dual meaning: information and intelligence. *Joho* is something that is believed in, admired, and feared. The Japanese desire to gather, analyze, report, and share information has been one of the driving forces of Japan's economic success over the last 50 years. This cultural predisposition toward information and intelligence appears to be stimulated by three key factors (Ikeya & Ishikawa, 2001):

1. *Information is not taken for granted.* Within the Japanese culture, information represents power and authority. Companies tend to evaluate and promote personnel based on an employee's ability to gather and analyze information.

2. *Group loyalty is highly valued.* This is a legacy of the Bushido culture, in which extreme loyalty to the overlord in Samuri society was demanded and expected. Group loyalty is seen to secure the position of a senior individual while creating a comfortable feeling of doing the same thing as others (that is, peer identity and acceptance). For Japanese business people, obtaining valuable information—despite bureaucratic obstacles—is the ultimate demonstration of their value and loyalty to the group.

3. *"Uncertainty avoidance" is emphasized.* This is the result of a legacy of an isolationist policy in a highly homogeneous society—most families have only Japanese roots. In this single-race culture, it is much easier to create a common system based on mutual agreement and understanding. The underlying assumption is that because the Japanese share a racial and cultural background, they can easily understand each other within a common context. As a result of this cultural past, Japanese people don't like uncertainty or ambiguous situations and therefore have a strong interest in investigating and eliminating uncertainties.

In Japan, CI is seen to be part of everyone's job because it is widely recognized that employees who obtain *Joho* about competitors will help ensure their own company's survival and success. Even within functional groups, there are many unofficial CI people scanning for information in the internal as well as external environment.

For example, it is known that those attending trade shows typically follow up with extensive analysis of a competitor's new product features and pricing, even if this is outside their own area of responsibility. Detailed reports are presented to a wide audience within the organization. Reverse engineering is seen as a daily activity, while the marketing department will continually gather information from dealers regarding end-users' preferences and competitors' activities. However, as with all organizations across the globe, there is a downside to this frantic pace of information collection. The Japanese have an intense and diverse information-gathering process, but unless management has created a special information system, the information is usually not well organized. The gathered information tends to be stored separately by individual groups in a fragmented way.

In the past, benchmarking was an important part of CI activity in Japanese companies and involved learning, analyzing, modifying, and adopting the successful strategies of Western companies to narrow the technology gap following World War II. Recent change in benchmarking activity from a focus on quality to a focus on value has shifted the influence of benchmarking to become more strategically focused, with a greater emphasis on analysis.

On the other hand, for a Westerner attempting to collect information on Japanese organizations, several limitations arise that have a strong impact on the quality of CI available for decision-makers. The first limitation is that 96% of competitive information is available only in Japanese (Stern, 1997). There is also a low computer usage by government and industry bodies as compared to Western economies. Additionally, there is also poor information disclosure.

Other factors that impact the effective collection of information in Japan include these:

- Rivalry between different types of reporters
- Ethics—a burden of doing overseas business, but not a domestic driver
- Limited means of resolving mistakes in business relationships
- Poor intellectual property protection (Effective competition to a foreign product or service usually appears within two years)

The emergence of several countervailing factors, however, is beginning to foster a climate that is more conducive to effective information collection:

- The emergence of useful Japanese language databases for news, patents, and trademarks
- Positive image of foreign-induced information technology (IT) market shifts

In Japan (Ikeya & Ishikawa, 2001), key government organizations have played a significant and critical role in supporting the nation's CI activities in business, particularly in the industrial and technology area. The two main government departments are METI (Ministry of Economy, Trade, and Industry) and JETRO (Japanese External Trade Organization).

METI has a legacy of coordinating, supporting, and sometimes leading business interests in Japan, and it has multiple departments involved in business-related activities, among them these:

- *Small- and Medium-Enterprise Agency.* This agency is responsible for promoting the growth and development of small and medium enterprises (SMEs) and seen as the driving force of the Japanese economy.

- *The Research Office.* This office provides early warning signals, competitor monitoring and assessment, strategic planning, and strategic and tactical decision-making advice. It surveys business trends, structure, and other related economic issues.

Conversely, JETRO is seen as a world-class business CI agency. It focuses predominantly on gathering information related to import and export and provides an early warning of opportunities and threats, competitor monitoring, and assessment in terms of international trade. These activities significantly benefit private companies, especially general trading companies (*sogo-shoshas*). These companies have wide, far-reaching global networks and sophisticated support systems. In Japan, this strong collaboration between government and business organizations is expected to continue.

The Japan Chamber of Commerce and Industry (JCCI) also provides information that is focused on delivering an early warning of opportunities for local businesses, along with practical information on such areas as government policies and projects. Information is also shared within each local chamber of commerce.

The Keidanren and Nikkeiren are two of Japan's most influential trade associations. These were formed by a group of individual companies that provide personnel and collect and disseminate information from and to the business societies that they represent.

As long as Japanese companies maintain their information-intensive culture, there will be support for CI activities from either government or other sources. The key issues for Japanese companies today are similar to those of CI units in the West—the need for a more organized and systematic approach for both information-collection and analysis.

CONCLUSION

While this chapter has only briefly reviewed two different Asian societies, there are some common issues and techniques that Westerners should be aware of when carrying out CI activities in the Asian region. Table 8.2 is a suggested four-step process in line with the CI flowchart referred to in Figure 8.1. Together, these tools will guide CI practitioners as they operate their way through the CI process in Asia.

In light of the differing cultural factors in Asia, these four steps provide a broad guideline for undertaking CI in Asia. Information sources,

Table 8.2
Issues for Conducting CI in Asia

Step 1: Planning and Direction —Defining Requirements (What is it that you are seeking to learn and know?)	• The need for sensitivity with regard to cultural, societal, regulatory, legal, and economic factors by country • Awareness that intuitive social and cultural considerations can often be lost in translation and cross-border comparisons • In Asian cultures, contextual clues are often provided through body language and may contradict spoken words. • The need to understand the role of government in the support given to local companies and the level of market control • The need to understand the network and web of interconnected businesses and relationships.
Step 2: Planning and Direction —Resourcing the Project (How are you going to get the information you need? What is the budget?)	• This requires an initial focus on the knowledge that is currently available internally to your organization. This knowledge may include internal relationships and contacts in a particular market in Asia. • It is important to establish a solid base for initial analysis in order to develop and leverage further search strategies and appropriate contacts • Good local interpreters and contacts are a necessary expense for understanding local nuances • Maintain an awareness of global issues and diversity at all times • Possess active reading and listening skills with an open and patient disposition. Remember the three Ps of CI in Asia–Patience, Perseverance, and Politeness.

Step 3: Collection–Now What?	• The need to focus on each particular market in its own right is paramount. Issues that may need to be addressed include
	   ○ Domestic market size
	   ○ Growth potential for specific products and services
	   ○ Local consumer tastes
	   ○ Structure of marketing channels and pricing
	   ○ Background of individual families
	   ○ Projected developments of local governments
	   ○ Actual financial strength of corporate groups and their member companies
	• Assuming one market is the same as the other may be detrimental to the analysis being undertaken. Remember four key cultural criteria:
	   1. The role of close human relations in acquiring good intelligence information
	   2. The bureaucratic approach to local market information
	   3. The intensive use of human resources
	   4. The use of intermediaries
	• Document as much as possible, including future areas for investigation.

Step 4: Analysis and Presentations–So What? What does this all mean for us?	• Ensure size and scope perspectives of each market can be maintained • Maintain acceptance and understanding of local traits when drawing a conclusion from the analysis. If necessary, split areas into sub-regions to encourage familiarity with the idiosyncrasies of each market. • Reports and presentations must be tailored to the audience, domestic or foreign, taking into account cultural and societal norms. • Understand that the relationships developed with local contacts, whether customers or suppliers, in undertaking any CI project in Asia need to be maintained and ongoing.

managerial styles, and local cultures are key issues that impact heavily on any CI output and cannot be judged in the context of Western approaches. Each step in this four-step process will alert the CI practitioner to the nuances in each market.

The importance of Confucian values adds a particular dimension to any project where there is respect for authority, family, and group orientation, as well as a preference for personal relations. Outside the firm, close personal ties between families and linkages among top executives across organizations may form an exclusionary community, leading to higher entry barriers and limited information access (Fleisher, 2002).

The challenges that CI professionals face in Asia are mainly based around bridging differences in languages, understanding, culture, positions in history (inherited positions as well as those resulting from colonialism), and perceptions and experiences of previous engagements or transactions.

Collecting information in Asia requires a CI mindset that takes into account the need for sensitivity in approaching each market and the need for awareness of cultural and socioeconomic variations. No two markets in Asia are identical, and CI must be done on a country-by-country basis. The CI professional has to remain alert to the idiosyncrasies of each market and at the same time be aware of the impact of cultural and country factors on the analysis itself.

Exploring how the Asian mindset impinges the ability to effectively collect, analyze, and utilize CI demands an understanding of how individual and organizational mindsets can be changed—and that is another chapter.

REFERENCES

Asia-Pacific Editorial Consultants. (2000). "Beyond the Bamboo Network." September 15. http://www.asiafeatures.com/business/0009,1315,01.html.

Dugal M., and J. Prescott. (1997). "CI Lessons from India and Korea," pp. 31–36 in *12th Annual SCIP Conference Proceedings*, San Diego, CA, May 28–31, 1997, Alexandria, VA. Society of Competitive Intelligence Professionals.

East Asia Analytical Unit, Australian Department of Foreign Affairs. (1995). "Overseas Chinese Networks." Barton, ACT, Australia: Australian Department of Foreign Affairs.

Fleisher, C. (2002). "CI in Asia: Comparisons with Western Practice," in proceedings of Canadian Association of Security and Intelligence Studies Annual Conference, September 2002, Ottawa, Canada.

Ikeya, N., and H. Ishikawa. (2001). "The Japanese Intelligence Culture." *Competitive Intelligence Review* 12(4): 51–56.

Stern, J. (1997). "CI and the Introduction of Foreign Business in Japan," pp. 229–239 in *12th Annual SCIP Conference Proceedings*, San Diego, CA, May

28–31, 1997, Alexandria, VA: Society of Competitive Intelligence Professionals.

Wang, Y. (2002). "Gathering/Analyzing Information and Avoiding Pitfalls in China," pp. 213–215 in *15th Annual SCIP Conference Proceedings*, Cincinnati, OH, April 3–6, 2002, Alexandria, VA: Society of Competitive Intelligence Professionals.

9

The Internet Will Continue to Revolutionize International Competitive Intelligence Practices

Kelly Mah

The Internet, as we know it today, has significantly changed competitive intelligence (CI) practices over the past decade. Likewise, future impacts of the Internet will again fundamentally change how information is processed, improving all aspects of the CI process. The objective of this chapter is to analyze the areas of international CI that have been impacted by the Internet and to determine how they will be affected in the future. With the rapid evolution of Internet technologies, it is critical to understand its impact on the CI process. Future capabilities will enable business executives and CI professionals around the world to leverage the tools and technologies that provide a distinct advantage over their competitors, leaving the laggards and late adopters at risk of being left behind.

This chapter will primarily focus on the business area of CI (otherwise known as "business intelligence"), since most of the current research originated from business sources. However, many of the impacts mentioned in this chapter can also be applied beyond the business world into government, military, and economic CI.

THE COMPETITIVE INTELLIGENCE PROCESS

The CI process has been defined in several different ways by different authors. This chapter will use the CI process that is illustrated in Figure 9.1.

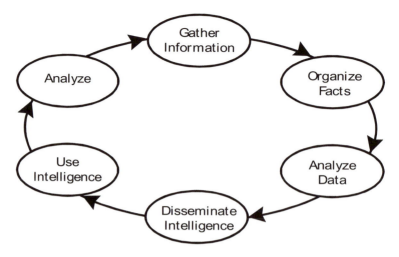

Figure 9.1 The CI Process (*Source:* Clarke [2001]).

CI Process Phase 1: Analyze CI Needs

Typically, the starting point of the CI process has been to evaluate a business's information needs and objectives. This often requires the involvement of senior management within the business to ensure the CI objectives are aligned with the corporate strategy and goals. This provides CI practitioners with a clear understanding of what information should be gathered, analyzed, and disseminated for use. Furthermore, this phase of the process also enables CI user groups to provide feedback and to evaluate the effectiveness of the information that has been provided.

CI Process Phase 2: Gather Information

In the past, primary and secondary information was typically gathered by actively pulling data from various sources. Finding primary sources of information involved obtaining the information directly from the source, which often included annual reports, interviews, and direct observations. Collecting secondary sources involved obtaining information secondhand through such sources as newspapers, magazines, books, and other edited media. This was very time consuming and expensive, requiring both human interaction and physical storage of the paperwork. CI professionals were bogged down with photocopying, clipping articles, and searching through mounds of paperwork to extract information morsels. Recent techniques have become much more efficient, relying on electronic information available through the Internet; however, human CI is still critical to gathering information.

CI Process Phase 3: Organize Facts

Once the information is available, CI practitioners can sort the facts into reasonable and logical categories that should enable quick and easy retrieval and reuse. The categorization should be very intuitive, so that other practitioners and users can quickly find the information they are looking for. If people can't find the information, there is no value in keeping it. In the past, facts were typically organized in a central location, such as the company library or the CI Department, where people had to seek assistance from someone who knew the filing system. Today, the information is distributed much more widely in different locations and the information retrieval processes tend to be self-service based. The techniques used to organize the facts can still vary greatly, from simple physical filing cabinets to an elaborate system of networks and databases. Whether simplistic or complex, the approach should be suitable for each specific CI environment, since the cost of implementation and support will increase as the level of complexity increases. Furthermore, the organization of the data should facilitate cross-cultivation of facts that would assist in the data analysis.

CI Process Phase 4: Analyze Data

The analysis of the data is the distinguishing factor between CI capabilities among different organizations. Analysis involves the correlation of data to bring to light new information that otherwise would not have been evident. This could involve the study of market trends or competitor signals where one could reasonably predict (with high probability) a particular outcome. This phase of the CI process also includes packaging the information in a useable and concise format. If practitioners cannot understand the analysis, they won't use the information; worse, they may use the misinterpreted information to make a critical decision. Traditionally, the strength of a CI practice has been as strong as the analyst's ability to provide the key findings in a timely and relevant manner.

CI Process Phase 5: Disseminate Intelligence

Once the information is analyzed and key findings have been documented, CI practitioners must get the right information to the right people at the right time. Competitive intelligence is very time sensitive and can become obsolete in a matter of hours. In the past this was very difficult, particularly across great distances and time zones. As teleconferences and faxes became more utilized, however, information could be quickly routed to a few select individuals. Fortunately, the pervasiveness of e-mail has greatly improved the practitioner's ability to disseminate intelligence, although this still does not ensure that the information will be used. A single e-mail among a sea of other e-mails may easily be overlooked and disregarded by a busy executive.

CI Process Phase 6: Use Intelligence

In order for business executives and CI practitioners to use CI effectively, the fundamental question "so what?" must be addressed. Simply knowing a trend or several facts will not suffice in today's world of information overload. Business leaders must understand the implication and the potential applications of the CI in order to make timely and strategic decisions. A good CI report will often describe the recommended action(s) that should be taken as a result of the information. Often, the likelihood of the information being used to make key decisions is largely dependent on the CI professional's previous track record of providing accurate intelligence and recommendations. The Internet can serve many functions here, such as updating of intelligence and conferring with colleagues on possible scenarios and last-minute changes to assumptions.

CURRENT IMPACT OF THE INTERNET ON INTERNATIONAL CI

Today's use of the Internet has primarily affected three phases of the CI process: phase 2 (gather information), phase 5 (disseminate intelligence), and phase 6 (use intelligence). The key Internet impacts have been through access, speed, and security of information.

Access to Information

The Internet has provided global access to information. Today anyone with Internet access, from anywhere around the world, can log on to gather and disseminate information at any time. This flexibility has provided international CI professionals with an enormous amount of information that was not available a decade ago. Small- and medium-size firms all over the world now have access to competitive information that was once only available to large international corporations with sizable budgets. Presently, direct research can be conducted from across the world with a click of a mouse. CI professionals in Japan can easily log on to Canadian local news websites to find pertinent local information, or they can log on to a competitor's website to view upcoming job openings that may signal their future corporate strategy or product direction.

The Internet also provides a wide variety of information, from real-time news services to content-rich websites and brutally honest discussion groups (Imperato, 1998). Paid sources of information are also available on the Internet for industry or competitive information. The prices for these services have fallen dramatically, since the cost of the information can be spread across many users around the world. The wide usage of the Internet has dramatically reduced the costs while increasing the quality and quantity of CI, particularly when the intelligence is used for key product and strategic decisions.

Unfortunately, with the overwhelming amount of information available, it is often difficult to discern valuable information from irrelevant data. Also, since information on the Internet is generally unregulated, its accuracy is often questionable and dependent on the reputation of the source of the website. Furthermore, many have become overly dependent on the Internet for CI and have fallen prey to "Net Disease, a condition that allows otherwise rational business people to think that CI begins and ends with the World Wide Web" (Klein, 1999). As a result, valuable human sources of information are easily overlooked.

Speed of Information

The global availability of information and Internet technologies has increased the rate at which information can be gathered and disseminated around the world. Internet "push" and "pull" methods (McClurg, 2001) have been created to automate the information-gathering process. "Push" methods include client or browser-based services, e-mail alerts, and personalized web pages; "pull" methods often refer to Internet search engines, web crawlers, and intelligent agents.

Advancements in computer processing capabilities and Internet bandwidth have allowed quicker downloading of information from the Internet. Researchers can search and download information on patents and court filings instantaneously, rather than waiting to receive requested documents. All these developments enable CI professionals to compile and disseminate competitive information more economically, efficiently, and effectively than ever before.

The current technology, however, has failed to produce automated tools to effectively analyze data, apply intelligence, evaluate the effectiveness of CI, and provide feedback. As a result, skilled CI professionals are still considered critical resources, but they are often the constraints on obtaining optimal CI performance throughout the CI process.

Security of Information

Internet security has always been an area of great concern. As corporations integrate supply chains and grow heavily dependent on computers, the Internet proved to be a vulnerable access point to those systems. According to a Forrester report, "The 2001 CSI/FBI Computer Crime and Security Survey shows that the average per-incident loss from computer-based theft of proprietary information has grown 466%, from about $1 million to about $4.5 million in the past five years . . . the weakest security link in the supply chain can bring down the whole team" (Prince, 2001). Organizations across the globe have spent billions of dollars trying to prevent their intellectual capital and proprietary information from getting into the wrong hands. International CI practitioners play a critical role in ensuring the information that they receive and disseminate remains strictly confidential.

Large ethical debates have occurred within the CI community as a result of Internet security. Unfortunately, CI professionals around the world have different codes of ethics for obtaining and utilizing competitive intelligence. Some believe that if the information is accessible, it can be utilized. Although there are many reasons for Internet security violations (political, financial, criminal, or just for the challenge), it is up to each CI professional's moral ethics (which vary greatly among CI practitioners) to determine the use of the competitive information.

FUTURE IMPACT OF THE INTERNET ON INTERNATIONAL CI

Despite the bust of the dot.com economy and the September 11, 2001, terrorist attacks in New York and Washington, both the Internet and business intelligence (BI) will continue to grow. As Forrester Research predicts, "The technology slump will end in Q1 2003 . . . double-digit growth won't resume until 2004" (Temkin, 2002).

In light of the anticipated growth of the U.S. technology sector (see Figure 9.2), this chapter predicts that the Internet will have implications across the entire CI process, and will bring international CI practices to a whole new level. As indicated in Table 9.1, this new international CI process will be defined by the following characteristics: universal access to information, virtual global communities, online collaboration, counterintelligence, and new emerging technologies.

Universal Access to Information

Accessibility to competitive information will continue to grow as Internet technologies continue to evolve. The development and universal adoption of third- or fourth-generation telecom technology, personal digital assistants (PDAs), and other wireless technologies will enable real-time information-gathering, organizing, and dissemination from anywhere in the world. Soon, sales representatives in Hong Kong, for example, will be able to gather information from a competitor's new product at a trade show, file the information in a database from their PDA, and disseminate the information to a product development team lead in New York. This capability

Table 9.1
Internet Impact on the International CI Process

International CI Process	Current Internet Impact			Future Internet Impact				
	Access	Speed	Security	Universal Access to Information	Virtual Global Communities	Online Collaboration	Counter-intelligence	Other Emerging Technologies
Analyze Needs				X	X	X	X	X
Gather Information	X	X	X	X	X	X	X	X
Organize Facts					X	X	X	X
Analyze Data				X	X	X	X	X
Disseminate Intelligence	X	X	X	X	X	X	X	X
Use Intelligence	X			X	X	X	X	X

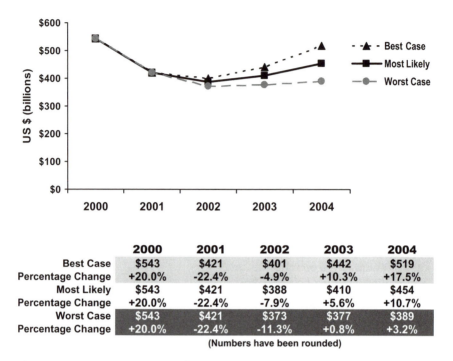

Figure 9.2 Forecast: U.S. Tech Recovery Scenarios, 2002 to 2004 (*Source:* Temkin [2002]).

will greatly reduce the lead time of information processing by eliminating the need to find a suitable location to log on to a PC with access to the Internet. In addition, as electronic devices become smaller, lighter, and more economical, the ability to discretely harvest human competitive information in the field will dramatically increase. Furthermore, as the Internet becomes more pervasive, analysts will be able to access information from collaborative international sources (internally and externally), to assist them in the data analysis. Moreover, end-users from around the world can apply the intelligence, evaluate and provide feedback on the effectiveness of the CI, or submit new CI requirements through a secured website, video streaming, or Voice over Internet Protocol (VoIP).

An obstacle the IT industry currently faces is excess capacity in the existing backbone infrastructure, in light of the downturn in the technology sector. This has prevented many corporations from further investments in third- or fourth-generation technologies. In order to facilitate universal access to information, the Internet infrastructure must also have higher bandwidth to facilitate real-time information transfers. Furthermore, until economies of scale can bring the prices down (as happened with the introduction of cellular phone networks), the initial cost of the technology will be very expensive. Until the technology becomes affordable to the common consumer or small business, CI professionals will have to rely on the existing infrastructure and tools to perform their tasks.

Virtual Global Communities

The Internet will create virtual global communities that focus on CI. These already exist in the form of Internet discussion groups through chat rooms and news groups. However, within enterprises, global CI communities can use groupware (e.g., Lotus Notes, Wide Area Networks, Local Area Networks, and Virtual Private Networks) to gather and disseminate information from around the world. The information can then be taken locally (or corporately) to impact future strategy, product development, or mergers and acquisitions. These virtual communities can also share techniques and lessons learned across the CI process to assist other CI professionals within their virtual global community.

Currently, virtual global CI communities are still in the infantile stage of evolution. Many corporations do not have CI departments and have not yet invested in global CI networks. As a result, CI professionals must take the initiative to develop their own communities inside and outside of their formal organizations in order to leverage each other's skills and experience. Furthermore, CI practitioners must become familiar with the emerging groupware technologies to facilitate these virtual communities.

Online Collaboration

Online collaboration is already taking place within the business world today. Marketspaces and portals are being used as focal points within cyberspace for the purpose of collaboration. This trend should continue to impact different areas of business, including the international CI process. Virtual CI communities should take advantage of this infrastructure to gather and disseminate international competitive information. Portals can also be used to organize facts gathered from the CI process and to provide a central repository for CI evaluation, feedback, or new requirements; this will enable registered users from around the world to access and input information. Also, as corporations continue to expand their electronic integration throughout the supply chain, CI professionals should utilize this information to verify that suppliers and customers remain as allies.

As the virtual global CI communities progress, subject matter experts from around the world will evolve. The community should leverage its expertise and potentially develop virtual mentorship programs that focus on each area of the CI process, especially in the more challenging areas of data analysis and the application of intelligence in decision-making.

"Webinars" (interactive seminars held over the World Wide Web) are an effective and efficient means of collaboration among virtual think-tanks, which should enable CI communities around the world to share the latest and greatest developments within their profession at a fraction of the cost.

The difficulty with online collaboration is that a complex infrastructure must first exist before the CI community can capitalize on the tools and network. This often takes significant time, money, and resources, which are difficult to obtain if senior executives do not see the value in CI. Furthermore, for organizations and individuals to participate in collaboration, a threshold of trust is required within the relationships; this is very difficult to obtain without some form of initial human interaction and relationship.

Counterintelligence

Forrester Research predicts that information warfare will continue to evolve as organizations increase in complexity (from individuals to tribes and ultimately to nations) with increasingly complex motives (Prince, 2000). In order to combat the information warfare, CI professionals will need to be integrated and coordinated to ward off these multi-leveled attacks. CI professionals may need to be involved with traditional security as well as IT security practices to ensure that all CI is protected. It is conceivable that international CI professionals will have to engage in proactive counterintelligence (a concept similar to "ethical hacking"), where CI professionals will try to conduct comprehensive audits to prove that proprietary information is being protected, not only in physical locations but, more important, on the Internet. Counterintelligence affects each stage of the CI process, since competitors can potentially target all Internet access points of a firm.

The challenge for CI professionals is that they are typically not involved with either computer programming or security, which forces them to team up with other professionals in order to provide effective counterintelligence. Furthermore, CI professionals will be battling on a new front, which will initially disadvantage them against those who have been hacking on the Internet for many years. As a result, CI professionals must adapt to the new challenges and become more flexible in expanding their existing roles.

New Emerging Internet Technologies

Although it is impossible to point out all the emerging Internet technologies, several innovative products are being developed that will certainly have a significant impact on international CI. These include open standards, artificial intelligence, and online multi-language translators.

Open Standards

A recent trend within the information technology industry has been to move towards open standards. Open standards allow all technologies to connect and integrate, allowing IT to become more modular. Open standards originate with a technology company or individuals who open their source code or technology to the public to be used or modified without compensation. As users refine the source code or technology, the adoption becomes more prevalent. Eventually, the industry will adopt the technology as an open standard, just as VHS tapes or DVDs have become industry standards within the entertainment industry. Similarly, Linux and Java technologies have brought open standards to the enterprise. Today XML (extensible mark-up language) and web services allow information and applications across business lines to be shared. As open standards continue to evolve in the technology industry, it is conceivable that fully integrated systems will exist through which it will be possible to extract information easily from anywhere within an organization. All functions will be integrated so that the system appears seamless to the end-user of the application. With respect to the CI process, this would improve information-processing throughout an organization, since the CI practitioner would no longer have to go to several different systems to extract information from multiple sources, nor enter information in multiple databases. Instead, imagine the capability to capture the inventory levels or prices of a competitor's product from a store shelf, search your own company's inventory planning system to determine your product availability, and then—depending on the amount of inventory in transit—being able to reduce your prices to undercut your competitor. Most impressively, all this would be completed on your PDA while on location at a retail store.

Artificial Intelligence

Although intelligent agents or "bots" are available today to assist CI professionals in gathering information on the Internet, they are still relatively new and limited in their capabilities. Future versions of intelligent agents will incorporate the latest artificial intelligence algorithms and technologies to "automatically learn customers' information needs, collect key information from remote sites, cluster into similar topics, and deliver it directly to clients anywhere in the organization" (Boureston, 2000). In addition, artificial intelligence has the potential of analyzing data to find hidden relationships and disseminating the resulting intelligence to the appropriate departments within an organization.

Online Multi-language Translators

Online multi-language translators are already available on the Internet. As the global community continues to integrate, more sophisticated language translators will surface. These online translators will extend beyond English, French, Spanish, and German to more complex languages like Russian, Arabic, Hebrew, Chinese, and Japanese. With the assistance of artificial intelligence, proper grammar and tense could also be translated. This will enable the international CI community to translate online information in any language instantaneously, opening an enormous floodgate to new communities and offering information that is not available today. This too can be applied throughout the CI process, from analyzing CI requirements through to analyzing the effectiveness of the CI application.

The main barrier to these innovations is finding the correct balance between the cost of development and demand. Unfortunately, the development of Internet technologies has dramatically slowed since the recent slowdown in the dot.com Internet technology sector. Investors are not willing to fund such research and development (R&D) without valid proof that the concepts are profitable. Until then, these emerging technologies and tools will remain on the wish list of the CI community.

CONCLUSION

The Internet will continue to revolutionize international CI practice. This chapter assessed the current and future impacts of the Internet with respect to the international CI process. The Internet's current impact has primarily been limited to the "gather information," "disseminate intelligence," and "use intelligence" phases of the CI process, specifically through improvements in the access, speed, and security of information. The Internet will ultimately transform every phase of the CI process in the future, raising CI practice to a new level. This will be achieved through the universal access to information, virtual global communities, online collaboration, counterintelligence, and other evolving technologies.

CI professionals around the world should be aware of these emerging tools and technologies so that they can be early adopters and embrace the changes that will ultimately revolutionize how CI is processed. This may mean updating one's skills on a specific technology or becoming a leader of a virtual global community. Those who fail to accept or join the new revolution may find that their skill sets have been rendered as obsolete as the typewriter and record player.

Business executives from around the world must take responsibility for influencing the future evolution of CI on the Internet. They must ensure sufficient support and funding for its continued development. Ultimately, it is the organization that utilizes CI most effectively that will secure a competitive advantage over others. As the business world and society become more dependent on information, CI will become increasingly important to business success. Having the right information in the hands of the right people at the right time will enable executives to make the critical decisions necessary to stay ahead of the competition.

Companies of all sizes and from all areas of the world should take advantage of the technologies and tools mentioned in this chapter. This will enable them to compete on the next level—a superior competitive plane that will be within the grasp of tomorrow's technologically enhanced international CI process. With the evolution of technology and the Internet, the world has definitely become smaller. Global competitors are appearing from out of nowhere. A case in point is the fact that India is now a leading software development source for the world—a reality few would have accurately predicted. Lines of businesses are also becoming increasingly blurred. For example, grocery stores are selling banking services, household electronics, and gasoline. As these examples indicate, competition will continue to grow fiercely as the pace of globalization accelerates. Companies that invest in developing a technologically advanced international CI process will be well placed to navigate the future challenges and opportunities ushered in by globalization.

REFERENCES

Boureston, J. (2000). "Using 'Intelligent Search Agents' for CI." *Competitive Intelligence Magazine* 3(1): 32–36.

Clarke, D.E. (2001). "Competitive Intelligence in Service Industries," pp. 222–237 in C.S. Fleisher and D.L. Blenkhorn [eds.], *Managing Frontiers in Competitive Intelligence*. Westport, CT: Quorum Books.

Imperato, G. (1998). "Competitive Intelligence—Get Smart!" *Fast Company*, 14: 269. http://www.fastcompany.com/online/14/intelligence.html.

Klein, C. (1999). "Overcoming 'Net Disease.'" *Competitive Intelligence Magazine* 2(3): 29–32.

McClurg, R. (2001). "Using the Internet for Gathering Competitive Intelligence," pp. 61–76 in C.S. Fleisher and D.L. Blenkhorn [eds.], *Managing Frontiers in Competitive Intelligence*. Westport, CT: Quorum Books.

Prince, F. (2000). "B2B Information Warfare." *TechStrategy Report* (May). Cambridge, MA: Forrester Research Inc.

Prince, F. (2001). "When to Share Supply Chain Secrets." *TechStrategy Report* (September). Cambridge, MA: Forrester Research Inc.

Temkin, B.D. (2002). "Tech Recovery Update: The Tipping Point in 2003." *TechStrategy Brief* (October). Cambridge, MA: Forrester Research Inc.

10

The Legal Playground: Conducting Competitive Intelligence on a Global Basis

Michelle S. Stever

Competition is a global force and businesses that fail to recognize this will not survive. As a result, it is essential that competitive intelligence (CI) professionals learn how to obtain information about their foreign competitors and foreign markets. Since CI focuses strictly on legal and ethical means of collecting data, CI professionals must understand how to legally obtain information in numerous countries. If they do not understand the legal environment, their actions will cause severe economic and legal consequences for the business as well as for themselves.

The goal of this chapter is to provide the CI professional with a general overview of the global legal environment. It begins by briefly discussing the role of ethics and the importance of establishing a global mindset. Next, the chapter takes a macro approach to the legal challenges facing the CI professional. Finally, the Trade Related Aspects of Intellectual Property Rights (TRIPS) and the Economic Espionage Act (EEA) are discussed. Essentially, this chapter helps CI professionals avoid legal pitfalls in obtaining CI in a global environment. It does not, however, provide a summary of all international laws or country-specific laws that the CI professional should know.

COMPETITIVE INTELLIGENCE: AN OVERVIEW

CI is comprised of three main elements: the collection of data through legal and ethical methods, the analysis of data, and the creation of new intelligence. Corporate espionage, in contrast, is the collection of information through illegal and unethical means such as wiretapping, theft, bribery, fraud, deceit, and misrepresentation. The goal of both is to influence strategic development and management decisions in order to increase profitability.

Since competition is globally based, the distinction between CI and corporate espionage is important. Businesses engaging in corporate espionage face global repercussions from their actions. The consequences could include the deterioration of the firm's global reputation and creditability. This impairs the ability of the business to enter new markets and attract new international partners. Given the speed with which global communication technologies can spread news of unethical corporate conduct, engaging in corporate espionage in international markets will result in swift and often fatal consequences. For these reasons, it is imperative that the global CI practitioner have an understanding of the global legal environment.

DEVELOPING A GLOBAL PERSPECTIVE

Before CI professionals examine the legal issues involved in global CI, they must develop a global approach to CI. It is common, however, for individuals to hold an ethnocentric view of the world. That is, people assume that their cultural, legal, and ethical perspectives are shared beliefs throughout the world. Ethnocentricity, however, often encourages incorrect assumptions. The CI professional must appreciate that different cultures, religions, morals, and governments distinctly affect the construction of laws in various countries around the world. "Globally minded professionals recognize that they must not only understand the orientations of the customers, competitors, and team members, but must also understand the basis for their own particular cultural beliefs" (Simpkins, 1998). Ultimately, such a geocentric view of the world is required to conduct global CI.

What is considered legal and ethical behavior in North America may not be considered legal or ethical in Europe, Asia, or South America. To illustrate this, consider how the Chinese and Western cultures influence their respective systems of law. Chinese "tradition is based on a collective view of property rights, whereas Western culture considers rights based on individuals" (Tao & Prescott, 2000). In China, "new intellectual property is considered a gain for society in general," whereas intellectual property is individually protected in Western culture (Tao & Prescott, 2000). These two diverse views produce very distinct and contrasting laws in these societies. Once CI professionals understand the origins of their own culture and of foreign cultures, they will be prepared to conduct global CI.

Another example that illustrates cultural differences is the treatment of fraud. Fraud is "to assume the identity of another in order to obtain information, knowing that the subject would not ordinarily answer you if your true identify were known" (Ehrlich, 1998). In his 1998 study, Chuck Klein highlights how the social acceptance of fraud varies across countries. Three CI professionals were hired to obtain competitor information in the United States, Britain, and Italy. The American and British professionals were extremely careful not to misrepresent themselves. The Italian professional misrepresented himself by lying about who he was and why he needed the information. By American and British standards, the Italian professional committed a fraudulent act. However, based on Italian culture, the actions were acceptable. When questioned about his actions, the Italian practitioner responded, "That's how we do it [competitive intelligence] in Italy!" (Klein, 1998). Although this is an isolated case, it does force the CI professional to recognize that CI practices vary across countries.

LEGAL PERSPECTIVE: BACKGROUND INFORMATION

It is unreasonable to expect the CI professional to understand all the laws that affect CI on a global basis. Laws are not only country-specific, but they may also vary from region to region in each country. The legal environment is complex and even with the most clearly defined laws it is the court's interpretation of the law that will determine how the law is enforced. Despite this variable interpretation, corporations are "obligated to know the legal danger zones in the competitive intelligence collection process" and, therefore, must make a reasonable effort to understand them (Duffey, 2000).

Despite the best research and legal advice, gray areas of the law will emerge. Unclear laws require CI professionals to use their judgment. In order to assist their CI professionals with these gray areas and to promote a consistent approach to CI, businesses should create their own code of ethics. Codes of ethics help to align the CI professional's judgment with corporate policies. Properly trained CI professionals can identify and avoid situations that may put them at legal risk (Horowitz, 1999). The focus of CI is to conduct only legal activity, but in the absence of clearly defined laws, CI professionals must refer to their company's code of ethics.

Legal Departments

CI professionals need additional resources to interpret foreign laws. Therefore, businesses that require global CI should expect to require legal advice as early as possible in the CI process (Sammon, Kurland, & Spitalnic,

1984). Businesses may choose to establish an internal legal department or to obtain legal advice as needed from an external law firm. Early legal preparation is critical in CI. Lawyers may be unfamiliar with the target country's laws, and they will need to complete additional research before providing any legal advice. Businesses should also encourage their CI professionals to contact their legal department if they are unsure about the legality of their actions (Fuld, 1988). Overall, early preparation prevents unwelcome legal problems.

PROCEED WITH CAUTION

CI Professionals and Their Employers or Customers

CI professionals' actions legally impact both the business and the CI professionals. They are not always protected by the businesses they work for, and can be held personally liable for any damages that they cause. Furthermore, the CI professional's legal rights are not consistent throughout the world. To conduct global CI, CI professionals must be cognizant of the personal risk associated with their work.

The contrast between Western and Asian laws highlights how the personal risk in completing CI varies across the globe. In the United States and in Canada, citizens are awarded specific rights to protect them from undue harm in the legal process. The U.S. Bill of Rights and the Canadian Charter of Rights and Freedoms ensure that people are presumed innocent until proven guilty. In these countries, the legal process is established to determine the individual's guilt or innocence. Some countries, however, have laws that are not based on a presumption of innocence. Case in point is a 1997 incident in South Korea in which an American employee of Litton Guidance and Control Systems was accused of obtaining classified military information. This information pertained to the military's intent to purchase Airborne Warning and Control Systems Aircraft. In South Korea, the accused waits in detention until the trial begins and "there is no presumption of innocence, right to bail, or trial by jury in Korea" (Ehrlich, 1998). In this situation, it was unclear if the information obtained was classified (Ehrlich, 1998). However, the CI professional was subject to the Korean laws and waited in jail for his trial.

In addition to reduced civil liberties, the CI professional can be held financially liable for damages caused. For example, in 1996 the U.S. government passed the EEA. The EEA's purpose is to govern trade secrets under federal law and impose financial liability on individuals and businesses for obtaining trade secret information through illegal means.

The financial liability under the EEA is severe. For example, if the individual is found guilty of obtaining trade secret information through illegal means, the courts can impose a penalty of 15 years' imprisonment and fines up to US$500,000. For the business, the court may impose fines up to US$10 million (Duffey, 2000). As of 1998, there were four cases tried under the EEA. In all four cases the defendants were individuals, not businesses (Pagell, 1998). Essentially, the activities the EEA criminalizes "had always been prohibited under state law and/or inconsistent with SCIP's [Society of Competitive Intelligence Professionals] code of ethics" (Horowitz, 1999). However, the CI professional must be aware of the personal and financial consequences of violating laws in the data collection process.

Media Test

In addition to corporate and professional codes of ethics, CI professionals can also use the media test to guide their actions. The media test simply asks, "Would I want the activities that I am performing to be exposed by the media?" If you do not want to see what you are doing reported in the front-page headlines of your local newspaper, do not do it" (Sammon, Kurland, & Spitalnic, 1984). While the CI professional's actions may be legal, the general public may perceive the actions as unethical and harmful. Since information is rapidly communicated across the globe, smart competitors will use these communication tools to publicize the CI professional's activities, especially if the CI professional's home country will condemn his or her actions. The media's impact on the competitive environment is enormous and its influence may "make a company wonder why it ever got into the intelligence process in the first place" (Sammon, Kurland, & Spitalnic, 1984). Overall, the media test helps CI professionals avoid activities that may cause personal and financial damages.

Legal Liability and Independent CI Consultants

Procter and Gamble's (P&G) highly publicized debacle, in which their independent CI consultants conducted dumpster diving activities to obtain information about Unilever, highlights two significant CI lessons. First, the media test is powerful. P&G's problems arose from the fact that the public perceived the CI to be "unfair, inappropriate, sleazy, and illegitimate" even though the actions were legal (Prescott, 2001). Second, businesses hiring third parties to conduct their CI are criminally and civilly liable for the actions of those third parties. Corporate liability is not removed by hiring a third parity.

In a global scenario, the CI professional may not have legitimate and established connections with industry experts in foreign countries. Businesses may need to hire professionals who originate from the target country. These third parties, who are familiar with the laws in the foreign country, are better prepared to complete CI in their nation. However, it is critical that the third party understands that illegal activity is unacceptable, that they understand the business's code of ethics, and that the media test be utilized.

P&G incurred significant financial damage and global embarrassment as a result of its third party's actions. P&G was required to pay US$10 million to Unilever in addition to allowing "an unusual third party audit to settle the matter" (Society of Competitive Intelligence Professionals, 2001). In order to protect against this damage, thorough background checks on any professional hired will determine if the professional's previous actions are consistent with the business's approach to CI. Remember, the purpose of hiring independent third parties is not to skirt around the law but, rather, to obtain information though legal and ethical means.

Liability for the action of third parties flows back to the business in two ways. The first is through tort law. Tort law "aims to compensate the victim and to put the monetary loss on the party best able to bear it" (Ehrlich, 2002). Second, "liability may follow through criminal law, which is designed to punish the wrongdoer, to exact retribution, and to deter future misbehavior" (Ehrlich, 2002). Employers are liable for on-the-job torts committed by their employees, and the corporation's liability is not dependent on the corporation authorizing or instructing the employee to commit these actions (Ehrlich, 2002).

For subcontractors, the law is less clear. Interpretation of liability depends on whether the third party is considered an independent contractor or a professional agent, in which trust is implied in the relationship. Again, these relationships are subject to interpretation. Essentially, the corporation that hires a third party should ensure that the third party is aware that no illegal activity is authorized and that the third party is aware of the company's ethical standards. Overall, a business that hires a third party and implies that illegal actions are acceptable will be liable for the action of third parties (Ehrlich, 2002).

Legal Jurisdiction

"Jurisdiction," an important legal term in global CI, is the power of the state to prescribe, adjudicate, and enforce its laws and judgments (Ehrlich, 1998). CI professionals who obtain information about a competitor in another country via e-mail, mail, or telephone can be held criminally or civilly liable if the information was obtained illegally. Generally, countries exert their authority within their own sovereign area (Ehrlich, 1998). However, through the objective jurisdiction principle, countries can exert their legal authority for offenses that occur outside their sovereign territory. Through the protective jurisdiction principle, most states will exert their authority if the acts committed abroad affect the security or vital interests of their state (Ehrlich, 1998).

The United States does recognize foreign countries' objective jurisdiction. The United States is a member of the Hague Service Convention, "a multilateral treaty that provides a means for serving legal process abroad, in other member states" (Ehrlich, 1998). As a result, it is fairly easy for an American to be served with a summons issued by a foreign court. The service of a summons represents the beginning of a civil case. Regarding criminal activity, foreign countries can request that the accused be delivered to their country through an extradition treaty, that the accused be deported, that the accused be prosecuted in the home country, and that the accused may be obtained though abduction or trickery (Ehrlich, 1998). In general, it is not uncommon for a U.S. citizen to be challenged by a foreign court through a civil case, but it is less likely that the citizen would be extradited and prosecuted on criminal charges (Ehrlich, 1998). In either case, country borders do not necessarily bind laws.

Legal Interpretation

Despite all reasonable efforts to comply with the law, the courts may have a unique and unexpected interpretation of the law. A good example to illustrate this conceivable scenario is the experience of du Pont. Although this example occurred in the late 1960s, its lesson is still relevant in the current legal environment. Du Pont's competitor hired a photographer to take aerial pictures of the construction of du Pont's new factory. Du Pont developed a highly secretive but unpatented process in the methanol plant that could be identified by the aerial photographer. The process would not be exposed after the construction was complete. Du Pont learned the identity of the photographer's client by taking the photographer to court. At the time, the photographer's actions were defined as improper but not illegal. The court determined that "improper will always be a word of many nuances, determined by time, place, and circumstances" and, as such, the court ruled that under this situation, the photographer's actions were not only improper but also illegal (Sammon, Kurland, & Spitalnic, 1984).

The photographer believed his actions were legal based on his interpretations of the law. However, the judge concluded differently. The court ruled that "one may use his competitor's secret process if he discovers the process by reverse engineering applied to the finished product; one may use a competitor's process if he discovers it by his own independent research; but one may not avoid these labors by taking the process from the discoverer without his permission at a time when he is taking reasonable precautions to maintain its secrecy (Sammon, Kurland, & Spitalnic, 1984). This example highlights that the law and its enforcement is subject to the interpretation of the judge who presides over it. In other words, even if one believes that one's actions are legal but the activity is still questionable, it is best to error on the side of caution. There is no guar-antee that the judge will support one's actions and, at any rate, the legal and public costs of a lawsuit should be avoided.

In another example, gray zones in Chinese law are extensive. James Stratton (1998), a writer for the U.S.-China Business Council, notes, "For-eign executives in certain industries must be careful, when trying to obtain business information, not to overstep China's vague boundary between commercial research and alleged criminal activity. One of China's haz-ardous peculiarities is its broad definition of state secrets, which can in-clude economic and financial information that is considered public in the West." While CI professionals may believe they are acting in ethical and legal ways, it is ultimately under the judge's authority to decide if the ac-tivity is reasonable. Despite all attempts to act in accordance with the law in China, in "few other countries is there such a thin line between com-mercial research and alleged criminal activity" (Stratton, 1998).

Legal Challenges: Capital Intense

Challenging the law is expensive. It is not only financially expensive, but it also negatively impacts the business's reputation. Negative publicity generated through a legal battle is difficult to overcome. If the public views the business's actions as unethical and illegal, even though the courts may determine that the activities were legal, the firm's profitability will be reduced through lost sales. The costs of litigation are immense, and all reasonable efforts should be made to avoid such situations.

Common, but Not Legal

Some investigative activities are more acceptable and common in some countries than others. For example, bribery, which is defined as providing an incentive or "something of value to induce a person to disclose confi-dential information," is more common outside North America (Ehrlich, 1998). Areas where bribery, especially in the government, is more preva-lent include Africa, Asia, Latin America, and the former Soviet Union (National Journal Group, 2002). Businesses competing in these countries should recognize that although this activity occurs, businesses should not participate in it. Remember the media test.

Seek Out Competitive Intelligence Professional Associations for Help

A CI professional does not establish an excellent reputation by obtain-ing degrees or diplomas. Rather, CI professionals obtain excellence be-cause of their networks, understanding of the industry, and ability to

collect information legally. In the global perspective, CI professionals are disadvantaged when they do not know how to obtain public information in foreign countries. For many countries, such as Brazil or those located in the Middle East, public information is not as extensive as it is in North America. In an effort to avoid breaking any laws while collecting information, CI professionals should seek assistance from other CI professional associations. For example, the South Africa Institute of Competitive Intelligence is firmly established in South Africa. China recently established its Society of Competitive Intelligence of China (SCIC), and there is a Society of Competitive Intelligence Professionals in Japan. CI professionals can refer to these organizations for assistance in completing and understanding the legal environment in foreign countries. In fact, SCIC "will strive to provide legal consultation for its members to ensure that their CI practices are within the legal framework" (Changhuo, Qingjiu, Luhong, & Shan, 1998). Global CI professionals should be aware of these public sources of information and seek assistance from them in completing their CI activities.

TRADE SECRETS AND INTELLECTUAL PROPERTY RIGHTS

International competition has increased the need for global cooperation in trade and the protection of intellectual property rights. Through the World Trade Organization (WTO), member nations have joined together to provide protection in these areas. This protection is provided for both foreign and domestic businesses operating in member countries. It is through TRIPS that member nations obtain minimum standards from which to build their own legal framework.

As of January 1, 2002, the WTO was composed of 144 member nations. These members must comply with the standards established in TRIPS. Two conventions form the basis of TRIPS: the Bern Convention, which deals with copyrights, and the Paris Convention, which includes trade secrets and unfair competition. At a minimum, most patents are protected for 20 years and industrial designs are protected for 10 years. TRIPS provides the minimum standards that each country must enforce in their legislation, and the TRIPS council monitors its members to ensure compliance (World Trade Organization).

Since the legal system varies globally, countries establish their own legislation to enforce the TRIPS standards. Each country must ensure that the legal penalties are severe enough to deter violation of the law. Members of the WTO include the United States, Canada, India, and Germany. Members currently in a transition period, meaning they have been given time to adjust their laws to comply with TRIPS, are Chile, China, Mexico, and Poland (World Trade Organization).

What TRIPS means for the CI professional is that countries are working together to protect against theft of trade secrets and unfair competition. Although TRIPS only imposes the minimum standards that members must uphold, the CI professional must be aware that there is some global protection against intellectual property and trade secret violation. For the CI professional, it is more important to know that information is legally protected than to know the severity of the punishment imposed by each country.

Trade Secrets

As a WTO member, the United States must comply with TRIPS standards. As discussed earlier, the United States has extended its protection of trade secrets through the EEA. The United States has estimated that it lost about US$24 billion–US$100 billion annually because of the black market for proprietary information (Pagell, 1998). Since the United States is one of the largest world markets, it is important that "anyone practicing any type of competitive intelligence . . . be aware of the Economic Espionage Act" (Pagell, 1998). The EEA identifies illegal activities as computer hacking, wiretapping, misrepresentation of self, deception to obtain information, and bribery. The act provides a very broad definition of trade secrets. Trade secrets can include financial or economic information, plans, formulas, procedures or codes that are either intangible or tangible. This list is not exhaustive. As with TRIPS, the owner of the trade secret must make a reasonable effort to protect the information in order for the trade secret to be protected under the EEA (Pagell, 1998).

Other countries also recognize the need to protect trade secrets. Germany recently expanded its confidentiality law, Law against Unfair Competition, to protect against the acquisition of trade secrets; and France, Japan, and Taiwan established trade secret legislation prior to the EEA (Pagell, 1998). Although China is a collectivist state, its government is establishing laws that are similar to North American competition laws (Changhou, Qingjiu, Luhong, & Shan, 1998). The Chinese government is establishing antitrust laws and trade secret protection laws in order to provide a more competitive market and to provide CI professionals with legal standards (Changhou, Qingjiu, Luhong, & Shan, 1998). As countries become more developed and information becomes more accessible, it is foreseeable that these countries will also enhance their trade secret legislation in order to protect their economies and their businesses.

CONCLUSION

Preparing for the legal CI environment on a global basis is not an easy task. The legal environments are complex, but similarities among countries

can be established, especially through TRIPS. CI professionals must take sufficient measures to protect themselves and their businesses from unnecessary and costly legal battles. Good preparation will prevent costly mistakes, allow the company to protect its reputation, and produce competitive information that will positively contribute to the firm's strategic development and profitability.

REFERENCES

Changhuo, B., T. Qingjiu, D. Luhong, and X.Y. Shan. (1998). "The Developing Chinese Competitive Intelligence Profession." *Competitive Intelligence Review* 9(4): 42–47.

Duffey, W.S., Jr. (2000). "Competitive Information Collection: Avoiding Legal Land Mines." *Competitive Intelligence Review* 11(3): 37–53.

Ehrlich, C.P. (1998). "A Brief CI Compliance Manual." *Competitive Intelligence Review* 9(1): 28–37.

Ehrlich, C.P. (2002). "Liar, Liar: The Legal Perils of Misrepresentation." *Competitive Intelligence Magazine* 5(2): 11–14.

Fuld, L. (1988). *Monitoring the Competition: Finding Out What's Really Going On over There*. New York: John Wiley & Sons.

Horowitz, R. (1999). "Competitive Intelligence and the Economic Espionage Act." *Competitive Intelligence Review* 10(3): 84–89.

Klein, C. (1998). "Cultural Differences in Competitive Intelligence Techniques." *Competitive Intelligence Magazine* 1(2): 21–23.

National Journal Group. (2002). "Corruption: Report Ranks Bribe Payers and Receivers." *UNWire: United Nations Foundation* (October 27). Washington, DC: National Journal Group. http://www.unfoundation.org/unwire/util/display_stories.asp?objid=5555.

Pagell, R. (1998). "Economic Espionage." *Database* 21(4): 23–30.

Prescott, J.E. (2001). "The P&G Dilemma: Espionage and Ethics." *Competitive Intelligence Magazine* 4(6): 22–24.

Sammon, W.L., M.A. Kurland, and R. Spitalnic. [eds.] (1984). *Business Competitor Intelligence: Methods for Collecting, Organizing, and Using Information*. New York: John Wiley & Sons.

Simpkins, R.A. (1998). "The Global Mind." *Competitive Intelligence Magazine* 1(2): 34–36.

Society of Competitive Intelligence Professionals. (2001). "P&G–Unilever Settlement Distinguishes CI from 'Dumpster Diving.'" *Competitive Intelligence Magazine* 4(6): 6–7.

Stratton, J. (1998). "The Straight and Narrow." *The China Business Review* 1–2: 24–29. http://www.chinabusinessreview.com/9801/stratton.html.

Tao, Q., and J.E. Prescott. (2000). "China: Competitive Intelligence Practices in an Emerging Market Environment." *Competitive Intelligence Review* 11(4): 65–78.

World Trade Organization. "Frequently Asked Questions about TRIPS." Geneva, Switzerland: World Trade Organization. http://www.wto.org/english/tratop_e/trips_e/tripfq_e.htm.

GLOBAL COMPETITIVE INTELLIGENCE MANAGEMENT

11

A StratCom Model for the Practice of International Competitive Intelligence

Attila L. Lendvai

INTRODUCTION

"Know your enemy; know yourself even more."

—Sun Tzu

"Fear we broadsides? Nay! We have cannons of our own!"

—William Shakespeare

There are few quotations from antiquity that, when taken in tandem, better capture the spirit of competitive intelligence (CI). Moreover, few figures from history better embody the spirit of strategy and communications than Sun Tzu and William Shakespeare. This connection shouldn't come as a surprise to a practitioner of CI, since the foundation of CI is, in fact, strategy and communications. At its very core, CI is essentially linked to strategy, and its practice relies intensely on efficient communication (Fuld, 1995). If either the strategic analytical component or the communicative actionable component is missing, professionals agree: it's not CI. In effect, as the quotations opening this chapter suggest, CI is a function, application, and shining example of a broader discipline . . . Strategic Communications (StratCom).

At this point, one might ask why it is important to place CI under the broader umbrella of StratCom. Is CI not its own discipline? For chief executive officers (CEOs) and CI practitioners alike, it is often difficult to "contextualize" the practice of CI, describe it to the uninitiated, convince them of its merits, and, indeed, know exactly where to "put" the CI function in an existing organizational structure. Furthermore, there are various "CI conundrums" afoot in the field that have largely eluded definitive solutions and the formation of best practices. This chapter explores one such CI conundrum, namely, how the practice of global CI differs from domestic CI, and makes the case that a StratCom approach gives the CI professional a simple yet solid foundation on which to erect a CI structure and realize very real and practical advantages, even in the contentious realm of international CI.

Understanding CI as StratCom can actually help answer this current CI conundrum, that is, how does the practice of global CI differ from domestic CI? Considering the rate of globalization, one may observe the conspicuous shortage of literature on global CI as ironic; but considering the typical narrow focus of CI-related literature, a shortage of global CI literature is understandable. Exploring the topic purely from a CI perspective produces varied and vague results—at best, a statistically insignificant survey of various international companies and their respective CI tactics. This "top down" approach is ineffective because CI is fundamentally linked with strategy; and asking how the manifestations of international strategies differ from domestic strategies (and one another) produces textbook volumes of explanations, models, structures, and cases. A StratCom approach, in contrast, examines international CI from the "bottom up" within a framework of international strategy and communication, and provides a context in which models of global CI practice can actually be developed—a foundation on which global CI can actually be practiced. With these models in hand, CI practitioners are better aware of how CI fits into the StratCom flows engendered by a particular global strategy and its supporting organizational structure. As a result, CI professionals will be able to make better decisions about what CI tools and tactics are most appropriate for their particular global organization and compare how these may or may not differ from purely domestic CI.

THE ROTARY ENGINE MODEL OF CI

It is useful to begin work from a basic understanding of CI from a StratCom perspective. At its core, StratCom stipulates that strategy and communication are not mutually exclusive, since each relies heavily on the other. Communication is dependent on listening (research, awareness, analysis, pattern recognition, etc.), and strategy is dependent on implementation (engaging, negotiating, convincing, motivating, etc.). Given the connection of CI to strategy and reliance on communication, CI practi-

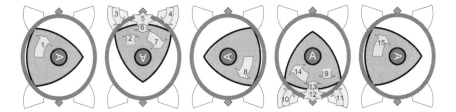

1. The CI professional 'A' initiates a forward momentum toward a source.
2. The momentum of the CI initiation causes pressure on the source (compression) – the necessary environment for inputs to be harnessed (combustion).
3. Essential information inflows (oxygen).
4. Essential but different information inflows (gasoline).
5. The inflows are combined with the 'spark' of analysis (ignition).
6. The force of the analysis pushes back on the CI initiative (energy conversion).
7. The momentum is forward, so the CI is pushed forward, around the axis of the CI professional, with greater momentum; the CI engine's output increases.
8. The CI professional 'A' moves forward with more momentum toward another source.
9. More momentum in the CI engine creates more urgent pressure on the source (compression) – a more urgent environment for inputs to be harnessed (combustion).
10. Essential information inflows (oxygen).
11. Essential but different information inflows (gasoline).
12. The inflows are combined with the 'spark' of analysis (ignition).
13. The force of the analysis pushes back on the CI initiative (energy conversion).
14. The momentum is forward, so the CI is pushed forward, around the axis of the CI professional, with even greater momentum: the CI engine's output increases even more.
15. The CI professional 'A' moves forward with even more momentum toward another source, etc.

Figure 11.1 The Rotary Engine Model of CI.

tioners, in particular, should agree that the successful development and deployment of any business strategy depends greatly on effective and timely StratCom, of which CI is an integral part. CI can be likened to an engine that powers strategy; but not just any engine, the StratCom model of CI is based on the Wankel Rotary Engine. The distinction between a conventional internal combustion engine and a rotary engine is the fact that oscillating pistons in the former are replaced by spinning rotors in the latter, thus allowing the rotary engine to harness inertia and momentum to a much greater degree than a conventional piston engine. The significance of this analogy, outlined in Figure 11.1, should be immediate and striking to the CI practitioner. The rotary engine model suggests that CI gains momentum over time, with the CI practitioner absorbing each consecutive "spark" and increasing the output of the CI engine accordingly. As momentum increases, the pressure and urgency exerted on inputs also increases; however, these increasing pressures are counterbalanced by the fact that the CI practitioner can safely encounter multiple "misfires" without the whole CI engine "seizing up."

Having accepted the simple yet significant StratCom model of CI as a rotary engine that powers strategy, the next step for the CI professional must be to determine how best to position the CI engine in the vehicle.

CONFIGURING THE CI ENGINE

How should a CEO or CI professional configure the CI engine in a business? Just as in the power train in a vehicle, the configuration depends on the size of the vehicle, its purpose, its environment, the competition (think auto racing), the driver's preference, and many other factors. Once again, the answer to the question of how to configure the CI engine in a business, domestic or otherwise, emerges from an appreciation of StratCom. What is the environment the business faces? What are the organizational structures, resources, and management preferences in support of the strategy? These issues apply regardless of the business—domestic or global—and are the first steps to developing a strategy, to which the CI engine must be married. Since the management preferences, resources, and competitive environments—all components of strategy—differ vastly among companies, seeking a StratCom model of CI on their basis alone would be precarious.

In their thorough benchmarking study representing information about the organizational strategies of 569 companies, Lackman, Saban, and Lanasa (2000) make recommendations based on organizational structure, specifically "the functions of the CI process within 16 leading intelligence companies." Their recommendations deal with matching specific CI functions and characteristics to existing functions in an organization, thereby suggesting "best fit." Organizations—especially international ones—can be defined by area divisions as well as functional divisions, however, suggesting that the CI professional must think about "organization" in broader terms. The following are fundamental international organizational structures and potential CI configurations that "best fit" those structures.

CI Configurations in an International Division Structure

An international division structure usually comes into being when a domestic firm branches out into international markets. The rationale for this organizational structure is logical, allowing the international division to grow as international sales grow, without distracting domestic managers focused—as they should be—on the mainstay domestic market. From a CI perspective (assuming that the firm has a CI engine operating domestically), the development of an international division poses interesting challenges. The CI engine may be very well tuned to the domestic competitive environment, but it may be completely out of touch with the international marketplace. Does the CI engine expand its scope of inputs to include global CI, and how does this process take place? If the growth in international business is gradual, then the existing CI engine can and should expand and adapt accordingly, beginning with the very first strategic explorations of international markets. As an essential component of the global strategy development process, the CI function will benefit from learning. Over time, the CI needs of the international division may necessitate a profound expansion of the CI engine, or the establishment of a dedicated international CI unit. Both of these configurations are illustrated in Figure 11.2.

An acquisition of a foreign firm or a joint venture may necessitate the establishment of a fairly robust international division—with equally robust CI needs—almost overnight. In such a case, it would be prudent for the firm to set up a specialized CI taskforce to assist in the exploration and due diligence process, thereby forming the hub of a subsequent international CI team from the very inception of the international initiative. The point is that the CI configuration supports the development of strategy and evolves according to the evolving organizational structure that supports said strategy. If a firm outgrows its international division structure and adopts a new organizational structure that better supports its evolving global strategy, the CI engine must evolve as well.

CI Configurations in an Area Division or Multidomestic Structure

Area division structures are a possible choice in organizational development around a firm's international strategy. "As international sales

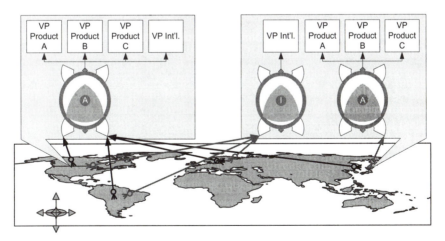

Figure 11.2 International Division CI Configurations.

grow as a percentage of total company sales, many successful companies evolve out of an international division structure and create an area division structure" (Beamish, Morrison, Rosenzweig, & Inkpen, 2000). This structure sees a decentralization of strategy crafting, execution, and decision-making authority and shifts power to multiple regional markets where the firm actually competes. The StratCom foundation of CI is once again reinforced, since CI is not only inextricably linked to strategy, but its inputs and outputs (through communications) must service the needs of multiple strategically relevant stakeholders—from managers to engineers (Dugal, 1998). As a result, the CI engine must shift with the organization to multiple regional markets, resulting in multiple CI engines serving the CI needs of regional managers, research and development (R&D) departments, marketing, and so on. At the same time, each area CI engine must report to the centrally located international CI engine serving the VP international division (refer to Figure 11.3).

For the CI professional, there is great merit to adopting this particular StratCom-based CI configuration, since it addresses multiple issues related to international CI. Decentralized CI engines can very much take the pulse of the markets in which they operate. Multiple CI engines around the world, each immersed in the language, culture, media, and network of particular regions can readily support the local management with domestic issues, but they can also act as a gatherer, filter, and translator of CI for head office. Properly executed, such an in-house global CI network would likely provide CI of a quantity and quality that no single centrally located CI engine could provide. The centrally located CI node

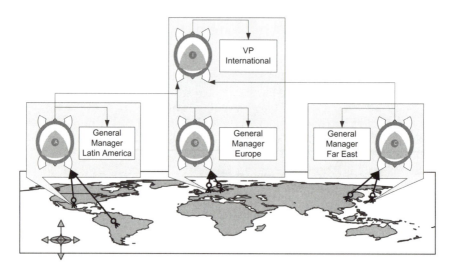

Figure 11.3   Area Division/Multidomestic CI Configuration.

would filter and distribute relevant CI downward, warning regional managers of outside threats beyond the scope of their area CI departments, or sharing best practices used by their colleagues around the globe. What may be the ideal model for international CI, however, is increasingly incongruent with the consensus best practice of international strategy. The ever-advancing wave of globalization, bringing with it reductions in tariffs and elimination of trade barriers, is allowing more and more international companies to shift away from an area divisional or multidomestic structure and back to a more centralized organization, repatriating most, if not all, strategic decision-making and cutting costs by eliminating duplication of effort across regions. The CI function is not immune to these effects, and the practitioner of international CI must be prepared for change.

CI Configurations in a Global Product Division Structure

A global product strategy divides a company into divisions based on product (or service). Typically, product strategies are set centrally for the world market by separate management teams organized by product division. This international structure has the strategy crafters and global decision-makers centrally located at head office. It is generally accepted that the CI professional needs to be in close proximity to the CI customers (users). Both the CI configurations in Figure 11.4 place the CI engine in the same physical location as the relevant decision-makers. The distinction between the two configurations is simply whether or not a single CI department is capable of generating valuable CI for multiple global product lines at once. With many multinational corporations (MNCs)

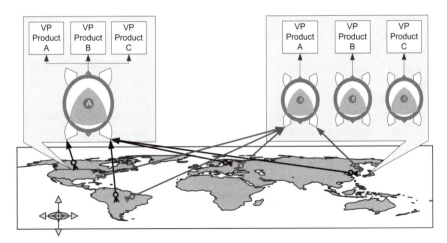

Figure 11.4 Global Divisional CI Configurations.

participating in a broad spectrum of products and services, the task of collecting and analyzing data alone may be too much for a single CI engine, particularly if the product divisions have stark dissimilarities. "MNCs, including ITT, Matsushita, General Electric, Grand Metropolitan, Philip Morris, and Mannesmann have highly diversified operations that lend themselves to distinct industry analyses and diverse business unit strategies" (Beamish, Morrison, Rosenzweig, & Inkpen, 2000). For these companies, it may be prudent to organize multiple CI engines, each answering to the appropriate division strategist.

The downside of this second CI configuration is overall CI for the MNC. If each CI engine is locked into a specific divisional structure, who is taking care of CI for the company as a whole? Theoretically at least, the reason for having a multi-divisional international strategy is precisely because the success of the MNC is dependent on the competitiveness and success of each "silo"; but in reality, the senior executives of companies like General Electric and Procter and Gamble (P&G) do make strategic decisions for their respective firms as a whole (Pepper, 1999). This may justify another, hierarchically superior CI professional who oversees the divisional CI departments, conducts CI on an enterprise level, and reports directly to the CEO. Another approach might see the divisional CI professionals meeting as a team, conducting broad enterprise analysis, and presenting their CI collectively. This way, the MNC wins the best of both CI worlds: senior divisional VPs have custom-tailored CI for divisional product strategy, while the CEO receives packaged CI from a united CI team for conducting global corporate strategy.

CI Configurations in a Global Matrix Structure

Despite a firm's best efforts to assume a global divisional structure, the reality for such firms is that global divisions most often assume some presence in geographically distributed and socioculturally and economically differing local areas. The emerging international structure known as a matrix addresses this reality in a formal—but often flexible and dynamically changing—organizational structure. Business is organized both by functional and area divisions, depending on the strategic directions of the various business units of the MNC. This means that strategic decision-making can at times be centralized and at times decentralized, depending on the best course of action from a strategic perspective. If the CI engine is to continuously support strategic decision-makers, it too must assume a matrix configuration (shown in Figure 11.5). The sum benefits of the area divisional CI configuration can thus be harvested by a firm that is otherwise in a divisional structure.

This is precisely what has been achieved at P&G, whose hub-and-spoke approach to CI demonstrates an MNC that treats CI as

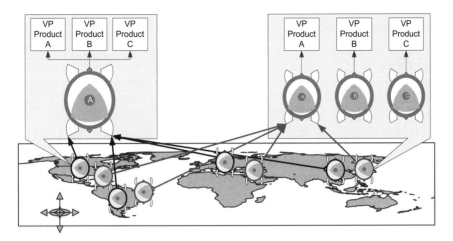

Figure 11.5 Matrix CI Configurations.

StratCom—inextricably linked to the service of strategic and communicative needs of the firm, at all levels:

> We now have seven "global business units." In addition, we have market development organizations, which you might think of as regions, plus a global business service organization, which brings together services. We have representatives and linkages between our central corporate business intelligence unit with each of those, and we're seeking advantages you'd expect, both from what is in the hub and what's in the spoke. The hub is important to provide the benefits of scale purchases, to have a common mission across the whole organization, standardized processes, and so on. At the same time, the spoke is terribly important for specific, flexible knowledge in the individual business units, and ownership of the activity in the individual business units.
>
> *John E. Pepper, 1999*

With a corporate endorsement by P&G, is it possible that the CI matrix configuration, what John Pepper calls the "hub and spoke," is the be-all-and-end-all model for international CI? If only it were that simple. Like all the international CI configurations discussed thus far, the matrix configuration is the best fit for a matrix organizational structure (just as John Pepper's hub-and-spoke model seems like a good, flexible configuration for P&G). In reality, there are far too many international organizational structures to arrive at one all-encompassing international CI configuration.

Joint Ventures, Affiliates, and Other International Structures

There are numerous other international structures that must be considered, since they do not necessarily fall inside the box of the four configurations discussed so far. Organizational structures such as joint ventures, affiliations, partnerships, and the like can see multiple autonomous bodies participating in the strategic development and execution of an enterprise—domestic or international in nature. Even a simple supplier or value-added reseller relationship can involve an international strategy—and a simple international organization—and so in a very basic way, even a computer company selling in a single domestic market requires an international CI configuration, since its components are of international origin. In all cases, the CI function must be married to the strategy and corresponding organization; however, since there are literally an unlimited number of permutations and combinations, there is no way to define an all-encompassing international CI configuration. Indeed, even the organizational categories discussed so far can be tweaked and tinkered with, such that the corresponding CI configurations will also reflect the nuances and eccentricities of particular international firms and/or their affiliates, partners, and broader business network (P&G's "hub and spoke" for instance).

The potential for infinite complexity in international CI configurations may just be why CI professionals have shied away from writing more about international CI. The four distinct models of international CI proposed thus far in this chapter do differ from domestic CI models in as much as their scope is global, but how "fundamental" is this difference; what of the other differences (if any); and what about this notion that even a domestic firm may need to do some international CI? In the end, as in the beginning, the answers to questions regarding the framework of CI can be found by observing its foundations—in this case, seeking the StratCom patterns among all the CI models discussed thus far and comparing them with those found in domestic CI. The result is the *Value Chain Model of CI.*

THE VALUE CHAIN MODEL OF INTERNATIONAL AND DOMESTIC CI

Let us recap how far we have come in our StratCom model of international CI. First, we explored the similarities between StratCom and CI, recognizing that both are born out of a union of strategy and communications. Next, we explored how CI is an engine that gains momentum as it gathers and analyzes a greater number and frequency of inputs. Then, we explored common configurations of the CI engine in the strategy vehicle—the particular organizational framework chosen to support the international strategy. We suggested particular CI configurations that seem to fit common international organizational structures, and in each case, we noted that no matter how complex or convoluted the organizational structure, the CI function must fit into said structure, thereby staying linked to the underlying strategy the complex structure supports. Finally, we discovered that, in addition to MNCs, international structures include a near infinite number of permutations and combinations of firms, governments, affiliates, suppliers, manufacturers, and the like, each executing its own strategy, each an international entity in its own right, as it participates in one or more extended organizational networks with other entities. In other words, by looking beyond the firm—even beyond the MNC—we find a second international organizational structure in support of strategy. Simply put, we find *value chains*.

The value chain is a beautiful model for understanding both international and domestic CI because it is, after all, universal. In one way, shape, or form, all business relies on some value chain or another. As complex as any given value chain might be—particularly in the global economy—business people take heart knowing for a fact that all value chains are doable; it's simply a question of logistics. Each stakeholder contributes to the value of the evolving product, and extracts some reward for doing so (although the payoff may be delayed until the ultimate product is finished and sold). Although the Rotary Engine Model for CI still applies (after all, it is the CI function that converts inputs into useable CI, gaining momentum and increasing the urgency of, and demand for, inputs), the Value Chain Model of international CI feeds the engine, and illustrates in real terms both how complex and how doable international CI can be. Consider Figure 11.6, a depiction of a complex international CI value chain.

The key points a CI practitioner should take away from this model are as follows. Multiple sources of information can be located anywhere in the world. These sources can be anything from suppliers to agents to affiliates to trade associations and publications. Some sources may provide internally completed CI, encapsulating P&G's hub-and-spoke model; but these CI engines could also belong to outside entities such as suppliers who might share bits of useable CI with customers, especially if the customer reciprocates or if CI sharing furthers the likelihood that the customer will continue to buy (or buy in greater quantities). As the CI engine rolls along the CI gathering process, it gains momentum and adds to an increasing quantity or quality of useable CI. Multiple sources can contribute to the CI value chain at different stages and in different ways so long as the CI engine can tap them; or, to express it from the sources' point of view, so long as sources have access to the CI value chain.

Actual value chains, international or otherwise, are generally complex structures involving numerous players each having their own agenda. They work because of the very fact that they are value chains

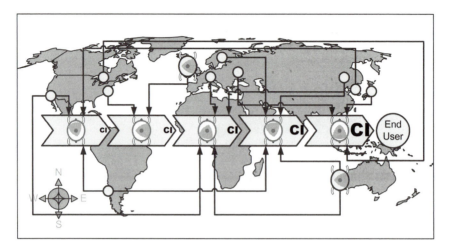

Figure 11.6   The Value Chain Model of International CI.

and so culture, language, and all the other conceivable obstacles to execution are overcome by the common notion that participants who input value will extract at least as much value in return. Still, the logistics of bringing a value chain together to produce a useable product at the end is no small challenge. One company, Descartes, has managed to tap into the logistics of value chain management from a networking software angle. Descartes's software allows multiple participants in a value chain to gain access to key information and documentation allowing them to execute their inputs and extract outputs according to pre-agreed terms. The Descartes networked logistics model is a good one from a CI perspective.

CI is, after all, information converted into actionable intelligence. As such, it is easily transported in the twenty-first century by telephone, fax, Internet, courier, and the like (Aker, 1998). There is no reason why a CI engine of any kind—domestic or international—would avoid using technology (even if it is in as basic a form as e-mail) when constructing the framework of a highly flexible CI value chain. Like a sea urchin's tentacles, the electronic network allows sources to be easily captured and drawn into the CI engine, where their inputs are converted to CI. In addition, we know that if a value chain is to work, it must also return value in the way of outputs to those who input. In other words, the same information technology network used to collect information can also be used to disseminate it (Rosen, 1998). The key here is that information is on a need-to-know basis. The CI value chain eventually produces actionable intelligence for the firm, but this is not necessarily what is desired by participants in the value chain. Consider the following case in point: chipset supplier X provides information to PC motherboard manufacturer A on a competitive motherboard manufacturer B. Manufacturer A uses the information, compounds it with other sources, and eventually produces valuable CI—from a motherboard manufacturer's point of view. The CI produced does contain information on the competitor's chipset supplier Z, however, and this information is made available to supplier X. From a networking perspective, such collaborative *quid pro quo* on the CI value chain is easily accomplished. With technologies from Open Text to Lotus Notes, Internet-based access with multiple access levels can ensure that only pertinent and relevant information is exchanged between parties. Furthermore, by constructing a CI value chain in this way, the CI practitioner receives information classified according to areas of interest, greatly reducing time-consuming sorting and cataloguing of raw data. If Descartes can automate real-life value chains of immense complexity, scale, and distance across vast cultural and geographical divides complete with payment, physical execution, and fulfillment, then surely a CI practitioner—appreciative of the StratCom foundations of CI—can establish a knowledge-based CI value chain using the appropriate CI configuration, technology-based tools, and existing business relationships along a real, established, and readily accessible value chain.

THE REAL VALUE OF THE STRATCOM MODEL OF CI

So how does this differ from domestic CI? How does an international value chain differ from a domestic value chain? Apart from distance, language, culture, currency, and trade-related issues, value chains do not fundamentally differ from one another. Likewise, CI is a knowledge-based activity intrinsically related to strategy and communications. International CI differs from domestic CI only in those ways that international strategy differs from domestic strategy. There are numerous nuances, rules, tariffs, guidelines, cultural notes, language issues, and other factors to take into consideration, but as long as the CI professional—or the CEO establishing a CI function—understands the three simple StratCom-based principles outlined in this chapter, the differences between domestic and international CI prove marginal at best.

First, CI operates as a rotary engine that gains momentum as it functions, increasing the rate and pressure for valuable inputs and subsequent forward momentum (outputs). Next, the CI engine is inextricably linked to strategy and must adhere to the organizational structures that support said strategy. Finally, in the absence of a definitive best fit model of CI, the CI practitioner can turn to the Value Chain Model. Grafting CI to the existing value chain—whereby numerous diverse and remotely located sources provide inputs over time, extracting some value in return for their contributions—leads to the development of a technology and process framework for enabling and streamlining a logistics network for the execution of CI. These three elements, in tandem, constitute the StratCom model of CI—international and domestic. Thus, the "great CI conundrum" of international versus domestic CI is easily overcome by the CI practitioner by embracing the StratCom foundations of CI and following a few simple steps:

1. When initializing any CI function, look first at the value chain of your organization.

2. At every point along the value chain of the organization, there will be one or more key individual(s) with something of value to contribute to (and gain in return from) your CI function; identify these individuals and manage relationships with them carefully.

3. Expand the scope of the CI function using the points of the value chain as primary nodes of subsequent levels of your CI network. An example of this would be to leverage the local networks of your foreign suppliers or distributors, either through direct introductions or using your reliable primary sources to relay information gathered from third parties.

4. Use technology—that is, use every communicative vehicle at your disposal, from paper-based communications to print, radio, TV, courier, and snail-mail, as well as electronic mediums. Too often, CI practitioners take for granted that technology means hi-tech; the CI practitioner who understands the Value Chain Model of CI knows that in most value chains, low-tech is far more pervasive than hi-tech, and that their CI function is no different.

5. Follow the KISS principle (as every engineer is taught: "Keep It Simple, Straightforward"), every value chain, no matter how complex, is obviously doable if it exists; CI professionals need not complicate their lives unnecessarily.

CONCLUSION

No longer relegated to the niche corners of marketing or human resources, the StratCom model of CI presented in this chapter positions the CI function along the very backbone of a business—the value chain itself. No matter how complex that value chain may be, the StratCom model gives the CI practitioner a simple, bottom-up, and real-world approach to CI that results in a hard, codified backbone, whose stakeholders and participants understand its value, and whose CI professional(s) use CI logistics to overcome any obstacles in the way of creating and extracting that value. The CI practitioner still requires "soft skills" and "the CI toolbox" (explored more fully in other chapters); but as is the case with any value chain, tremendous opportunities exist for CEOs and CI professionals alike to expand their StratCom frame of mind and develop their own enhancements to their CI value chains, be they continuous improvement, just-in-time delivery, or other processes that will improve their CI value chain. The bottom line is this: an appreciation of the StratCom foundations of CI opens a world of opportunity for innovation on the part of CEOs and CI professionals alike, free to construct, on a simple yet strong foundation, advanced CI functions that will potentially give their firm a competitive edge.

REFERENCES

Aker, B. (1998). "An Information Technology Blueprint for Conducting Competitive Intelligence." *Competitive Intelligence Magazine* 1(3): 25–28.

Beamish, P.W., A.J. Morrison, P.M. Rosenzweig, and A. Inkpen. (2000). *International Management: Text and Cases.* New York: Irwin/McGraw-Hill.

Dugal, M. (1998). "CI Product Line: A Tool for Enhancing User Acceptance of CI." *Competitive Intelligence Review* 9(2): 17–25.

Fuld, L.M. (1995). *The New Competitor Intelligence: The Complete Resource for Finding, Analyzing, and Using Information about Your Competitors.* New York: John Wiley and Sons.

Lackman, C.L., K. Saban, and J.M. Lanasa. (2000). "Organizing the CI Function: A Benchmarking Study." *Competitive Intelligence Review* 11(1): 17–27.

Pepper, J.E. (1999). "Competitive Intelligence at Procter & Gamble." *Competitive Intelligence Review* 10(4): 4–9.

Rosen, L. (1998). "Capturing and Sharing Competitive Intelligence: Microsoft's Intranet." *Competitive Intelligence Magazine* 1(2): 9–12.

12

The Location and Organization of the Competitive Intelligence Function in a Multinational Corporation

Michelle Murray

The global marketplace is becoming highly integrated with many multinational enterprises (MNEs) directing their resources toward global opportunities as the key drivers for growth. For example, Eli Lilly, Avon, Kellogg's, and Sun Microsystems derive approximately 40% of their gross sales from their foreign operations (Peter & Donelly, 2000). Foreign markets are taking on a greater strategic importance, and efforts to compete effectively in these arenas are being made through appropriately organized operations and marketing. Effective competitive intelligence (CI) to guide global efforts can be generated only by a deep understanding of regional cultures and environments. The ability of employees involved in the CI function to understand regional differences is often affected by the location and organization of the CI function within the organization.

This chapter will examine whether the CI function should be located centrally or regionally within a multinational company. A decision on the organization of any function within an MNE needs to balance the need for local responsiveness against the efficiencies of global integration. For the CI function, this balance is complicated by the need to be located close to key internal customers (decision-makers). The optimal degree of formality of a CI function and the effect that the underlying corporate structure may have on the CI function location decision will also be a major focus of this chapter.

The objective of the chapter is to create an understanding about the advantages and disadvantages of different locations of elements of the CI function within the corporate organization. Based on this understanding, the principles of this chapter may be applied to effectively locate the CI function to suit a firm's corporate organization and resources.

The current models of multinational organizations will be elucidated in order to illustrate how CI efforts and responsibilities can be most effectively organized and located to fit within these corporate structures and nurture the development of a CI culture. Effective global CI will be linked to a firm's optimal corporate structure to facilitate their marketing and strategic advantages. Key implementation considerations for CI organizational design will be established. There is no "correct" structure of the CI function within the organization, but as different CI structures are practiced, this guide may bring perspective to the choice of a particular one.

This chapter will examine the requirements of organizational structure for CI function success, explore the need for formalization of the CI function, and define the multinational corporate structures within a company. It will also discuss the resulting CI organizations to shadow the underlying need for CI products and communication that may be caused by different corporate structures. Interviews with executives of two MNEs and examples drawn from a literature review will be presented to illustrate the concept of shadowing the corporate organization as well as the organization of actual CI functions.

This chapter will not address the issue of whether the corporate structure of the case study companies are effective but, rather, will try to show that the CI organization does shadow the corporate structure or stated strategy. The success of the CI organization within the companies falls outside the scope of this chapter because of the complexity of separating out the impact of other key success factors on measurements of performance.

ORGANIZATIONAL REQUIREMENTS FOR SUCCESSFUL CI FUNCTIONS

Adequate CI human intelligence can be collected from a firm's employees to answer 70%–90% of intelligence requests by senior management (Sawka, Francis, & Herring, 1995). This information-gathering is one of the important activities of the CI function as described by the intelligence cycle that includes the following five phases: needs assessment; planning and direction; information storage and processing; analysis and production; and dissemination (Herring, 1998). Each phase of the intelligence cycle is necessary to create and add value to CI. In an MNE, internal customers and intelligence cycle phases may be separated and organized into different parts of the corporate structure. This organization of phases may make it more difficult to successfully complete the intelligence cycle due to the varying regional relevance of CI information, barriers to communication and understanding, and loss of the momentum between phases if there is a diffusion or imbalance in the location of the necessary CI function.

All the phases of the CI cycle are important, but the collecting, analyzing, and storing phase using the capabilities of a well-located CI library is a strategic asset for a CI function (Lackman, Saban, & Lanasa, 2000). The success of the CI function is strongly linked with CI leadership, personnel, and CI culture, but structure can directly influence these contributing factors. Structure has an influence on reporting relationships, budgets, and the types of projects assigned (Lackman, Saban, & Lanasa, 2000).

The most important result in centralizing or decentralizing the CI function is to ensure close alignment with the Chief Executive Officer (CEO) or other key senior management with responsibility for business strategy. Successful CI programs need a direct reporting relationship to leadership and decision-makers who support the core tenets of CI. Support will be gained only if tailored CI reaches them in a timely fashion and in the most effective communication media according to their needs (Sawka, Francis, & Herring, 1995).

FORMALIZATION OF THE CI FUNCTION

As structure and organization can impact on the performance and effectiveness of any function within a firm, it can impact on the CI function (Sawyer, 1999). In actual practice, CI functions are organized in a variety of structures mirroring the organizational diversity of MNEs. The CI function can be completely decentralized throughout subsidiaries, centralized in the parent company, or arranged in a hub-and-spoke fashion. Also, within these different arrangements of locations, CI can be formalized as a separate department or integrated informally within other job functions as more of a diffuse process.

Studies have shown that an increasing number of large MNEs have formalized the CI cycle within their corporate structure (Groom & David, 2001). Some firms, such as Motorola, have hired outside intelligence experts to conceive and create their formal CI department (Franklin, 2002). A formal structured CI function yields optimal results, but in actuality, many companies still do not have any formal structure and use a more informal CI process based on integrating the CI responsibility within the job of existing employees knowledgeable about their industry. (Groom & David, 2001). This can be a result of serious resource limitations or lack of awareness of the benefits of CI. The level of formalization of a CI process structure can be based on globalization of its industry, organization of its decision-makers and resources, geographic information needs, resources available, and anticipated demands. If the demand for CI is forecasted to be high, a more formal, organized structure is needed. Conversely, if the demand is low, the needs may be met by including CI in existing job responsibilities.

A proposed tool for planning the location and formality of a CI function is to match the structure to the organization of the corporation. This consistency should result in better service to the internal customers, ease of communication, close working relationships with decision-makers, and, ultimately, a CI functional strategy that is patterned after the corporate strategy and culture inferred by its structure.

CORPORATE STRUCTURE MODELS

This refresher of basic corporate structure models is meant to form the basis of an understanding of the advantages and disadvantages inherent to each type of underlying MNE structure. A similarly organized CI function that *shadows* the corporate structure and its decision-makers will experience the same challenges. To describe the degree of centralization and organization of an MNE, the term "multidomestic" (more broadly defined as geographical organization), "global corporation" (subdivided by product or function), or "hybrid organization" is used to define organizations (Peter & Donelly, 2000; Crossan, Fry, & Killing, 2002). Examples of different structures are outlined in Figure 12.1. Most MNEs are organized in a centralized and decentralized hybrid of different activities in the value chain. Centralization is usually focused on the core, routine operations of the value chain, whereas decentralization is more suited to deal effectively with strategic issues (Suutari, 2001). The MNE organizational structures and their respective strategic advantages and limitations are outlined in Table 12.1.

A global company competes with a vision of a unified global market with foreign subsidiaries and divisions interdependent by centralization for operations and strategy. A global strategy is more risky because it requires a stable organizational structure that may be inflexible to changes in global markets and customer needs (Peter & Donelly, 2000). The benefits of a global structure include economies of scale and scope. A global structure is more difficult to create than a multi-domestic, as it requires extremely good communication, global management processes, and a multi-cultural and flexible employee population (Peter & Donelly, 2000). These implementation challenges would be equivalent to the difficulties facing a centralized CI department.

A global structure and strategy are more favored by a company depending on the extent of the globalization of its industry. The measures of industry globalization are economic factors (e.g., rising product development costs, host country sourcing costs), market factors (e.g., product life cycle

Table 12.1
Advantages and Disadvantages of Different Organizational Structure Types

Multinational Enterprise	Advantages	Disadvantages
Global – Product	• Focus on each product line resource needs and performance • Can tailor the product line to regional needs better than functional due to focus	• High cost and heavy duplication of functional groups for each product line • No economies of scale or scope • Lack of communication in functional groups • Overall view of performance not transparent • Multiple contacts across divisions for external customers
Global – Function	• Good communication and resource allocation within functions • Allows efficiencies of scale	• Poor and slow communication /coordination • Lack of sensitivity to local markets
Multi – Domestic	• Responsive to local market diversity • Easier collection of market intelligence (Bajaj &Fernando, 2000) • Good for customizable products • Intense focus on a new market • Natural communication between functions and product lines.	• Generally poor communication among regions • Slow global product introductions • No global efficiencies of scope or scale • Decisions may be based on preserving autonomy rather than profit.
Hybrid	• Flexible scope • Responsive to local needs and global issues • Importance of organizing elements is equal to achieve even performance	• Complex • May lose focus • Reporting and ownership ambiguity • Slow decisions

[shelf life] and type of products, homogeneity of market needs, ability to globalize distribution channels), environmental factors (e.g., favorable government regulations, communication infrastructure), and competitive factors (e.g., opportunities to preempt a competitive product, extent of competitive firm global structures) (Peter & Donelly, 2000). A company's organizational structure will also depend on the standardization of its products, how different the foreign cultures are from the domestic culture, and the company's ability to actually implement a global structure (Peter & Donelly, 2000).

To balance the attributes of decentralized multidomestic and centralized global structures, a hybrid structure (hub-and-spoke) is an alternative (Society of Competitive Intelligence Professionals, 1999). This hybrid structure has centralization of responsibility for the functions that lend themselves to a global orientation but allows the opportunity for regional customization and flexibility (Peter & Donelly, 2000). This approach requires a high level of collaboration and division of responsibility between parent and subsidiary compared to other models.

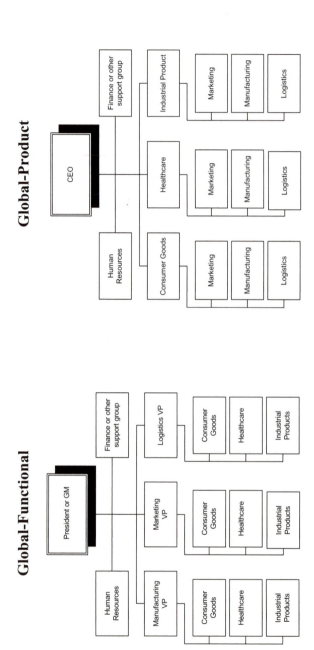

Global-Functional

Global-Product

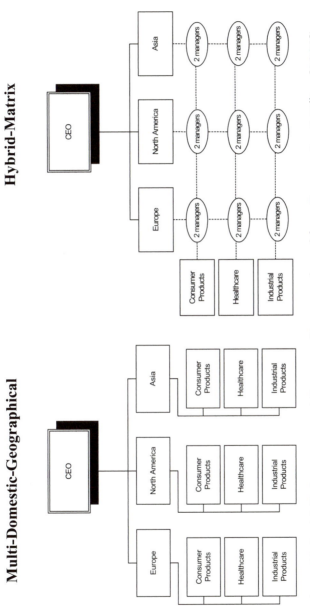

Figure 12.1   MNE Organizational Structures (*Source:* adapted from Crossan, Fry & Killing [2002]).

CI FUNCTION SHADOWING OF CORPORATE STRUCTURE

Global companies base their preference of global suppliers on their understanding of globalization factors, consistency of output, single point of contact, and the ability to gain service in regions where there is no regional supplier representation (Montgomery & Yip, 2000). This explanation can be fit to the CI process and internal customers. As the internal customers become more global in focus and create a global structure, they will value global CI suppliers with one point of coordination. The global CI output will help them manage their global issues.

To serve unique organizational needs closely, a shadow CI organization should match the formal corporate structure (Ashton, 1997). Table 12.2

Table 12.2
MNE Shadow CI Organizational Options and Key Implementation Considerations

Multinational Enterprise	Shadow CI Organization Options	Key Implementation Considerations
Global – Product	• Centralized unit with groups performing CI for each product group management, CEO, and corporate senior management • Possibly some decentralized groups in regional areas.	• Provides wider product focus • Need formal & informal horizontal communication mechanisms among divisions • May need to appoint regional coordinator or president to tie divisions together • Requires strong global strategy
Global – Function	• Centralized unit with groups performing CI for each functional group management, CEO, and corporate senior management	• Good for narrow product focus and small companies • Standardized products needed • Need formal & informal horizontal communication mechanisms
Multi- Domestic	• Decentralized groups performing CI in the geographic units of the company for all product and function types. Less focus on CEO and corporate senior management.	• Evaluate actual level of need for locally customized products and distinct local conditions • Investigate any opportunities for global economies of scale and scope • Requires strong global strategy
Hybrid	• Collaborative groups with centralized CI unit and specialists located within the corporate operating groups / corporate organization (multi-domestic, product or function division).	• Deciding on extent of hybrid - front end or back end (centralized regionalization) (Bajaj & Fernando, 2000) of CI group but some decision power resides with parent location and multiple reporting levels • Ownership, reporting and responsibility need to be clearly defined • Requires both global & regional strategy • Design mechanisms for expediting decisions

contains some options on where a shadow CI process might fit within each organizational structure type and the key implementation considerations of different global CI structures. To be effective, CI knowledge must be able to bridge hierarchical, functional, diagonal, and distance barriers to reach the appropriate decision-makers. Generally, information and influence flow vertically through reporting relationships with the greatest ease, but horizontal flow across groups will happen only with committed encouragement (Crossan, Fry, & Killing, 2002). Technological innovations in communications have eased horizontal communications to help fill the communication gaps created by pure global and multidomestic structures.

If a central unit is to be used, the CI function should be divided up by geographical areas allowing for the narrow scope of focus on a region (Robertson, 1998). It is not always necessary to have a completely centralized CI unit when the underlying corporate structure is centralized. A highly centralized CI function focused solely on long-term industry performance requires significant resources that are usually only found in the largest and most committed of companies. These centralized CI functions are historically more sensitive to layoffs compared to decentralized CI functions located within divisions and business units that are accessible by a wider set of key management for strategic and tactical information (Giese, 2002). Often, a decentralized, limited structure CI function with a central core coordinator who is responsible for the intelligence cycle is the most efficient use of resources and produces the most meaningful outputs (Clarke, Herring, Papp, Rosenkrans, & Tessun, 1999). In a decentralized organizational structure, the CI function must be focused (formalized) on filling strategic management requests prior to routine, short-term, tactical requests in order to maximize their value with senior management.

For all types of underlying corporate structures, a diffuse or informal CI process may be evident due to a lack of understanding about the value of CI or a belief that the best CI is done by those currently in job functions with expert industry knowledge. Also, due to resource limitations within the corporation, a diffuse structure may be a common occurrence. An emerging trend in decentralized, informal organization is the "knowledge cell." The knowledge cell membership is dispersed throughout the organization but communicates regularly on a focus theme or topic (Ashton, 1997). Knowledge cells have had some successful applications in gathering and interpreting data and in forming strategy, but this organizational structure does not allow for quick responses to CI requests and so has only a long-term planning focus. A diffuse CI process occurs when the CI process is not formally structured and is part of other job responsibilities with the communication following established reporting relationships to senior management (Ashton, 1997). This complete lack of structure is not recommended because CI can lose both focus and executive support and can suffer from a lack of prioritization. This is especially evident when a CI role is bundled with a market research responsibility (Lackman, Saban, & Lanasa, 2000).

ACTUAL CORPORATE ORGANIZATION OF THE CI PROCESS

In 1989, a benchmarking study was done on a sample of leading companies to understand the formalization of the CI function in organizations. This study revealed that formal, organized CI capabilities were relatively new (four years old on average), tended to have decentralized CI processes located within marketing and strategic planning departments, and had an average of three employees assigned to CI activities (Groom & David, 2001).

From the literature, the experience of Procter and Gamble (P&G) in 1999 provides an example of the development of an organization with a hybrid hub-and-spoke CI network (Society of Competitive Intelligence Professionals, 1999). Prior to 1999, the P&G CI function evolved from a highly centralized CI department to decentralized regional business units. The resulting performance of these decentralized regional CI functions was unsatisfactory. This led, in part, to P&G's 1999 restructuring of its corporate processes and culture to be able to meet the increasing demand for nimbleness and global marketing. This restructuring moved corporate processes from four geographic areas into a global organization subdivided by three product divisions (global product organization) (Crossan, Fry, & Killing, 2002). In order to meet the new demands of this centralized structure and yet retain the ability to collect regional CI, the CI process became a hybrid, hub-and-spoke network (Miller, 1999). The hybrid structure has a global director with responsibility for benchmarking and communicating CI to executives, cross-functional global strategy forums, and global information centers. The global information centers are linked into the organization to encourage better collaboration. The Global Knowledge Network (internal intranet) disseminates information to all P&G employees with only sensitive areas restricted (Miller, 1999).

An additional example from the literature involves the organization of CI within Lexis-Nexis. Lexis-Nexis has a global product corporate structure. There are ten dedicated CI employees located in decentralized locations within the product and regional business units. There is no central, formal CI function for coordination. The CEO manages a strong communication network to support the CI employees. The emphasis on regional locations of the CI functions may be explained by the product characteristics of legal and business software that have a strong need for regional customization. All employees have access to the CI output by internal intranet and intelligence is disseminated through e-mail and meetings (Gieskes, 2000).

Ericsson has a well-deserved reputation as a leader in the gathering and dissemination of business intelligence data. Ericsson has recently reorganized to form a matrix organization with global functional organization for resource roles, geographic organization for sales and marketing (reporting to the CEO) and global product organization for business units and product development (reporting to the Chief Operating Officer [COO]) (Ericsson Corporation, 2001). Ericsson has leveraged an information technology (IT) solution to establish a coordinated, global CI network to serve its complex organization. The Internet portals facilitate the CI process by centrally coordinating information-gathering, storage, and retrieval; networking 100 global CI analysts (located within the various substructures of Ericsson) with project responsibility and provision of tools for specific and broad dissemination (Ormerod, 2002).

3M provides an example of an informal organization of CI similar to the concept of knowledge cells. The 3M corporate structure is a hybrid, hub-and-spoke organization. CI at 3M has transitioned from a formal, centralized department to a multi-disciplined approach in which employees from a division's manufacturing, research and development (R&D), marketing, sales, and a variety of other functions take a team-based approach to data-gathering and analysis on specific topics (Miller, 2000).

Pittsburgh Plate Glass (PPG) also uses cross-functional knowledge cells within each business unit but has formally addressed the need for executive management support. PPG is organized through a matrix corporate structure but has heavier emphasis on a global product structure. The knowledge cells have a formal, reporting relationship to the centrally located Chief Information Officer (Miller, 2000).

To extend the knowledge of current practices and highlight that there is no single preferred structure, two companies were asked about the current organization of the CI department or process within their corporation. The scope of the examination was bounded by the location of a subsidiary or parent company within Canada. Most of the companies contacted had the parent company or North American regional parent located within the United States. All the sources and companies requested to remain anonymous.

The first company interviewed was an MNE with a hybrid organization (sales and distribution by region; product and other corporate functions were structured by global product organization). The firm competes in the consumer goods industry with global subsidiaries and the parent company in the United States. The CI process is informal and diffuse in Canada and focuses on AC Nielsen market data, the purchase of which is initiated from within the marketing department. Other global subsidiaries gather more detailed intelligence on their regional environment, but the corporate CI function is very centralized. The main CI function is structured to deliver CI from a uniform global product focus. All CI except sensitive material is available to all employees through an intranet. The lack of formal CI in Canada may possibly be attributed to the proximity of the Canadian subsidiary to the U.S. parent company as well as to a lack of perceived difference between U.S. and Canadian intelligence needs (Anonymous, 2002a).

The second company interviewed was a high-tech MNE based in Canada with two subsidiaries located in Europe and Asia. The company is organized in a hybrid, multidomestic structure with strong centralization of certain functions (notably financial and research functions) reporting to a global CEO. Within the parent company, product groups further subdivide the operational structures. This company has been in operation for approximately 25 years. At the time of the contact, all CI efforts were limited to the parent company, but they were diffused throughout the sales and marketing areas with no formal structure. Currently, there are plans to organize a centralized, formal CI function within the next year. As the CI function matures within the parent company, it is very conceivable that decentralized CI functions will be created (Anonymous, 2002b).

CONCLUSION

The interview and literature examples of CI functions in organizations attempting to shadow corporate organizations illustrate the merit of locating and organizing the CI function based on the characteristics underlying the structures of MNEs. Corporate structure is usually a reflection of the multinational's global strategy, culture, and power distribution. By shadowing the MNE structure, the success of the CI function is able to secure better access to CI leadership, decision-makers, and applicable human intelligence, allowing the creation of intelligence that is responsive to regional issues. During planning and implementation, the challenges, resource needs, and benefits of each type of CI organization must be carefully balanced to meet the organizational requirements for successful CI.

There are some obstacles to using the multinational's structure as a guide to locating and organizing the CI function. If the industry is being redefined, or if the corporation is unsure about which structure it should be using, or if it is in the midst of transition, it will be difficult to identify the appropriate aspects of organization against which to shadow the CI function. In these circumstances, the employees charged with the CI function should help formulate the organizational change strategy. In this way, they are in a position to monitor progress and provide CI on industry globalization and input on striking a balance between local responsiveness and global efficiencies to support recommendations of a suitable structure. As new organizational structures are implemented, the CI process can be organized and located to meet the emerging demands.

High-caliber CI will result in improved performance for a corporation. There are measurable benefits from investing in a formal and structured

CI function. Many suggestions for measurements have been proposed, but a 1995 study by the University of North Texas found that companies that place a high emphasis on CI earned an average of US$1.24 a share annually versus losses of US$0.07 per share sustained by companies that did not emphasize CI (Franklin, 2002). Cliff Kalb, senior director of strategic business analysis at Merck, credits their CI efforts for allowing the company to proactively strengthen their market position against the introduction of a competitive new drug. This position has resulted in US$150 million to US$200 million in revenues over the past three years (Franklin, 2002). Additional evidence was gathered about the value of a formal CI process defined as having a separate group of employees performing CI, frequent competitor analysis and a dedicated number of employees for CI analysis. It was found that companies with advanced formal CI monitoring processes had a higher return on assets than companies with primitive CI systems (Sawka, Francis, & Herring, 1995).

By instituting a formal CI process that suits the degree of centralization of the MNE structure, the CI intelligence cycle will have a better fit with the organization. Consequently, each phase of the intelligence cycle will be more effective in delivering high-caliber CI.

REFERENCES

Anonymous. (2002a). Interview conducted on 02/12/2002.

Anonymous. (2002b). Interview conducted on 02/05/2002.

Ashton, W.B. (1997). "Future Directions in Competitive Technical Intelligence," pp. 477–509 in W.B. Ashton and R.A. Klavans [eds.], *Keeping Abreast of Science and Technology: Technical Intelligence for Business.* Columbus, OH: Battelle Press.

Bajaj, J., and R. Fernando. (2000). "Why Regionalization Didn't Meet Expectations." *Medical Marketing and Media* 35(5): 98–108.

Clark, C., J.P. Herring, J. Papp, W. Rosenkrans, and F. Tessun. (1999). "Developing Process and Infrastructure to Meet Management's CTI Needs: A Roundtable Discussion." *Competitive Intelligence Review* 10(3): 4–18.

Crossan, M.M., J.N. Fry, and J.P. Killing. (2002). *Strategic Analysis and Action.* Toronto, ON: Prentice-Hall.

Ericsson Corporation. (2001). "Ericsson Strengthens Management Structure and Appoints Chief Operating Officer." Press Release, August 17. http://www.ericsson.com/press/archive/2001Q3/20010817-1044.html.

Franklin, D. (2002). "Spies like Us: Creating a Competitive Intelligence Shop Is Easier than You Might Think." *Time Magazine* 159(12): B12.

Giese, D. (2002). "A Bright Future for CI through Competitive Affairs." *Competitive Intelligence Magazine* 5(2): 21–24.

Gieskes, H. (2000). "Competitive Intelligence at LEXIS-NEXIS." *Competitive Intelligence Review* 11(2): 4–11.

Groom, J.R., and F.R. David. (2001). "Competitive Intelligence Activity among Small Firms." *S.A.M. Advanced Management Journal* 66(1): 12–20.

Herring, J.P. (1998). "What Is Intelligence Analysis?" *Competitive Intelligence Magazine* 1(2): 13–16.

Lackman, C.L., K. Saban, and J.M. Lanasa. (2000). "Organizing the Competitive Intelligence Function: A Benchmarking Study." *Competitive Intelligence Review* 11(1): 17–27.

Miller, S.H. (1999). "CI of 'Singular Importance' Says Procter & Gamble's Chairman." *Competitive Intelligence Magazine* 2(3): 5–7.

Miller, S.H. (2000). "Competitive Market Intelligence Takes Varied Forms; Offers Key Lessons." *Competitive Intelligence Magazine,* 3(1). http://www.scip.org/news/cimagazine_article.asp?id=234.

Montgomery, D.B., and G.S. Yip. (2000). "The Challenge of Global Customer Management." *Marketing Management* 9(4): 22–29.

Ormerod, P.H. (2002). "How Ericsson Turned Its Workforce into Intelligence Gatherers." *Competitive Intelligence Magazine* 5(1): 27–29.

Peter, P.J., and J.H. Donelly, Jr. (2000). *A Preface to Marketing Management.* Toronto, ON: Irwin McGraw-Hill.

Robertson, M.F. (1998). "Seven Steps to Global CI." *Competitive Intelligence Magazine* 1(2): 29–33.

Sawka, K.A., D.B. Francis, and J.P. Herring. (1995). "Evaluating Business Intelligence Systems: How Does Your Company Rate?" *Competitive Intelligence Review* 6(4): 22–25.

Sawyer, D.C. (1999). "Inside Job: Organizational Structure as Competitive Saboteur." *Competitive Intelligence Magazine* 2(1): 45–46.

Society of Competitive Intelligence Professionals. (1999). "Face to Face: John Pepper and Susan Steinhardt." *Competitive Intelligence Magazine* 2(4): 35–38.

Suutari, R. (2001). "Organizing for the New Economy." *CMA Management* 75(2): 12–13.

13

Best Applications of Global Competitive Intelligence: Macro-Level Scanning and Cultural Analysis

Scott A. Lapstra and Victor Knip

In a world that is experiencing an increasing trend toward globalization, competitive intelligence (CI) is a useful tool for companies to study and understand competitive opportunities and threats not only at home but also abroad. To support global aspirations, many firms are developing global CI programs to successfully navigate the competitive challenges of foreign markets. A core component of many global CI programs is a macroenvironmental analysis of a nation's social, technological, economic, environmental, and political (STEEP) environments. Many global CI programs, however, are not realizing their full potential because of a flawed approach to STEEP analysis—inattention paid to the pervasive impact of national culture on each competitive variable of the macroenvironment.

This chapter explores the fundamental flaw of ethnocentrism that lies at the root of this inattention to cultural diversity and so often plagues the transition from a domestic CI program to a global CI program. Reasons are offered as to why it is so easy for aspiring multinationals to fall into the trap of ethnocentrism. Next, arguments are provided to invalidate the concept of ethnocentrism. In particular, the pioneering work of Geert Hofstede is used to show that, despite globalization, distinct national cultures are enduring. A working example of the impact of cultural diversity on a hypothetical STEEP analysis is provided to underscore the very real potential for drawing incorrect strategic inferences from global macroenvironmental analysis due to ethnocentrism. To prevent such problems and to optimize a global CI program, recommendations are offered to build cultural awareness into the firm's CI capability.

CURRENT THOUGHT ON GLOBAL CI

Although the CI literature does reference the importance of global capabilities in corporate CI programs, new literature on specific applications of global CI is rather limited. Literature on global CI very often deals with intelligence issues as they pertain to individual countries or regions and, to a lesser extent, the importance of global intelligence or particular applications of global CI. Most often, global CI is identified in association with external scanning techniques that are practiced in conjunction with ongoing CI functions.

In almost all the current literature on CI, however, it is widely recognized that foreign markets and competitors need to be monitored and evaluated. Although this statement may seem obvious in a world that is increasingly global, two themes do emerge as central to the application of global CI in most of the literature: the importance of macro-level scanning, and explicitly attending to cultural analysis in evaluating threats and opportunities.

THE ISSUE OF CULTURAL ANALYSIS
AND MACRO-LEVEL SCANNING

It is very easy for CI professionals to fall into the trap of assuming that very little distinguishes domestic and global CI. Due to their ethnocentric attitudes and misperceptions around the impact of globalization, this trap catches many CI professionals unaware. The typology of centrism (Perlmutter, 1965) describes the three basic dominant attitudes that people hold toward foreign cultures (Calof & Beamish, 1994):

- *Ethnocentrism.* Often referred to as a home country orientation, ethnocentrism is an attitude that assumes that foreign cultures are inferior to the culture of the domestic market. In CI, this translates into analytical approaches that are rooted in the home country's culture and disproportionately suited to the domestic market.

- *Polycentrism.* Often referred to as a host country orientation, polycentrism is the converse of ethnocentrism. It is an attitude that assumes that different countries have different cultures and that foreign cultures are superior in terms of guiding behavior in foreign markets. In CI, this translates into analytical approaches that are totally customized toward the requirements of each particular market.

- *Geocentrism.* Often referred to as a world orientation, geocentrism is an attitude that is a compromise between the ethnocentric and polycentric extremes. In CI, this translates into analytical approaches that attempt to balance sensitivity to country-specific cultural differences with the demands of cost efficiency, global commonality, and opportunities for cross-national sharing of ideas, intelligence, and analytical approaches.

Many CI professionals, especially those who were born and raised in Western countries, fall prey to the dogma of ethnocentrism. By virtue of being inculcated in Western culture since birth, they assume that Western culture is the optimal operating model. It is very difficult for a person to change cultural frames past adolescence—so much so that the cultural environment of one's youth often becomes the cultural frame for a person's whole life.

Ethnocentrism for Westerners has been reinforced by the end of the Cold War and the seemingly unchallenged spread of U.S. culture around the world. The Hollywoodization of global culture, the spread of U.S. brand names into every corner of the planet, the confirmation of English as the language of commerce—all these factors may contribute to ethnocentrist attitudes. Despite these reinforcements providing impetus for ethnocentrism, this common attitude toward foreign cultures is untenable.

DISPUTING UNIVERSALITY AND ETHNOCENTRISM

The term "globalization" is often misinterpreted as a powerful force that is ushering in a new era of homogeneity across all countries. There is a solid body of academic research, however, that disputes the assertion by ethnocentrists that global culture is assimilating into convergence around a universal Western model.

Perhaps the strongest argument disputing the universality of global culture is found in the pioneering work of Geert Hofstede (1980, 2001). His book *Culture's Consequences: Comparing Values, Behaviors, Institutions, and Organizations across Nations* is a fascinating exploration of the enduring cultural differences among the nations of the world. His work has much validity in that the aforementioned book is one of the top 100 cited sources in the *Social Science Citation Index*. Further, his conclusions on global cultural heterogeneity have been validated by rigorous statistical analysis and verified by many cross-cultural studies conducted by others since the original publication of his work in 1980.

Hofstede's (2001) definition of culture is refreshingly simple: "the collective programming of the mind that distinguishes one group or category of people from another." These mental programs are developed in people at a very early age at home and then reinforced while growing up through school and again as an adult through various organizations and social institutions. The important implication of this research for global CI professionals is that these mental programs drive the different values held by people from different cultures.

In measuring global cultural heterogeneity across the countries of the world, Hofstede (2001) determined five dimensions of culture:

1. *Power Distance:* the degree to which the culture will accept inequality in the distribution of power
2. *Uncertainty Avoidance:* the degree to which the culture is comfortable with unstructured situations, ambiguity, and uncontrollable elements
3. *Individualism versus Collectivism:* the degree to which the culture organizes individually or into groups
4. *Masculinity versus Femininity:* the degree to which the culture emotes "tender" feminine or "tough" masculine characteristics
5. *Long-Term versus Short-Term Orientation:* the degree to which the culture pursues immediate versus delayed gratification in satisfying needs, tastes, and preferences

The differences among countries on these five dimensions of culture have shown a remarkable consistency that has been statistically validated and replicated by many other studies. Hofstede's (2001) research "identifies five main dimensions along which dominant value systems in more than 50 countries can be ordered, and that affect human thinking, feeling, and acting as well as organizations and institutions, in predictable ways." Figures 13.1 to 13.5 capture the essential conclusions of the mountains of research conducted to support Hofstede's central thesis that each culture is unique.

To demonstrate the ease of slipping into an ethnocentric mindset, recall the first country that you searched in Figures 13.1 to 13.5. It is not surprising that most readers are drawn first to their country of residence, their country of birth, or that of their parents or forefathers. This natural tribal tendency of human nature to find a common geographical or cultural reference point underscores the strong pull of ethnocentrism. The central message of Figures 13.1 to 13.5, however, is that each country has its own unique, enduring, and equally valid culture. Therefore, it is very important that global CI professionals conduct macro-level scanning through the lens of cultural sensitivity.

POWER DISTANCE			
Quartile 1 (highest acceptance of power inequality)		**Quartile 2**	
• Malaysia (1) • Guatemala (2/3) • Panama (2/3) • Philippines (4) • Mexico (5/6) • Venezuela (5/6)	• Arab countries (7) • Ecuador (8/9) • Indonesia (8/9) • India (10/11) • West Africa (10/11) • Yugoslavia (12) • Singapore (13)	• Brazil (14) • France (15/16) • Hong Kong (15/16) • Colombia (17) • El Salvador (18/19) • Turkey (18/19)	• Belgium (20) • East Africa (21/23) • Peru (21/23) • Thailand (21/23) • Chile (24/25) • Portugal (24/25) • Uruguay (26)
Quartile 3		**Quartile 4** (lowest acceptance of power inequality)	
• Greece (27/28) • South Korea (27/28) • Iran (29/30) • Taiwan (29/30) • Spain (31) • Pakistan (32) • Japan (33)	• Italy (34) • Argentina (35/26) • South Africa (35/36) • Jamaica (37) • United States (38) • Canada (39)	• Netherlands (40) • Australia (41) • Costa Rica (42/44) • Germany (42/44) • Great Britain (42/44) • Switzerland (45) • Finland (46)	• Norway (47/48) • Sweden (47/48) • Ireland (49) • New Zealand (50) • Denmark (51) • Israel (52) • Austria (53)

Figure 13.1 Differing Power Distance Indexes (rank in brackets) among nations (adapted from Hofstede, 2001).

UNCERTAINTY AVOIDANCE			
Quartile 1 (highest acceptance of uncertainty)		**Quartile 2**	
• Greece (1) • Portugal 02) • Guatemala (3) • Uruguay (4) • Belgium (5/6) • El Salvador (5/6) • Japan (7) • Yugoslavia (8)	• Peru (9) • Spain (10/15) • Argentina (10/15) • Panama (10/15) • France (10/15) • Chile (10/15) • Costa Rica (10/15)	• Turkey (16/17) • South Korea (16/17) • Mexico (18) • Israel (19) • Colombia (20) • Venezuela (21/22) • Brazil (21/22)	• Italy (23) • Pakistan (24/25) • Austria (24/25) • Taiwan (26)
Quartile 3		**Quartile 4** (highest avoidance of uncertainty)	
• Arab countries (27) • Ecuador (28) • Germany (29) • Thailand (30) • Iran (31/32) • Finland (31/32) • Switzerland (33)	• West Africa (34) • Netherlands (35) • East Africa (34) • Australia (37) • Norway (38) • South Africa (39/40) • New Zealand (39/40)	• Indonesia (41/42) • Canada (41/42) • United States (46) • Philippines (44) • India (40) • Malaysia (36) • Great Britain (47/48)	• Ireland (47/48) • Hong Kong (49/50) • Sweden (49/50) • Denmark 51) • Jamaica (52) • Singapore (53)

Figure 13.2 Differing Uncertainty Avoidance Indexes (rank in brackets) among nations (adapted from Hofstede, 2001).

INDIVIDUALISM VS. COLLECTIVISM			
Quartile 1 (highest individualism)		**Quartile 2**	
• United States (1) • Australia (2) • Great Britain (3) • Canada (4/5) • Netherlands (4/5) • New Zealand (6) • Italy (7)	• Belgium (8) • Denmark (9) • Sweden (10/11) • France (10/11) • Ireland (12) • Norway (13)	• Switzerland (14) • Germany (15) • South Africa (16) • Finland (17) • Austria (18) • Israel (19)	• Spain (20) • India (21) • Japan (22/23) • Argentina (22/23) • Iran (24) • Jamaica (25) • Brazil (26/27)
Quartile 3		**Quartile 4** (highest collectivism)	
• Arab countries (26/27) • Turkey (28) • Uruguay (29) • Greece (30) • Philippines (31) • Mexico (32) • Yugoslavia (33/35)	• Portugal (33/35) • East Africa (33/35) • Malaysia (36) • Hong Kong (37) • Chile (38) • Singapore (39/41) • Thailand (29/41) • West Africa (39/41)	• El Salvador (42) • South Korea (43) • Taiwan (44) • Peru (45) • Costa Rica (46) • Pakistan (47/48)	• Indonesia (47/48) • Colombia (49) • Venezuela (50) • Panama (51) • Ecuador (52) • Guatemala (53)

Figure 13.3 Differing Individualism vs. Collectivism Indexes (rank in brackets) among nations (adapted from Hofstede, 2001).

MASCULINITY VS. FEMININITY			
Quartile 1 (most masculine)		**Quartile 2**	
• Japan (1) • Austria (2) • Venezuela (3) • Italy (4/5) • Switzerland (4/5) • Mexico (6)	• Ireland (7/8) • Jamaica (7/8) • Great Britain (9/10) • Germany (9/10) • Philippines (11/12) • Colombia (11/12)	• South Africa (13/14) • Ecuador (13/14) • United States (15) • Australia (16) • New Zealand (17) • Greece (18/19) • Hong Kong (18/19)	• Argentina (20/21) • India (20/21) • Belgium (22) • Arab countries (23) • Canada (24) • Malaysia (25/26) • Pakistan (25/26)
Quartile 3		**Quartile 4** (most feminine)	
• Brazil (27) • Singapore (28) • Israel (29) • Indonesia (30/31) • West Africa (30/31) • Turkey (32/33) • Taiwan (32/33) • Panama (34)	• Iran (35/36) • France (35/36) • Spain (37/38) • Peru (37/38) • East Africa (39) • El Salvador (40) • South Korea (41)	• Uruguay (42) • Guatemala (43) • Thailand (44) • Portugal (45) • Chile (46) • Finland (47)	• Yugoslavia (48/49) • Costa Rica (48/49) • Denmark (50) • Netherlands (51) • Norway (52) • Sweden (53)

Figure 13.4 Differing Masculinity vs. Femininity Indexes (rank in brackets) among nations (adapted from Hofstede, 2001).

LONG-TERM VS. SHORT-TERM ORIENTATION			
Quartile 1 (Long-term orientation)		**Quartile 2**	
• China (1) • Hong Kong (2) • Taiwan (3) • Japan (4) • South Korea (5)		• Brazil (6) • India (7) • Thailand (8) • Singapore (9) • Netherlands (10)	
Quartile 3		**Quartile 4** (Short-term orientation)	
• Bangladesh (11) • Sweden (12) • Poland (13) • Germany (14) • Australia (15)		• New Zealand (16) • United States (17) • Great Britain (18) • Zimbabwe (19)	• Canada (20) • Philippines (21) • Nigeria (22) • Pakistan (23)

Figure 13.5 Differing Long- vs. Short-Term Orientation Indexes (rank in brackets) among nations (adapted from Hofstede, 2001).

WHY CULTURAL AWARENESS IS CRITICAL IN GLOBAL CI

From a business perspective, ethnocentrism is dangerous. In a study (Calof & Beamish, 1994) of 38 Canadian multinationals, researchers found that those companies with a geocentric orientation enjoyed more than a 100% greater export intensity (international sales and domestic sales) than their ethnocentric and polycentric peers. Clearly, these results show the advantage afforded to global firms in adopting a geocentric mindset—a significant determinant of which is a well-developed global CI capability that is culturally aware.

Almost any firm can do the hard, quantitative, secondary-sourced global CI research—this is rapidly becoming a hygiene factor—necessary but insufficient to secure competitive advantage. However, a significant portion of the competitive advantage that global CI is able to deliver comes from the ability to correctly interpret weak or ambiguous signals in the macroenvironments of different markets. This capability is inextricably linked to a strong cultural awareness when doing CI. Cultural awareness will fine-tune the corporate radar, enabling the global CI function to pick up the ambient signals while they are still leading indicators. To companies that have not developed cultural awareness as a core competence, these weak signals will seem like "white noise" and they won't pick up the signals until they are lagging indicators. Moreover, without cultural awareness, CI analysts are prone to draw incorrect strategic inferences from the weak signals that they do pick up.

Although the concept of culture may seem very ambiguous and high level, its impact on the firm's bottom line is tangible. Figure 13.6 provides some examples of the very real difference that cultural awareness makes in conducting international-level STEEP analysis. As the examples suggest, CI analysts with different cultural frames will often make widely

Macro Scanning STEEP Element	Weak signal detected in national culture macro-environment	Possible conclusions drawn by global CI analyst born and raised in nation with low index rating on cultural dimensions in question (i.e, cultural frame)	Possible conclusions drawn by global CI analyst born and raised in nation with high index rating on cultural dimensions in question (i.e., cultural frame)
Social	Population in country is becoming disproportionately aged	CI analyst with a low Individualist Index (Fig. 13.3) cultural frame might conclude that this demographic trend represents little growth opportunity as most aged adults end up living with their children.	CI analyst with a high Individualist Index (Fig. 13.3) cultural frame might conclude that this presents a tremendous opportunity as most aged boomers will be looking to a new generation of retirement homes to support an active lifestyle well into their older years.
Technological	Radical new biotechnology on the cusp of commercialization	CI analyst with a low Power Distance / low Masculinity Index (Fig. 13.1, 13.4) cultural frame might conclude that views of nation under analysis are: • Biotechnology will be perceived as a threat to human health and environment • Biotechnology will be perceived as unethical • Commercialization decision will be government determined	CI analyst with a high Power Distance / high Masculinity Index (Fig. 13.1, 13.4) cultural frame might conclude that views of nation under analysis are: • Biotechnology will not be perceived as threat to human health and environment • Biotechnology will be perceived as ethical • Commercialization decision will be market determined
Economic	Opposition political party adds tax relief to its policy agenda prior to major election	CI analyst with a low Masculinity Index (Fig. 13.4) cultural frame might conclude: • Tax cuts for poor have a high chance of securing electoral victory • Dividend tax credits for corporations and wealthy have a low chance of securing electoral victory	CI analyst with a high Masculinity Index (Fig. 13.4) cultural fame might conclude: • Dividend tax credits for corporations and wealthy have a very high chance of securing electoral victory • Tax cuts for poor will not resonate very strongly with voting public
Environmental	Environmental scientists are on the verge of finding that a proprietary production process may be contaminating the local environment	CI analyst with a low Power Distance / low Uncertainty Avoidance / low Masculinity index (Fig. 13.1, 13.2, 13.4) cultural frame might conclude that a proactive socio-political strategy is optimal: • Expect grass roots activist groups to form • Focus on informing public stakeholders • Public sympathy can be expected for economically and socially weak victims • Expect government funding/disaster relief • Expect environmental legislation	CI analyst with a high Power Distance / high Uncertainty Avoidance / high Masculinity (Fig. 13.1, 13.2, 13.4) cultural frame might conclude that a 'wait and see' contingent socio-political strategy is optimal because: • Opposition from powerful grass roots activist groups can be expected to be minimal • Proactive communications to public might be perceived as admission of guilt • Heavy-handed environmental legislation not likely • Public sympathy for victims not large enough to sway key corporate or government decision-makers
Political	Rumors of a major government scandal – several ministers may be involved in major fraud case	CI analyst with a low Power Distance Index cultural frame (Fig. 13.1) might conclude that the impact of scandal will be a gradual change in form of government via proper democratic channels (resignations, investigations, bipartisan committees, elections, etc.). Probably little long-term oscillation between left- and right-wing party control — as a result, the center moderate party or coalition will resume normal political dynamics. Current policy regime will continue indefinitely.	CI analyst with a high Power Distance Index cultural frame (Fig. 13.1) might conclude that the impact of scandal could conceivably be a sudden change in government (civic revolution or political unrest/instability). This could result in a major swing to the left or right with the requisite threat to the current policy regime in the short term.

Figure 13.6 The Difference that Cultural Sensitivity Makes (adapted from generic inferences made by Hofstede, 2001).

divergent strategic inferences from the same macro-scanning information. Bear in mind that Figure 13.6 is not designed to display a rigorous set of rules that can be generalized across nations—they are just hypothetical speculations based on the inferences made in many cross-cultural studies. Nor is Figure 13.6 designed to indicate which strategic inference is correct or incorrect. Rather, the key insight to glean from the exhibit is the pervasive impact that culture exerts on international macro-scanning analysis.

For each STEEP element in Figure 13.6, the correct strategic inference depends on the country in which the STEEP element is playing out. Depending on the cultural background and frame of the CI analyst, very different conclusions might conceivably be derived. The correct strategic inference critically depends on the correct match between the cultural frame of the analyst and the actual location of the nation under analysis on the five cultural dimensions. Getting to the correct conclusion hinges, in large part, on culture. From this perspective, culture is no longer an ambiguous factor but, rather, is a very strong influence on the STEEP process and ultimately a determinant of very real and tangible strategic inference.

Sensitivity to cultural nuances should allow businesses to better understand foreign markets, foreign competitors, and their strategies (Simpkins, 1999). Many organizations fail because they are unable to read weak or ambiguous signals that are in their environments and markets (Fleisher, 2001). These subtle, but ever-present signals may best be uncovered and interpreted through the use of macro-scanning and cultural analysis as part of the global CI function to reveal competitive threats or opportunities. Through incorporating analysis that includes sensitivity to cultural variables, CI professionals will develop a more robust understanding of the competitive international environment. This broader cultural perspective is perhaps the most significant contribution of a global CI program, since it will likely reveal opportunities and threats in global markets that may have otherwise gone unrecognized or misunderstood.

HOW TO BUILD CULTURAL AWARENESS INTO A GLOBAL CI PROGRAM

There are several measures that international companies can undertake to develop and strengthen the cultural awareness of their global CI programs, among them investing in foreign market expertise and hiring diversity.

Invest in Foreign Market Expertise

The cultural dimensions of each country will in large part determine how any developments in the STEEP environment will play out. CI professionals who are attuned to the impact of culture on these variables stand a much higher probability of making the correct inferences and hence the most accurate strategic recommendations based on their global macroenvironmental scanning.

To a domestic analyst analyzing a foreign culture, however, deriving the correct strategic inference requires managing a very complex array of interactions on the five cultural dimensions. For example, not only is each country located at different positions along the five cultural dimensions, there are also many interactions among dimensions (e.g., individualist versus power distance; uncertainty avoidance versus long-term orientation); further, there are 3×3, 4×4, and probably 5×5 interactions as well. Add in the impact of cross-country or regional interactions, as well as the larger number of diverse developments that arise in the STEEP environment, and it is easy to recognize that the expatriate CI analyst would (1) become overwhelmed with the complexity of the required analysis and (2) probably make incorrect inferences.

Conversely, consider the CI analysts who were born and raised in the country or culture they are assigned to monitor. With a proper match between the national culture and the cultural frame of the analyst, much of this seeming complexity can be adequately handled by the innate cultural knowledge of the analyst. That is, the CI analyst in this scenario is not overwhelmed but, instead, is hard-wired to draw the correct inferences of the impact of national culture on the five STEEP elements. Delivering this correct match requires an investment in foreign CI analysts with innate knowledge of national culture by virtue of having been born and raised in the country under analysis. Ideally, a global firm should have a local CI professional on the ground in every major market in which the company operates.

Realistically, this may be cost prohibitive for smaller companies, so some less costly alternatives would be to invest in regional as opposed to nation-specific cultural expertise, find a local partner, or hire consultants familiar with the local market. These "cheaper" alternatives may prove more costly in the long term, however, because the value of specialized local knowledge provided by consultants may also be purchased by rivals. Further, given that many multinational companies have never recovered from competitive blindsides arising in the STEEP environment, the question "Can we afford to invest in foreign market expertise?" may be more properly phrased as "Can we afford not to invest in foreign market expertise?"

Hire Diversity to Leverage Innate Cultural Differences in People

The statistically verified data provided in Figures 13.1 to 13.5 provide a strong argument that each national culture is unique. Further, the nature

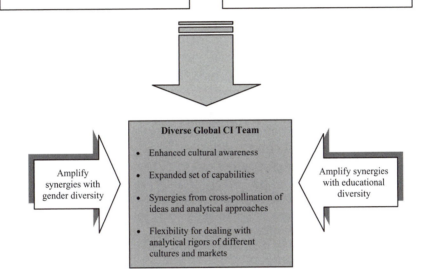

All-Western Global CI Team

- Prefer clarity & formal logic, consistency
- Adept at breaking problems into discreet, coherent components
- More attention to objects and classification
- Belief in controllability of environment
- Insistent on correctness of one belief over another when challenged by contradiction
- Focus on independence
- Attribute behavior to actors

All-Eastern Global CI Team

- Comfortable with contradiction regarding it as an indication that problem is being viewed from all perspectives
- Better able to see relationships among events
- More attention to relationships among events
- Belief in uncontrollability of environment
- Inclined to seek compromise when challenged by contradiction
- Focus on interdependence
- Attribute behavior to context

Diverse Global CI Team

- Enhanced cultural awareness
- Expanded set of capabilities
- Synergies from cross-pollination of ideas and analytical approaches
- Flexibility for dealing with analytical rigors of different cultures and markets

Amplify synergies with gender diversity

Amplify synergies with educational diversity

Figure 13.7 The Value of Diversity (Note: East/West cultural differences from Landry, 2003 and Nisbett, 2003).

of human development is such that our individual "mental programs" become hard-wired by the age of adolescence. Given that collective mental programs drive national culture, it is valid to assert that cultural differences are enduring or at least change very slowly. In light of this assertion, an effective way of raising the global awareness of the firm's global CI function is to hire as much diversity as possible.

Figure 13.7 provides an example of the benefits of leveraging cultural diversity by comparing the capabilities of a global CI team exclusively composed of analysts from Western cultures versus a global CI team exclusively composed of analysts from Eastern cultures versus a global CI team that is composed of a diverse mixture of both. Note the expansion of capability with the diversity of cultures. Imagine the synergy of diversity that would come from many cultures being represented on the global CI function. These synergies can be amplified by hiring gender diversity. Global CI functions should also be sprinkled liberally with people with various educational backgrounds such as philosophy, anthropology, sociology, history, and political science—all majors that may be more closely attuned to the subtle yet all-encompassing impact of differences in national cultures.

Increase Cultural Awareness of the CI Function

The two prior recommendations (investing in foreign market expertise and hiring diversity) will provide a great opportunity for existing CI staff to learn about new ideas and analytical approaches that are successful in the different global markets in which the firm currently operates or is targeting for entry. In addition to these ancillary benefits, several initiatives can be undertaken to develop a global mindset in the existing CI function, including

- cultural sensitivity training
- expatriate assignments
- diverse international project teams

Although this chapter has primarily focused on the macro-scanning phase of the global CI process, the entire global CI process should be embedded with cultural awareness.

CONCLUSION

Despite the illusion of cultural convergence seemingly induced by globalization, distinctive national cultures will persist. In order to maximize the effectiveness of the global CI function, the issue of cultural awareness must be explicitly managed. Multinational firms and firms with international aspirations would be well served to develop a global mindset in their CI functions that allows cultural awareness to permeate not only the STEEP macro-scanning process but every facet of the global CI process.

It is extremely interesting to note that after producing mountains of research, and developing a rigorous argument regarding the distinctness of national cultures, Hofstede (2001) concludes at the end of his 600-page treatise that "the popular business slogan 'Think globally, act locally' . . . is both naïve and arrogant. . . . No one, as this book has amply proven, can think globally. We all think according to our own local software. . . . The slogan should be 'Think locally, act globally'."

From the perspective of global competitive intelligence, this contrarian conclusion certainly provides food for thought. Perhaps the enlightened global corporation of the future will accept that cultural ethnocentrism is innate at the individual CI analyst level and, instead of trying to pretend that it doesn't exist, will exploit this dynamic for competitive advantage at the organizational level by building a culturally aware global CI function whose geocentric whole is greater than the sum of its ethnocentric parts.

REFERENCES

Calof, J.L., and P.W. Beamish. (1994). "The Right Attitude for International Success." *Business Quarterly* 59(1): 105–110.

Fleisher, C.S. (2001). "An Introduction to the Management and Practice of Competitive Intelligence," pp. 3–18 in C.S. Fleisher and D.L. Blenkhorn [eds.], *Managing Frontiers in Competitive Intelligence.* Westport, CT: Quorum Books.

Hofstede, G. (1980). *Culture's Consequences: International Differences in Work-Related Values.* London, UK: Sage Publications.

Hofstede, G. (2001). *Culture's Consequences: Comparing Values, Behaviors, Institutions, and Organizations across Nations.* Thousand Oaks, CA: Sage Publications.

Landry, J.T. (2003). "Books in Brief: The Geography of Thought." *Harvard Business Review* 81(6): 24.

Nisbett, R.E. (2003). *The Geography of Thought: How Asians and Westerners Think Differently . . . and Why?* New York: Free Press.

Perlmutter, H.V. (1965). "L'entreprise Internationale: Trois Conceptions." *Revue Economique et Sociale, Lausanne* 2: 1–14.

Simpkins, R.A. (1999). "The Global Mind." *Competitive Intelligence Magazine* 1(2): 32–36.

14

Knowledge, Skills, and Abilities of Domestic and International Competitive Intelligence Practitioners

Betty Toczydlowski

Competitive intelligence (CI) practitioners require various knowledge, skills, and abilities (KSAs). There are many similarities between the required traits for practicing international CI and those traits required for practicing domestic CI. The key difference, however, is the necessary knowledge of global information and how it applies to individual markets.

Due to the growth in global business, both small and large domestic firms are being forced to compete globally. Given this competitive reality, it is inevitable that the traits required for successful CI practitioners working in international firms will also become necessary for their counterparts at domestic firms. Therefore, firms wishing to develop competitive intelligence capabilities should build CI programs that have a global focus that encompasses both domestic and international competition.

This chapter will address the general traits necessary to practice both domestic and international CI. It will also expand on the additional knowledge required for global CI. A framework will be proposed that integrates knowledge management (KM) with developing actionable competitive intelligence. Lastly, application of this framework at Shell Services International will be examined.

CI KNOWLEDGE, SKILLS, AND ABILITIES

Competitive intelligence provides actionable recommendations resulting from a process that includes planning, gathering, analyzing, and disseminating information about the external environment. It is used to determine opportunities or developments that can potentially affect a company's competitive situation. The goal of CI is to provide organizations with a sustainable competitive advantage.

The CI cycle (Society of Competitive Intelligence Professionals, 2003a) outlines the stages necessary to produce actionable intelligence. These stages include

- obtaining CI requests
- collecting necessary information
- analyzing and synthesizing information
- communicating intelligence

Each stage of the cycle identifies the KSAs required by CI practitioners. These traits are similar to those necessary in the marketing function, where constant scanning of the external and internal environments is necessary for developing successful marketing strategies. Therefore, most CI practitioners are marketing directors or marketing research managers (Richard Combs Associates, Inc., 2000).

Obtaining CI Requests

The CI practitioner must be able to identify and extract the intelligence needs of decision-makers within the organization. Obtaining CI requests can be accomplished through verbal or written communications, interviews, or presentations. However, difficulties can arise when assessing the needs of managers of differing personality or psychology types, thereby resulting in potential conflict of opinions or requests between them. Hence, exceptional interpersonal skills are necessary to probe and extract precise requirements.

In addition to obtaining knowledge of internal and external company capabilities, awareness of the organizational structure, culture, environment, and key informants is necessary. This information will guide the objective practitioner in determining the company's CI needs through conducting a gap analysis. For instance, prior to initiating a CI program, the organization needs to complete a CI audit. The purpose of the audit is to determine existing knowledge of the external environment and thereby identify gaps of required knowledge (Malhotra, 1996).

Collecting Necessary Information

This portion of the cycle requires that the practitioner obtain knowledge through primary and secondary sources. There are numerous methods to access internal, external, primary, and secondary sources. This is where ethical research skills need to be developed and assumptions and hypotheses clarified. However, CI practitioners must recognize that meanings and understandings of ethical research vary among countries and cultures.

Primary research requires interpersonal communication skills and the ability to conduct interviews. Secondary research skills include Internet and intranet searching, database searching, and data mining and querying. Both types of research require persistence. Due to the potential for collecting large volumes of data, management of primary and secondary sources is necessary. In order to have confidence in the sources, data validation (testing) is required to recognize variances or inconsistencies. Specific knowledge and issues regarding counterintelligence and international and cultural issues must also be addressed.

According to John Nolan (in Miller, 2001a), a retired federal intelligence officer of the U.S. government, skills used in government intelligence operations can be applied to CI. Such transferable skills include source administration, elicitation, and psychological profiling. Source administration is the recording of specific individual knowledge for future reference. Elicitation (as opposed to interrogation) techniques can be used to acquire specific information without using direct questions. In addition, psychological profiling can help identify the leadership style of a potential company leader, or the leadership behavior of competitors under certain situations (Miller, 2001a).

Examples of information sources for CI include

- government agencies
- online databases
- Internet
- intranets
- other companies
- the investment community
- surveys
- interviews
- trade shows
- conferences
- drive-by or on-site observations.

Analysis and Synthesis of Information

Using various qualitative and quantitative analytical models in this stage will assist in developing inductive and deductive reasoning. Different analytical models can be used, depending on the CI needs. Throughout the analysis, gaps and blind spots need to be recognized. Many types of analytical models are used in CI, including those based on competitive, comparative, industry, financial, economic, and accounting principles and methodologies. Other models include personality profiling, benchmarking, case study, forecasting, risk assessment, marketing, and trend assessment (Miller, 2001b). In addition, organizational culture analysis may be conducted to predict the behavior of competitors based on cultural norms within the firm and an understanding of the personnel and leadership style.

Developing intelligence combines the preceding analysis with creative thought, strategic thinking, industry knowledge, observations, and experience. In doing so, the CI practitioner requires the ability to deal with ambiguity, such as inferring missing pieces of information to develop conclusions. Lastly, "paralysis by analysis" must be avoided by knowing when to stop the analysis and when to move forward with action. One can avoid this pitfall by adhering to strict timelines for analyzing various pieces of information; this structure is similar to the process used in project management.

Communicating Intelligence

The CI practitioner is required to organize findings using a format and present a breadth and depth of intelligence desired by the "client." This could be in the form of a report, presentation, e-mail, or any combination of these. The information dissemination needs to be persuasive, assertive, and diplomatic. Therefore, excellent communication, writing, and listening skills are required (Society of Competitive Intelligence Professionals, 2003b).

GLOBAL CI KNOWLEDGE

Due to the expansion in global business activity, international CI is increasing in importance. This is evidenced in the dominant position of European and Japanese firms in the U.S. patent system over the past 20 years. Furthermore, the Japanese are currently funding research programs at American universities as a competitive tool. As a result, Japanese and European firms have significantly increased their market share in various industries, namely, steel, automotive, home electronics, and ceramics. In addition, increasingly hostile competitiveness can potentially evolve into trade wars among rival economic blocs, thereby posing a threat to current global practices (Dreyfuss, 1994). As a result, vast amounts of additional global knowledge are required for the international CI practitioner. This primarily includes understanding the culture and regulatory environment of target countries.

Culture

Investigating a new culture requires a global mindset; understanding the social and political dynamics of countries is required for business success in overseas markets. For example, North American corporate culture is known for its short-term outlook in business dealings, thereby influencing decisions accordingly. In contrast, Japanese firms focus on long-term initiatives, where patience is key. Hence, knowing the impact of culture on business practices will allow the CI practitioner to make informed analyses. A historical background will assist in obtaining this knowledge, in addition to comparative and case study analysis (Werther, 1997). Specifically, global CI requires gathering information on sociological, educational, economic, political, and geographic criteria. These environmental factors can indicate competitive opportunities or threats (Sheinin, 1996).

Sociological Values

Sociological values relate to country attitudes toward success, authority, and cooperation between groups. Global CI practitioners need to understand the differences in cultural orientations between their own country and the new region in regard to customers, competitors, and team members. Visible orientations include behaviors toward things such as music, art, food, drink, dress, greetings, manners, trials, myths, and legends. In addition, religion, ethnic background, and history also contribute to cultural orientation. When assessing a foreign country, CI practitioners should be capable of adapting to the surroundings, without incorporating their own domestic culture (Simpkins, 1998).

Cultural perception can be influenced by eight criteria that consist of action, competitiveness, communications, environment, individualism, structure, thinking, and time.

- *Action* refers to the level of stress placed on working for the "experience" or to achieve a specific goal.
- *Competitiveness* for rewards occurs in some cultures, while others strive for cooperation to benefit relationships.
- The level of direct or indirect *communications* can vary. Due to an acceptance of shared experiences, some regions do not require much information exchange.
- Some cultures feel that the *environment* can be controlled to fit their needs, while others believe in fate or chance.

- *Individualism* refers to the level of importance that the individual has over the group.
- *Structure* refers to a society's dependence on predictability and rules.
- *Thinking* patterns for some can rely on experience or experimentation while others rely on theory and logic.
- A society's *time* emphasis refers to the acceptance of completing one task at a time or multiple tasks at once. In addition, *time* consideration includes the importance of punctuality, past orientation, present orientation, or future orientation.

Education Standards

Education standards reveal the competitive position in a particular location with respect to skills. These standards include the education level of the labor pool, training capability, skills transfer, and adaptability to technological changes.

Economic Policy

Economic policy reveals the development or limitations in the competitive environment. This includes information regarding a country's position on domestic business and foreign competition. As a result, one can determine the environmental support in a specific region. For example, information can be obtained by investigating customs or port records of imports and exports passing through a country. This can reveal to the major buyers and suppliers in a specific industry the amounts that are shipped and the parties involved (Gikandi, 2001).

Political Environment

The political environment reveals the support for free markets through laws that stimulate and protect competition. A country's politics includes foreign policy that dictates the level of trade with other countries. Other political issues include defense and national security, political stability, political organization, and flexibility in legal changes.

Geographic Information

Geographic information is used for marketing purposes in determining target population, language, and communication needs. The geographic environment determines the transportation requirements to reach consumers or other businesses within the country. Lastly, the availability of raw materials and energy to manufacture goods is required when assessing geographic conditions.

While conducting CI abroad, secondary sources can be helpful in gaining knowledge regarding the target company's local conditions. Country-specific business publications, journals, and newspapers are other sources for international information. Some examples of sources and information available on the Internet are provided in Table 14.1.

Based on cultural differences, the CI practitioner needs to be aware that the ease of collecting data will vary from region to region. For instance, although most marketing research techniques have become standardized across Europe since the formation of the European Union (EU), seven key areas have been identified as needing specific attention when gathering CI in Europe. These seven areas can also be applied globally within the country that is being analyzed and can be modified for local conditions. The following seven recommendations apply primarily to conducting interviews and gathering statistical data (Stanat & Seydel, 2002):

1. *Avoid face-to-face interviews.* This applies unless the practitioner has a lot of time and money or a complex interview to conduct. Telephone interviews are much cheaper and are widely accepted, even for durations of up to 40 minutes. However, competitor interviews are more productive face to face.

2. *Avoid interviewing in a non-native language.* Interviewing in English can be considered discourteous and can reduce the quality of information. Speaking in the native tongue is recommended.

3. *Avoid assuming that the EU and Europe are common territory.* Countries within Europe may possess more than one ethnic area and therefore will require specific attention in marketing products.

Table 14.1
Sources for Global Information

www.worldbiz.com	www.globalworkshop.com	www.odci.gov/cia/publications/factbook/
Business customs	Business meetings	Introduction
Business negotiations	Negotiating tactics	Geography
Business travel	Doing business	People
Import/exports	Business entertainment	Government
Industries and sectors	Social etiquette	Economy
Laws and regulations	Country information	Communications
Marketing	Travel tips	Transportation
Trade and investment	Useful contacts	Military
		Transnational news

4. *Avoid running projects in vacation periods.* Europeans take much longer vacations than their North American counterparts. The months of June, July, and August are common vacation periods, and the most popular vacation month depends on the specific country.

5. *Avoid interviewing from within the country.* For sensitive data, results have been better when calling from another country.

6. *Avoid assuming that definitions across Europe are the same.* European definitions are not necessarily comparable with U.S. definitions. This can include areas such as job titles, products, industry classifications, education classification, and social class.

7. *Avoid using a single data source.* Secondary information may reveal no relevant information or too much conflicting data that, therefore, needs to be cross-checked and verified where possible. Differences need to be explained and understood.

Regulatory Environment

Business practices in gathering CI vary among regions. Therefore, the CI practitioner needs to be aware of various legal, regulatory, and ethical issues (Klein, 1998).

Copyright and trade regulations can pose limitations to doing business overseas. One must also be aware of the various international tax rules and frequent tax rate changes. Rates can differ by region, product, or service (McDonald, 2001).

A country's privacy landscape can place limitations on gathering consumer and employee information. The CI practitioner needs to be aware of local regulations regarding protection of personal information. Limitations can be placed on "sensitive" information, where the definition of "sensitive" needs to be clarified among countries. This information can include health status, financial information, sexual orientation, religious affiliation, and membership in labor organizations. In addition, industry-specific and labor laws need to be included. In some cases, local privacy authorities monitor the collection and processing of personal information and may require strict adherence to local rules in the creation and maintenance of databases. Several international agreements contain restrictions to transferring information across borders, including the Safe Harbor agreement between Europe and the United States (Leizerov, 2001).

KNOWLEDGE MANAGEMENT

KM Systems

A KM system organizes the intellectual assets of a corporation. This includes recorded information, corporate experience, third-party information, and tacit knowledge of employees. KM consists of four steps to achieve enterprise knowledge: capturing knowledge, analyzing and cataloging knowledge, sharing knowledge, and creating knowledge (Adams, 2001).

KM can be implemented through developing an electronic database, or enterprise portal, that allows for information organization and retrieval. The architecture is an integrated database or knowledge repository. Typical interfaces are web-enabled and reside on a company's intranet. The proper information architecture design is a key component in creating knowledge. The design incorporates web development, library science, architecture, cultural anthropology, and literary theory. Planning a system requires deciding on grouping content, labeling, and navigation paths, where the ultimate goal is the integration of the company's content, strategy, and corporate culture. The result is an information architecture that provides employee access to knowledge and tools for information retrieval. To use the system effectively, employees need to be encouraged to find useful information when deemed necessary, rather than expected to learn vast amounts of knowledge.

In order for KM to work, a knowledge culture must be established within the organization. This can be accomplished by creating a networked organization that emphasizes communications and provides appropriate reward systems to reinforce information sharing (Skyrme & Amidon, 1997). Sharing of knowledge requires executive participation across business units. This communication is otherwise known as "T-shaped management," where information flow across business units occurs along the horizontal portion of the "T" (Hansen & von Oetinger, 2001). The vertical portion of the "T" represents communication within the specific business unit. This practice facilitates transferal of best practices and improves decision-making, thereby creating opportunities through cross-pollination of ideas. The shared information creates well-coordinated implementation and allows for increased strategic risk-taking (Hansen & von Oetinger, 2001).

The goal of KM and the electronic infrastructure is to provide content management that encourages employee interaction and knowledge creation. KM takes advantage of the explicit and tacit knowledge of employees to solve problems and create new knowledge. A knowledge-sharing corporate culture is enabled by the information exchange, thereby creating a learning organization. As a result, this knowledge stimulates the development of competitive intelligence.

Barriers to KM Systems

To create the desired structure for communication and generation of CI, successful implementation of a KM program requires senior management support. This entails significant long-term financial and human resource commitments.

Although physical electronic storage of information is inexpensive, the combination of creating, storing, maintaining, and obtaining access to databases requires financial and human resources. Recording every detail of knowledge can become a daunting task. Therefore, corporate information should integrate personal knowledge of specific individuals as records that are knowable, rather than being inundated with capturing all that is known. Records that are knowable would provide a high-level overview of personal knowledge topics that are of interest to the CI practitioner. For instance, CI practitioners or employees can be supplied with an index of individuals, complete with a summary of their knowledge on specific topics, or in other words, information that is knowable. The details of the topic would remain with the individual. If additional information is required, the CI practitioner can contact the relevant individuals. With such rules for capturing information, personal knowledge can be provided with limited information and hence, less structure. As a result, this procedure can save the company valuable time and money by limiting the maintenance of databases (Drott, 2001).

The desire to share company information across geographical boundaries creates technical challenges in developing a global information architecture. This includes developing interfaces that are operational in different languages, such as Asian character sets and different fonts. Applications need to be double-byte enabled or internationalized to allow expression of different languages. Also to be considered are the technical capabilities of the countries in question, such as bandwidth (Svetvilas, 2001).

Counterintelligence

A KM system must consider counterintelligence. Protecting company information is as important as gathering it. Both functions must be managed to maintain a competitive advantage. Counterintelligence can be accomplished by making employees aware of the importance of guarding sensitive information through monitoring published materials, paper shredding, cautiously selecting business partners, and encrypting electronic databases. Firms must be careful of public relations material and information disseminated over the Internet. Target information that can be used to benefit competitors includes trade and pricing data, investment strategy, contract details, supplier lists, planning documents, research and development (R&D) data, technical drawings, and computer databases

(Donaldson-Briggs, 2001). Other valuable target information includes sales figures, factory production, advertising campaigns, job postings, resumés, and salary structure (Rosner, 2001).

A firm's competitive advantage, and hence core competency, is its key to remaining successful. Therefore, the firm must review all available information on this competency so that proper protection can be exerted against theft. The experience of a former federal intelligence officer with the U.S. government, John Nolan, suggests that government counterintelligence skills can be transferred to business (Miller, 2001a). These skills require the counterintelligence professional to

- define protection requirements
- estimate vulnerabilities
- test penetration
- develop countermeasures
- employ countermeasures
- analyze data
- disseminate information

Unfortunately, uncertainty in world events has sparked the need for corporate counterterrorism in the twenty-first century. In order to develop a valuable corporate counterterrorism strategy, intelligence-gathering must encompass the following areas: global, national, regional, corporate perimeter, and corporate premises (Underwood, 2002).

INTEGRATING KM AND CI

Creating CI requires the integration of much knowledge and many skills and abilities. This chapter offers an integrated framework to indicate the necessary inputs for creating CI. The key integrating factor is knowledge management (KM), as shown in Figure 14.1.

The first step to CI creation is for the CI group or individual to identify the needs of senior management in order to apply efficient use of valuable research time. Upon completion of this crucial initial stage of needs assessment, the ensuing factors in the process of integrating KM and CI are shown in Figure 14.1 and discussed in the following three sections.

Collection and Information Factors of the CI/KM Framework

Data collection skills and abilities are used to obtain industry, global, and company information through primary or secondary sources. Industry

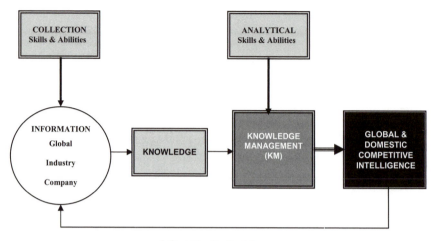

Figure 14.1 Framework for Integrating Knowledge Management and Competitive Intelligence.

information would include monitoring the actions of current and potential competitors, suppliers, and customers, as well as monitoring risk management strategies (counterintelligence) and other market conditions. Global information would include gathering necessary cultural and regulatory information on specific targets. Company information would include internal data such as organizational strengths and weaknesses, culture, capabilities, and available resources.

Knowledge and Knowledge Management (KM) Factors of the CI/KM Framework

Collection of data creates knowledge. In order to take advantage of this knowledge, the information needs to be filtered and organized into company-specific categories. A knowledge-management system is an electronic database that can store the relevant information. Intelligent agents are software packages that can automatically collect relevant secondary source data over the Internet. Other tasks of the knowledge management system would require manual input of primary source data or other secondary source data. Dissemination of the organized and filtered information can be provided though an intranet portal.

Analysis and Global and Domestic CI Factors of the CI/KM Framework

CI practitioners' analytical skills and abilities, together with the information available in the knowledge management system, create actionable global or domestic CI. Through proper dissemination, this intelligence is fed back as new company information. This is where action or inaction on the intelligence occurs.

APPLICATION OF THE KM AND CI FRAMEWORK: SHELL SERVICES INTERNATIONAL

This section will apply the proposed KM and CI framework to the operations at Shell Services International (SSI). SSI provides business services to the Royal Dutch/Shell Group entities. One of the services provided by SSI includes the Shell Services Company (SSC). This division focuses on information technology (IT) services and IT-enabled business solutions (Breeding, 2000).

SSI's competitive intelligence group was established in 1997. Its CI group wanted to make a transition from a state of "reactiveness" to one of "proactiveness" by the application of technology. Their vision for change (Breeding, 2000) stated the following:

Take SSI to a position of thought leadership in the application of competitive information and knowledge sharing to enable responsiveness.

The key to SSI's CI function is the implementation of a KM system. SSI maintains and disseminates information through its intranet site CI KnowledgeHouse. The key features of this system are its information reusability and self-access. SSI maximizes efficiency by automating much of the information collected during ad hoc requests and researching the weekly report "CI News-to-Go." Access is provided by the CI group and is obtained through justification of need. A complete summary of tasks completed within the KM and CI framework at SSI is provided in Figure 14.2. The CI KnowledgeHouse is composed of three components:

1. *Level Set Components.* Users can obtain a working knowledge of CI.
2. *Research Components.* Secondary and published information, including competitor profiles, are available here.
3. *Knowledge Management Components.* Users can share their knowledge here. This section includes "yellow pages" that contain a list of SSI people providing CI activities (information that is knowable).

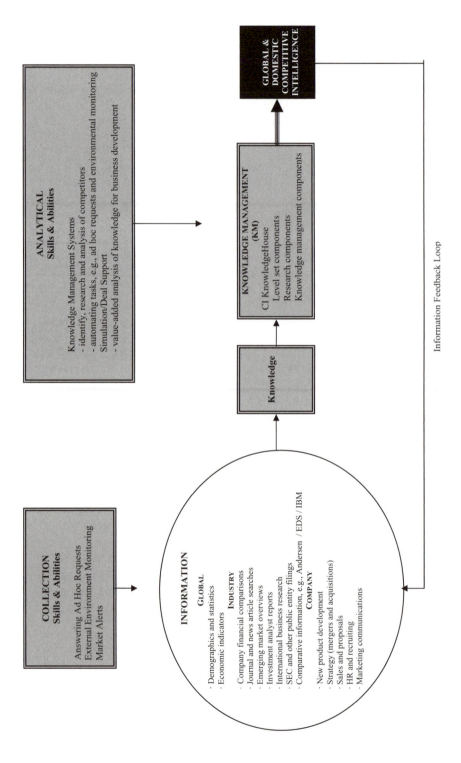

Figure 14.2 Framework for Integrating Knowledge Management and CI Applied to Shell Services International Inc.

The CI group continually evaluates the effectiveness of its activities using a 24-item evaluation model. The CI KnowledgeHouse has been integrated with five business intelligence topics, including competitor intelligence, customer and prospect intelligence, market intelligence, technical intelligence, and partner intelligence. The critical success factor has been maintaining relationships with the users of the information and marketing the system to these users. The result is a fully integrated CI and KM infrastructure that performs exceedingly well in practice.

CONCLUSION

The knowledge, skills, and abilities of domestic and international CI practitioners are differentiated by the additional knowledge required for successful competition in a global setting. The fundamental knowledge, skills, and abilities needed for collecting and analyzing data are transferable, regardless of the global scope of the firm. However, the additional necessity of obtaining global cultural and regulatory information for international CI distinguishes the knowledge, skills, and abilities required of international CI practitioners from those required of domestic CI practitioners.

This chapter offers an integrated framework that shows how KM can be used to leverage the knowledge, skills, and abilities of both domestic and international CI practitioners in order to facilitate the creation of actionable competitive intelligence. To produce knowledge, information is gathered through the collection skills and abilities of CI practitioners—a process that produces vast amounts of data that need to be organized by means of a knowledge management system. Through the use of KM systems, CI practitioners are able to use their knowledge, skills, and abilities to analyze, produce, and disseminate actionable intelligence. The outcome is a fully integrated KM and CI system working in concert to achieve the ultimate goal of providing organizations with sustainable competitive advantage.

REFERENCES

Adams, K.C. (2001). "Information Architecture Translates KM Theory into Practice." *KMWorld* 10(6): http://www.kmworld.com/publications/magazine/index. cfm?action=readarticle&Article_ID=1024&Publication_ID=50.

Breeding, B. (2000). "CI and KM Convergence: A Case Study at Shell Services International." *Competitive Intelligence Review* 11(4): 12–24.

Donaldson-Briggs, A.L. (2001). "Competitive Intelligence and Industrial Espionage." *Emerald Insight* (March 16): http://www.managementfirst.com/ knowledge_management/articles/espionage.php.

Dreyfuss, R. (1994). "Company Spies." *The Foundation for National Progress/Mother Jones* (May-June): http://www.motherjones.com/mother_jones/MJ94/dreyfuss.html.

Drott, M.C. (2001). "Personal Knowledge, Corporate Information: The Challenges for Competitive Intelligence." *Business Horizons* 44(2): 31–37.

Gikandi, D. (2001). "Gathering International Competitive Intelligence on the Web." *For Home Business.* http://www.4hb.com/0111intlcompetintell.html.

Hansen, M.T., and B. von Oetinger. (2001). "Introducing T-shaped Managers: Knowledge Management's Next Generation." *Harvard Business Review* 79(3): 106–116.

Klein, C. (1998). "Cultural Differences in Competitive Intelligence Techniques." *Competitive Intelligence Magazine* 1(2): 21–23.

Leizerov, S. (2001). "Finding Privacy Abroad." *Intelligent Enterprise* (October 4): http://www.intelligententerprise.com/011004/415trust1_1.shtml.

Malhotra, Y. (1996). "Competitive Intelligence Programs: An Overview." *BRINT Research Institute.* http://www.brint.com/papers/ciover.htm.

McDonald, P. (2001). "Global B2B: A KM Perspective." *KMWorld* 10(3): http://www.kmworld.com/publications/magazine/index.cfm?action=readarticle&Article_ID=997&Publication_ID=46.

Miller, S.H. (2001a). "Special Report: Learning from the Government Intelligence Community." *Competitive Intelligence Magazine* 4(4): 9–11.

Miller, S.H. (2001b). "Special Report: First CI Academic Conference Focuses on Skills." *Competitive Intelligence Magazine* 4(2): http://www.scip.org/news/cimagazine_article.asp?id=46.

Richard Combs Associates, Inc. (2000). "The Competitive Intelligence Handbook." Chicago, IL: Richard Combs Associates. http://www.combsinc.com/handbook.htm.

Rosner, B. (2001). "HR Should Get a Clue: Corporate Spying Is Real." *Workforce* 80(4): 72–75.

Sheinin, C.E. (1996). "Global CI: Assessing Global Competition." *Competitive Intelligence Review* 7(3): 86–88.

Simpkins, R.A. (1998). "The Global Mind." *Competitive Intelligence Magazine* 1(2): 34–36.

Skyrme, D.J., and D.M. Amidon. (1997). "Creating the Knowledge-Based Business." *David Skyrme Associates.* http://www.skyrme.com/pubs/kmreport.htm.

Society of Competitive Intelligence Professionals. (2004a). "Curriculum Modules for Educational Programs: The Competitive Intelligence Cycle." *Education and Events.* http://www.scip.org/education/module4.asp.

Society of Competitive Intelligence Professionals. (2004b). "Curriculum Modules for Educational Programs: Competencies for Intelligence Professionals." *Education and Events.* http://www.scip.org/education/module2.asp.

Stanat, R., and J. Seydel. (2002). "Conducting Business Intelligence Gathering in Europe: Seven Key Areas." *Competitive Intelligence Magazine* 5(6): 34–37.

Svetvilas, C. (2001). "Going Global: Domestic Web Sites Need Overhaul for International Markets." *Intelligent Enterprise* 4(1): 12–13.

Underwood, J. (2002). "Corporate Counter-Terrorism, Intelligence, and Strategy." *Competitive Intelligence Magazine* 5(6): 15–18.

Werther, G.F.A. (1997). "Doing Business in the New World Disorder: Assessing, Understanding, and Effectively Responding to the Challenges of Social and Political Instability within Emerging Markets." *Competitive Intelligence Review* 8(4): 12–18.

COUNTRY-, INDUSTRY-, AND PROCESS-SPECIFIC STUDIES IN GLOBAL COMPETITIVE INTELLIGENCE

15

The Application of the Global Competitive Intelligence Model to Sweden

Sandy Kokkinis

Today's business environment is increasingly impacted by the global economy. Maintaining a competitive edge requires knowing more about what competitors are doing across the world. Global competitive intelligence (CI) necessitates knowing what domestic and international competitors are doing in various parts of the world and why.

Whether the objective of CI efforts is to expand business presence or to assess the potential threats and opportunities that may arise from competing firms, it is important for CI practitioners to develop an international or global perspective. Many organizations are beginning to implement international CI efforts by trying to learn as much as they can about international situations, paying particular attention to the contextual meaning of global events and global firms' actions (Prescott & Gibbons, 1993). A global intelligence antenna should be developed by the CI function with the intention of obtaining a better understanding of what competitors can and will do (Prescott & Gibbons, 1993).

The basic process of CI tends to be similar across international borders. It begins with the gathering of basic data, then involves organizing that data into information, and finally analyzing that information so that it becomes actionable intelligence. There are differences across borders, however, and they must be recognized, understood, and managed to compete effectively in the global economy (Prescott & Gibbons, 1993). The first step in preparing to conduct global CI is to assess how CI is accomplished in the particular target country. Assuming that CI is practiced in target nations similarly to how it is practiced in the CI practitioner's home country is likely to result in wasted efforts and resources, not to mention inaccurate conclusions.

This chapter will begin by introducing a new global CI model that can be applied to explain how CI is pursued in other parts of the world. The model also helps to identify the differences that exist in various international environments. It is worth noting at this point that while the model can be applied to any country, this chapter will apply it to Sweden in an effort to demonstrate how it works. This application will therefore also provide an insight into how CI is conducted in Sweden.

THE GLOBAL CI MODEL (GCIM)

When conducting CI in a target country, it is important not to restrict all research efforts to hard data. Secondary sources, such as the Internet and web searches, have limitations that need to be recognized. At some point, a thorough assessment of the competitive landscape will require primary research and the exploration of soft data. A combined effort of addressing both hard and soft issues would be ideal and best serves global CI initiatives.

An understanding of the CI infrastructure within a country can be gained by examining both its internal and external environments. The Global CI model shown in Figure 15.1 can be applied in order to help provide this insight. This model helps develop an understanding of the CI culture or CI activities for a particular company within a target country. The aim is to identify how CI is provided. It highlights the possible differences that one may encounter.

The model begins with an evaluation of two basic dimensions: the internal and external environments. *Factors of influence* are then identified within each of these two dimensions. The *factors of influence* for the external environment dimension include political, economic, legal, and social as well as other contexts. For the internal environment dimension, the *factors of influence* include the organizational structure, people, management style or preferences, tasks, and resources. Each of these *factors of influence* plays a role in shaping the two dimensions. It is worth noting that some *factors of influence* play a larger role than others. For example, societal factors such as religion or gender roles may have a larger impact in a given country than other factors such as politics or economics.

The external environment defines the external culture for a particular country. In turn, the internal environment defines the organization's internal culture. Together, the internal and external cultures characterize and shape the CI culture or CI activities.

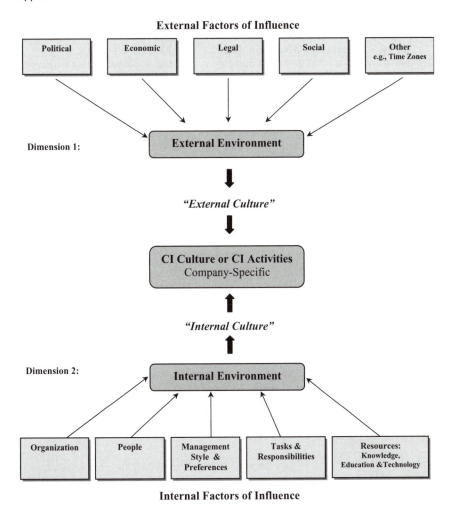

Figure 15.1 The Global CI Model (GCIM).

APPLICATION OF THE GLOBAL CI MODEL TO SWEDEN

External Environment

The political, economic, legal, and social dynamics of the country act as *factors of influence* that define its external culture and impact how CI is conducted. The impact of each *factor of influence* depends on its scope, magnitude, and role played within the country. Each *factor of influence* will reveal certain obstacles, limitations, and opportunities that will impact how CI is conducted.

Political Dynamics

Sweden has a stable political environment. This implies that CI professionals do not have to continuously monitor the country for unexpected changes to its political climate. The Swedish government supports CI practices (Kahaner, 1996), and it has made a commitment to CI initiatives by allocating resources to help firms develop their CI capabilities (Calof, 1998). In Sweden, intelligence is both highly regarded and respected. It is viewed as a national necessity (Kahaner, 1996), and Sweden has been able to establish a national culture that values information intelligence (Calof, 1998). For many years, government and industry have worked closely together in the development of intelligence products (Calof & Skinner, 1998). Sweden has had a historical tradition of networks of information-gathering activities (Calof & Skinner, 1998). An example of this historical tradition lies within the banking industry. The Swedish banks have played and continue to play a large CI role in the country. For example, SE Banken has implemented a computer-based system that does country analysis for its clientele. Customers are provided with hard and soft information on a country, including information on politics, stability, opinion changes, internal conflicts, and institutional legal changes (Dedijer, 1998).

CI Implications

Government support for CI activities indicates a clear buy-in from the upper echelons of the country, who understand the role and value of CI. Swedes view CI as a valid and legal business activity that is required to ensure competitive success. As such CI may be performed openly and freely in Sweden.

Economic Dynamics

Sweden is widely regarded as having one of the most knowledge-based economies in the world. In 2002, Sweden was ranked number 1 for the third consecutive year by the influential IDC and World Times Information Society Index (World Times, 2002; IDC Consulting, 2002). It has leveraged its advanced technological development, sophisticated infrastructure, and high general educational level to develop world-class knowledge-intensive industries in information technology (IT), telecommunications, biomedicine, and the so-called experience industries (design, music, fashion, art, media, tourism, etc.) (Swedish Institute, 2003). To support their knowledge-based economy, the Swedes invest heavily in the development of IT clusters such as their famous Wireless Valley and Telematics Valley. Their country invests 9.3% of its GDP in IT and telecommunications, more than any other nation (Europemedia, 2003). Sweden will probably not relinquish this knowledge-based dominance any time soon. Consider that in 1998, there were 600 Swedish IT companies, four years later, there were more than 1,000—despite the then-recent dot.com crash and recession (Europemedia, 2002).

Due to its small domestic market, Swedish companies have little choice but to export. As a result, Sweden is home to many successful multinationals, including IKEA, Volvo, Ericsson, Absolut, ABB, SAAB, and Astra Zeneca. This outward orientation continues as Sweden welcomes foreign investment and ownership with a very liberalized foreign investment policy regime. Essentially, foreigners have the same rights as Swedes to engage in business in Sweden. The government's Invest in Sweden agency provides general assistance to foreign firms wishing to establish a presence in the country. As a result of this favorable foreign investment climate, foreigners owned a majority stake in more than 3,000 enterprises in Sweden by the end of 2000. These enterprises employ more than 250,000 people—roughly 15% of Sweden's private-sector workforce (Economist Intelligence Unit, 2001). Further, in 2001, there were 7,821 firms with foreign ownership; this was up from 5,519 in 2000 (Economist Intelligence Unit, 2003). The increasing trend of foreign ownership underscores Sweden's openness to foreign economic involvement.

Contrary to common belief, the main driver of Sweden's economy is free enterprise. However, the state still owns or controls 25% of the economy through its ownership of shares and voting rights in 62 companies with an estimated 2002 combined revenue of SKr 334 billion (Economist Intelligence Unit, 2003). Currently, the Swedish government owns interests in a diverse array of industries, including banking, defense, telecommunications, mining, utilities, retail pharmacy, broadcasting, alcohol retailing, airlines, and postal services. In recent years, the government has introduced several deregulation and privatization initiatives (Economist Intelligence Unit, 2003):

- Partially privatized Telia, the state-owned telecommunications firm, reducing its ownership to 70.6%
- Decreased its holdings in its banking concern, Nordea, to retain 18.1% ownership
- sold its 25% interest in the defense firm Celsius
- Signed a letter of intent to sell off the banking subsidiary owned by the Swedish Post Office

In 1997, the Swedish Parliament passed legislation allowing for the sale of state-owned enterprises without parliamentary approval. That same year, the Swedish government also indicated its intent to sell eight state-owned enterprises, but to date it has sold only one. In the future, however, any sustained macroeconomic malaise and the attendant budget deficits, or an electoral victory for more conservative opposition parties, may induce accelerated pursuit of privatization of state-owned or controlled enterprises.

CI Implications

Sweden provides a very hospitable economic climate for CI in several ways. First, the country boasts a world-class technology infrastructure that will support two very important stages of the CI cycle: secondary CI research and dissemination of CI. Second, the outward orientation of Swedes and their favorable disposition toward foreign investment makes them very accepting of CI—a business activity that often precedes and helps to sustain foreign direct investment. Third, recent deregulation and privatization indicate that CI activities will become increasingly important in Sweden, as formerly state-owned or controlled enterprises must begin competing in an increasingly open free-market economy.

Legal Dynamics

The Swedish constitution gives citizens free access to official public documents (Anderson, 1995). All information that is of public record can be accessed either voluntarily or with the aid of officials, who are required by law to comply with requests for access. Access to any information is possible (Dedijer, 1998), although one regulation that may impact CI activity forbids the transferring of information without the permission of its owners (Oakes, 1999). In addition, the European Data Protection Directive (DPA) mandated all European Union (EU) members to adopt legislation that guarantees the rights of an individual's privacy and the control of the contents in electronic databases that contain personal information (McGonagle & Brogan, 2000).

CI Implications

In Sweden, CI activity must adhere to legislative requirements, and all personal information exchanged electronically must have the approval of the individual to whom the information pertains. This law must also be observed and enforced by any foreign companies when dealing with information on Swedes (Dedijer, 1998). However, since public information is readily and easily accessed, CI practitioners should have few, if any, difficulties in obtaining public information. On a national level, Sweden is an information-sharing nation. This helps to promote and encourage CI activities and, in turn, a CI culture.

Social Dynamics

Fully understanding how Swedes approach CI requires an understanding of Swedish society. On the surface, Sweden may appear to be culturally similar to North America. However, for the CI practitioner, even slight differences can be important and may prove costly if ignored. "The more similar a country is to your own on the surface, the greater the risk that you'll misjudge some crucial aspects of its culture" (Anderson, 1995).

Swedes value independence, honesty, and openness. They tend to favor agreement and consensus (Anderson, 1995). Swedes tend to be honest and straightforward people, and telling the truth is unquestionable (Anderson, 1995). Swedes respect straight talk and prefer to speak openly and directly. They prefer getting to the point and avoiding any unnecessary small talk (Anderson, 1995). A CI professional will be best served by keeping this in mind when collecting primary data from Swedish sources. Double meanings and ambiguity make Swedes uncomfortable. People who don't provide straight answers are perceived as devious and unreliable (Anderson, 1995). For the CI professional, a direct, straightforward approach would be the best to use in Sweden. Swedes prefer doing things, as opposed to talking about them (Anderson, 1995). Therefore, if meetings need to be scheduled, one must be sure to address the issues at hand, and not waste time.

The Swedish language should not be a barrier when conducting CI in Sweden. English is spoken and understood by everyone and should be the language used when dealing with Swedes. Additional advice to the CI professional is to ensure that one's approach is not too aggressive. In Sweden, the word "aggressive" carries negative connotations (Anderson, 1995). When engaging in conversations with Swedes, it is important to pay attention to what is being said. Sweden is a low-content culture; words have specific meanings, and the situational context plays an irrelevant role in the meaning of what is being said (Anderson, 1995).

CI Implications

Understanding how Swedes behave and how they communicate will help the CI professional's approach. A straightforward, honest, and direct style would be ideal. Learning what is valued in the culture will help one avoid mistakes and embarrassments.

Other Dynamics

Additional factors, such as time zones, must also be considered. For example, there is a seven-hour time difference between Toronto and Stockholm.

CI Implications

CI practitioners seeking primary source information must take the time difference into account before meetings and telephone conversations can occur if the CI is not actually being conducted in Sweden.

Internal Environment

Intelligence is an activity that relies on people and their willingness to contribute information (Hamilton, 1992). The soft data that is found within an organization is one important source of intelligence information (Hamilton, 1992). In order to tap into this source of information, the organizational culture must encourage information-sharing and promote inter-functional cooperation. To gain an understanding of CI practices in Sweden, an understanding of the internal environment is therefore required. An organization is shaped by its structure, people, tasks, management preferences, and culture. These dimensions act as *factors of influence* that define a company's internal culture.

Organization

A firm's organizational chart defines its organizational structure. It outlines the functions and roles of people in a given organization. A flexible structure allows for inter-organizational communication, collaboration, and cooperation. Such a structure would be ideal for the information-sharing aspects of CI. In Sweden, organizational structures tend to be flatter and team oriented. Matrix structures are common in Sweden, since Swedes are comfortable with multiple reporting structures. Work tends to be organized more horizontally than vertically (Anderson, 1995). Unlike North American companies, businesses in Sweden often lack a clear hierarchy. It is not uncommon to see fewer management levels in Swedish companies than one would find in other countries (Anderson, 1995).

Access to information is important to the people in Swedish organizations (Hamilton, 1992). Information is not viewed as a source of power in Sweden and is thus not reserved for a select few. Rather, information is seen as a viable and significant resource that should flow freely, be openly shared, and be openly thought about by everyone (Anderson, 1995). The sharing of information across the organization is seen as a means through which a company may survive and prosper. The sharing of knowledge and information is regarded as one way that individuals can increase their chances of success in Sweden (Anderson, 1995).

CI Implications

With a flatter matrix organizational structure and an emphasis on information-sharing, successfully implementing a CI project in Sweden is a very feasible prospect. Sharing knowledge and information is a common business practice in Sweden and can only serve to benefit any CI activities in this nation.

People

In Sweden, every employee is expected to understand and take an active interest in the entire organization, and not just in their individual responsibilities. This is referred to as "know-why" and is distinctively different from "know-how" (Anderson, 1995). The theory is that once people know why something has to be done, they usually find the best ways to do it on their own (Anderson, 1995). At work, Swedes strive for consensus and cooperation (Anderson, 1995). They also prefer to go directly to the source of information and thus frequently bypass the traditional hierarchy. Some cultures would see this as violating the corporate chain of command. Swedes simply don't see it that way. Whether something needs to be done, someone needs to be informed, or an employee simply needs information, Swedes feel the process should be as simple as possible (Anderson, 1995).

CI Implications

Sweden has a participative business environment, which helps create a positive climate for CI and helps promote a culture of information-sharing. If people understand why sharing information benefits the company as a whole, they are more willing to do so. This sharing therefore creates a CI atmosphere that is enriched by the input of all employees.

Management Style and Preferences

Swedish managers tend to think of themselves primarily as coaches and tend to delegate responsibility and authority throughout their organizations. Their aim is to achieve full participation in the decision-making process (Anderson, 1995). "Everyone, not just people with certain positions or job titles, has the right to make judgements, form conclusions, reach decisions, and then act, without asking management for permission" (Anderson, 1995). Swedish management practices are said to have small power distances. "Power distance" is the extent to which managers in a hierarchy feel they can and should control the behavior of others (Anderson, 1995). Organizational power is more equally distributed in Sweden than in many other nations (Leidner, Carlsson, Elam, & Corrales, 1999).

CI Implications

With a management style that encourages decision-making and the drawing of conclusions at all organizational levels, businesspeople in Sweden are well positioned to carry out all phases of the CI process with full support.

Tasks, Roles and Responsibilities

In Sweden, the roles within an organization are slightly different than they are in North America. For example, the role of supervisor does not exist in Sweden. The translation of the word in Swedish equates to probation officer and is subsequently viewed negatively (Anderson, 1995). When employees are given an assignment, it is assumed that they will be left on their own to complete it (Anderson, 1995). The CI activities that occur predominantly within Swedish organizations are those of data-collecting (Calof, 1998) and information-sharing. CI awareness is taught and reinforced through training and education and through continuous improvement efforts. For example, telecommunications multinational Ericsson states that it "works hard to improve its business intelligence" (Dedijer, 1998). CI initiatives succeed in environments where information can flow freely and where there is less local ownership by individuals in the organization (Leidner, Carlsson, Elam, & Corrales, 1999).

CI Implications

A foreign CI practitioner must be aware of the subtle differences in the roles and responsibilities within a Swedish organization. When information is required from key individuals within the organization, going directly to those responsible will likely yield the greatest and fastest results.

Resources

Information technology plays a large role in Sweden. There is an emphasis placed on computerization, and many Swedish companies have begun to systematize their business intelligence activities (Pettersson, 2001). Familiarity with e-mail and the Internet is prevalent. Sweden is becoming an information society, with goals to provide access to computers and Internet connections for everyone (Docere Intelligence, 2000). Sweden was one of the first countries to develop and introduce a web-based course in business intelligence, and Swedish companies continuously maintain the content of their information systems and adjust their content in ways that help management understand their individual businesses (Leidner, Carlsson, Elam, & Corrales, 1999). Data access and security concerns become more important to organizations such as those in Sweden, since they believe information should be open and accessible to all.

Sweden has been ranked as one of the most knowledge-based economies in the world (Marsh, 2001). A strong emphasis on training and education seems to prevail throughout most organizations. There are currently several companies that offer to do CI research, as well as provide training sessions, seminars, and workshops for managers and individuals interested in CI. There is clearly a business awareness of the benefits of CI and its value in maintaining a competitive edge. The Business Intelligence and Strategy Network of Sweden (BISNES) is a network that "holds conferences and courses, gives diplomas and publishes a Business Intelligence Review' (Dedijer, 1998).

In Sweden, the relationship between industry and academia is strongly maintained and reinforced (Anonymous, 2001). The practice of CI has been institutionalized for decades (Calof, 1999), and business schools in Sweden have incorporated CI into their curriculum. There is currently a CI program at the School of Economics & Management at Lund University in Stockholm, which is the only university that offers master's and doctoral degrees in CI (Kahaner, 1996).

CI Implications

Sweden's educational dedication to CI serves to elevate CI as a valid business discipline. It helps authenticate CI as a profession. In placing a strong educational focus on CI, it increases CI's relevance to the business community. In addition, specific CI training programs and degrees help create a pool of CI-versed individuals.

External and Internal Cultures

In order for CI to be effective, the corporate or internal culture defined by internal *factors of influence* must be supportive. These factors include management preferences, organizational structure, and resources that affect CI initiatives. This culture plays a large role in how CI is practiced, how companies view CI, how they use it, and what aspects of CI they see as being important. It affects how information is collected and what information is collected (Kahaner, 1996).

Equally important is an external culture that supports CI efforts. By exploring the external *factors of influence* such as political, social, and economic factors, one can draw conclusions of a country's "CI friendliness." Certain environments are more conducive to CI practices because these external factors allow practitioners to access information easily.

Once all *factors of influence* have been identified and their potential impact assessed, a picture of the internal and external cultures will begin to evolve. Together, they create a clearer portrait of the forum in which CI will be practiced. In this Swedish example, what emerges are participative external and internal cultures. Both emphasize the sharing and access of information, and such an environment facilitates the ease of CI in Sweden.

CONCLUSION

For the CI practitioner, the Global CI model presented in this chapter will help assess how CI is approached in a global context. It is a model that can easily be applied to any country, and it helps identify how factors in other countries will influence the practice of international CI. This perspective can only prove to be beneficial to CI practitioners when formulating strategies for projects that deal with foreign countries.

Unfortunately, one cannot deny the existence of individual cultural biases, which have to be taken into consideration when conducting global CI. Ethnocentrism must be avoided; CI cannot be approached with the mentality that "our way is the best way" of conducting CI. It is incorrect to assume that the approach used to practice CI in one's native country will work elsewhere in the world. The primary benefit of using the Global CI model presented in this chapter is that it will help the CI professional incorporate both global awareness and country-specific insights into international competitive intelligence.

REFERENCES

Anderson, B. (1995). *Swedishness*. Stockholm, Sweden: Postiva Seveirge.

Anonymous. (2001). "Sweden: Culture of Creativity." *Los Angeles Business Journal* (October 8): http://www.findarticles.com/cf_0/m5072/41_23/79254314/p1/article.jhtml?term=%22Sweden%3A+Culture+of+Creativity%22.

Calof, J.L. (1998). "Increasing Your CIQ: The Competitive Intelligence Edge." *The 1998 Economic & Technology Development Journal of Canada.* http://www.edco.on.ca/journal/item22.htm.

Calof, J.L. (1999). "Teaching CI: Opportunities & Needs." *Competitive Intelligence Magazine* 2(4): 28–31.

Calof, J.L., and B. Skinner. (1998). "Government's Role in Competitive Intelligence: What's Happening in Canada." *Competitive Intelligence Magazine* 2(2): 20–23.

Dedijer, S. (1998). "Competitive Intelligence in Sweden." *Competitive Intelligence Review*, 9(1): 66–68.

Docere Intelligence. (2000). "The Internet Market in Sweden: A Survey Conducted on the Assignment of the National Post & Telecom Agency." Stockholm, Sweden: Docere Intelligence.

Economist Intelligence Unit. (2001). Country Commerce: Sweden. *The Economist Intelligence Unit.* New York.

Economist Intelligence Unit. (2003). Country Commerce: Sweden. *The Economist Intelligence Unit.* New York.

Europemedia. (2002). "Swedish IT Industry Continues to Grow." *Europemedia* (March 25).

Europemedia. (2003). "Positive Signs for Swedish IT/Telecom Business." *Europemedia* (March 3).

Hamilton, D. (1992). "The Intelligence Imperative for Managers," pp. 59–69 in J. Sigurdson and Y. Tagerud [eds.], *The Intelligent Corporation: The Privatization of Intelligence*. London, UK: Taylor Graham Publishing.

IDC Consulting. (2002). *Information Society Index 2002: The Nordic Paragon?* http://www.idc.dk/products/Factsheets/Factsheets_2002/ISI.pdf.

Kahaner, L. (1996). *Competitive Intelligence: From Black Ops to Boardrooms: How Businesses Gather, Analyze, and Use Information to Succeed in the Global Marketplace*. New York: Simon & Schuster.

Leidner, D.E., S. Carlsson, J. Elam, and M. Corrales. (1999). "Mexican and Swedish Managers' Perceptions of the Impact of EIS on Organizational Intelligence, Decision Making, and Structure." *Decision Sciences* 30(3): 633–658.

Marsh, P. (2001). "Sweden Tops List of Knowledge-Based Economies." *Financial Times* 3(254): 9.

McGonagle, J.J., and C. Brogan. (2000). "Law & Ethics: The EU Directive and the British Data Protection Act: A Transatlantic Conversation." *Competitive Intelligence Magazine* 3(4): 45–48.

Oakes, C. (1999). "A European's Net View of U.S." *Wired News*. http://www.wired.com/news/politics/0,1283,21476,00.html.

Pettersson, U. (2001). "Creating an Intelligence System at the Swedish National Financial Management Authority." *Competitive Intelligence Review* 12(2): 20–31.

Prescott, J.E., and P.T. Gibbons. (1993). "Global Competitive Intelligence: An Overview," pp. 1–27 in J.E. Prescott and P.T. Gibbons [eds.], *Global Perspectives on Competitive Intelligence*. Alexandria, VA: Society of Competitive Intelligence Professionals.

Swedish Institute. (2003). *An Economic Miracle*. http://www.sweden.se/templates/CommonPage_2711.asp.

World Times. (2002). *The 2002 Information Society Index*. http://www.worldpaper.com/2002/feb02/isi.jpg.

16

A Comparison of Competitive Intelligence Practices in the United States and Mexico

Ross Kerr

Competitive intelligence (CI) helps organizational decision-makers make better decisions (Fleisher, 2001). In order to make good decisions, the vast majority of decision-makers in the United States expect intelligence that is based on a solid analysis of reliable, valid, and objective information obtained through ethical means. CI practitioners in the United States typically have access to a wealth of information through public sources such as industry regulators and trade associations (Robertson, 1998). Given the availability of inputs to the CI process, CI practices in the United States are reasonably well developed. Moreover, a relatively large body of literature has evolved on the topic of CI practices. The CI environment in countries outside of the United States, however, may be very different. Therefore, it might be reasonable to propose that the CI environment of a particular country is, in part, responsible for the prevalence of CI practices in that country as well as a contributing factor in the development of unique CI practices. The purpose of this chapter is to identify the key considerations to doing CI in Mexico and to compare and contrast those findings with U.S. CI approaches commonly used by practitioners and as published in the literature.

The chapter begins with a review of the CI literature related to CI practices in Mexico and the United States. Subsequent sections describe Mexico's external and internal CI environment, as well as current CI practices in Mexico (inputs, the transformation process, and outputs). Following these descriptions is a comparison of CI practices in Mexico relative to those in the United States. CI practices are reviewed from the perspective of local CI professionals in each country, who provide input into how they conduct CI. The final sections highlight some of the implications for CI practitioners and business managers, as well as potential areas of future research on this topic.

CI professionals will learn about the unique CI practices that are prevalent in Mexico and the specific skills required for conducting those practices; these skills may in fact not exist among current U.S. CI professionals. Business managers will learn that there are critical skills that should be part of the criteria for recruiting and selecting professionals to conduct CI in Mexico. Business managers will also learn what to expect after engaging a Mexican CI professional.

LITERATURE REVIEW

It should be no surprise that there is significantly more literature on CI in the United States than in Mexico. CI practices are more widely accepted and established in the U.S. business community than they are in the Mexican business community. As such, evidence for CI practices in Mexico is necessarily drawn from limited sources. Nevertheless, there has been a sufficient enough description of the Mexican and Latin American contexts, relative to CI practices, to allow for a general review and some conclusions.

In order to conduct a cross-cultural assessment of CI practices, assumptions must be made about the nature of CI in each country. One important assumption in this chapter is that the CI cycle is similar in both the United States and Mexico. The literature has provided no evidence to refute this assumption, moreover, there is some evidence to support it (Price, 2000). As such, this chapter compares the CI practices of each country on the basis of the CI process—or intelligence cycle—outlined here (Blenkhorn, 2001; Clarke, 2001; Herring, 1998):

- Planning and direction (Adler, 2000a)
- Gathering data (InfoAmericas, 2001; Baranauskas, 1998; Fuld, 1995)
- Organizing facts (Leidner, Carlsson, Elam, & Corrales, 1999)
- Analyzing information (Adler, 1999c)
- Disseminating intelligence (Adler, 2000b; Adler, 1999b)
- Making decisions (Adler, 2000b; Price, 2000; Adler, 1999c; Adler, 1999b)
- Revisiting information and analysis

From the literature, three elements of CI stand out as particularly useful for the purpose of conducting a comparative analysis between countries

(InfoAmericas, 2001). The first two elements may be referred to as the context in which CI is performed, which includes the internal and external environments. The external environment includes factors such as the availability and quality of government information, the reliability of the business press, and the development of industry associations. The internal environment refers to factors such as organizational structure, formal and informal authority, and corporate culture. The third element of comparing CI in different countries is an examination of the CI practices themselves.

Another valuable reference is the 1996 study conducted by the American Productivity and Quality Center (APQC), which developed a benchmark of CI practices. The results of the study provide criteria for evaluating CI practices against U.S. benchmarks. The study discovered seven key processes or mechanisms that define good CI practice (Prescott, Herring, & Panfely, 1998):

1. Evolving, yet stable, CI infrastructures
2. Decentralized-coordinated networks
3. Responsive information technology (IT) system operating as a learning system
4. Linkages
5. Customer-feedback-implementation linkage
6. Hypothesis-driven recommendations
7. Institutionalizing intelligence cultures

The literature therefore provides a framework for comparing and contrasting CI practices in the United States and Mexico and, to a limited extent, illustrates the CI practices used by CI professionals and managers in the Mexican context.

MEXICO'S EXTERNAL CI ENVIRONMENT

The Mexican business environment is benefiting from increased political stability and reduced economic volatility that is, in turn, encouraging growth in international trade. Mexico's improved status in the global marketplace has placed greater emphasis on the ability of domestic and international companies to conduct CI within the country. However, the business environment is not particularly conducive to practicing CI in the same manner as would be done in the United States. The external environment in Mexico has numerous dimensions that are important in terms of the focus of this chapter, and Figure 16.1 provides an overview of Mexico's external CI environment.

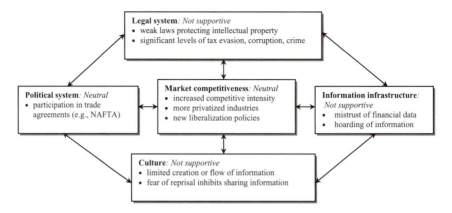

Figure 16.1   An Analysis of Mexico's External CI Environment.

Within Mexico's external environment, there is little support for CI efforts. Mexico's culture is characterized by few sources of reliable information and limited information flow from and between sources. The information infrastructure contributes directly to the lack of information in particular because industries with low wages encourage the hoarding of information to be sold to the highest bidder. The legal system exacerbates this issue through a lack of enforcement of any right to protect information. Meanwhile, the intensity of market competition is increasing due to higher levels of privatization and increasing numbers of free trade agreements within the Americas. Clearly, the market is shifting toward a more global competitiveness and there has been progress toward making improvements in each of the outlined areas. Mexico's CI infrastructure, however, is not currently in alignment with the direction in which the country is headed. CI efforts will be hampered until corrective action is taken to improve the external CI environment in Mexico.

Table 16.1 compares and contrasts the CI environment in the United States with that in Mexico. As shown in Table 16.1, there are significant differences between the external CI environments in the United States and Mexico. Specifically, this analysis highlights the low level of CI infrastructure that exists in Mexico relative to the United States. For example, Mexico has higher instances of crime and corruption that may go unpunished, as well as inadequate systems for encouraging the flow of reliable and valid objective information. Unfortunately, this information is a key ingredient to effective CI. These variations exist primarily as a result of the historical, political, and social development of the country (InfoAmericas, 2001).

It is important to note that changes are currently taking place in Mexico (Government of Province of Alberta, Canada, 2003). The level of

Table 16.1
Comparison of External CI Environment in the United States and Mexico

External CI Environment	United States	Mexico
Economic openness	High	Low
Level of privatization	High	Low
Intensity of competition	High	Medium
National support systems (economic, technology)	High	Medium
Information infrastructure	High	Low
Respect for intellectual property	High	Low
Acceptance of CI as a profession	Medium	Low
Legal protection	High	Low
Tax evasion	Low	High
Corruption	Low	Medium
Crime & security	Low	Medium
Elitism	Low	High

Sources: Government of Province of Alberta, Canada (2001); Lewandowski (1999); Adler (1999c); InfoAmericas (2001).

privatization is increasing in industries such as electricity, banking, transportation, and natural gas. In fact, the private sector is expected to drive expansion in telecommunication and electrical capabilities.

In general, the economy is becoming more open as a result of new liberalization policies from the government. The government is also expanding the scope of the Mexican marketplace by entering into bilateral and trilateral trade pacts with various Latin American nations—including nine free trade agreements—as well as establishing a *maquiladora* program with free zones and special incentives to attract manufacturing facilities.

The conclusion derived from this analysis is that the external CI environment in Mexico has some critical limitations for using CI as a managerial tool for decision-making, but it is beginning to head in a direction that could ultimately support the effective pursuit of CI within the next decade.

MEXICO'S INTERNAL CI ENVIRONMENT

Equally important to the context of conducting CI in any country is the internal CI environment. While larger firms in the United States may have a department dedicated to CI work, this level of commitment would be unusual in the Mexican context. Mid-size companies in both countries tend to hire CI firms for competitive intelligence services, and smaller companies will likely conduct CI on their own (Miller, 2001).

Table 16.2 summarizes the key variations and similarities between the structure of the CI functions in the United States and Mexico.

Table 16.2
Comparison of Internal CI Environment in the United States and Mexico

Internal CI Environment	United States	Mexico
CI infrastructure	Evolving, yet stable, CI infrastructures	Initial stages of development in terms of personnel, networks, and champions
Organizational structure	Decentralized-coordinated networks	Initial stages of experimentation
Information technology (IT)	Responsive IT system operating as a learning system	Not well developed
Link to business strategy	Linkage is a circular process	Primarily facilitated through informal information-gathering by executives; no formal linkage
Measures of effectiveness	Customer-feedback-implementation linkage	None
CI roles	Hypothesis-driven recommendations; business skills tend to be emphasized over broad knowledge of history, philosophy, and politics	Business skills and social science competencies such as a sense of history as well as understanding relevant social, political, and cultural contexts
Organizational culture	Institutionalizing intelligence cultures; supportive	Limited acceptance; neutral
Accreditation	Formal training provided from within the company as well as from third-party providers	No formal training; university academics are increasingly being used as business consultants
Ethics	Ethical behavior relative to high expectations; ethics is critical component of CI	Attention to ethics is increasingly viewed as essential to business success
Formal authority	Hierarchical structure	Hierarchical structure
Informal authority	Senior managers expect their subordinates to take charge of their field of responsibilities	Family-owned companies weaken middle-management decision-making and handicap the flow of information; centralized decision-making is evolving toward a more decentralized approach
Rewards	Based on quality and timeliness of analysis	No evidence

Sources: Adler (2000b); Boluarte (2001)[1]; InfoAmericas (2001); Lewandowski (1999); Prescott, Herring & Panfely (1998); Werther (1998).

Similar to the previous comparative analysis of the external CI environments, there are several interesting variations between the internal CI environments in the United States and Mexico. As Table 16.2 reflects, the CI environment in Mexico is in its infancy, and so CI is not widely accepted within Mexican organizations. For example, most organizations in Mexico do not have a formal CI infrastructure or linkage of CI to decision-making. Informal practices, such as decision-making and information-sharing, are also indicative of limited support for CI within firms. To be sure, this could also be said of the internal CI environment at many firms in the United States. However, it appears that, in relative terms, there is currently less support for CI in Mexico than exists in the United States.

One trend in particular indicates that this situation in Mexico may be changing. Attention to ethics is increasingly viewed as essential to business success (Adler, 2002). Ethical behavior is widely held as a critical component of CI in the United States. Thus, the trend toward adopting ethical practices may be an indication that the internal CI environment in Mexico is in fact approaching that of the United States and could ultimately support U.S. CI practices.

In the final analysis, however, the conclusion from the examination of the internal CI environment is consistent with the findings for the external environment. There are a number of critical issues in the internal environment that currently limit the effectiveness of CI practices in Mexico.

CONDUCTING CI IN MEXICO

As discussed, the external and internal environments provide the context for CI practices in each country. The next step is to examine the CI practices themselves.

Inputs

Information in Mexico is both scarce and full of errors. Adler (1999a) offers several reasons for this reality. First, there is a general lack of respect for intellectual ownership, which makes development of for-profit information more difficult. Second, capitalism in Mexico is developed on the basis of privileged access to information, such as information regarding which government actions will be taken. Third, there is a family business tradition whereby families hold business secrets to themselves. Fourth, official associations offer few statistics because their own membership fails to provide them with such figures. Finally, Mexico has a large informal economy (perhaps 20%–40% of the total economy, according to Adler [1999a]); which, of course, is not recorded in official statistics.

This finding is supported by other evidence, which identifies several important obstacles to conducting CI in Mexico (Price, 2000). First, only a tiny percentage of Latin American firms are publicly traded, so financial reporting is minimal. Second, modern industrial associations publish member profile databases, but their publications still fall short of developed-country standards. Third, business publications continue to focus on high-profile companies and often provide inadequate coverage of mid-size firms. Finally, information is closely guarded among top-level executives. The tone of secrecy may also be set by Mexico's political environment. For example, the Mexican government legally prohibits the public release of information about employees, their pay, and positions (Parker, 2001).

Although there is a lack of adequate information, research methods in Mexico follow a similar pattern to those in the United States. For example, secondary "desk" research, business-to-business research, consumer surveys, and focus groups are all viable practices. However, the effectiveness of most research practices is severely restricted by the internal and external CI environments. For example, social stratification makes it impossible to survey a true cross-section of society in one area, and the low rate of telephone penetration prohibits representative telephone samples (InfoAmericas, 2001).

Another method of gathering information in this difficult climate is to rely on third-party investigators. This is the preferred method because it affords an element of protection for the researcher, whose reputation could be ruined by undertaking unscrupulous gathering techniques. Clearly, there is an argument to support separating the more aggressive type of investigative research from mainstream competitive intelligence practices when conducting CI in Mexico.

A sales representative who has worked in the Mexican business environment for 20 years has several suggestions for gathering information.[2] The website (http://www.bancomext.com) offers valuable industry data and may be supplemented by the industry directories at the Mexican Trade Commission in many countries. Large companies with good financial results will have valuable information on their corporate website; however, companies with poor financial results are unlikely to have an updated website. The banks that lend to a particular company will often provide information in respect to the firm's financial status, and this information may be supplemented by data from Dun & Bradstreet, which has a representative office in Mexico. Finally, as more firms conduct business with Canada and the United States under the North American Free Trade Agreement (NAFTA), credit bureaus and export development agencies will become increasingly important sources of reliable and valid information.

The Transformation Process

Mexican managers have adapted to this information gap by relying on intuition for decision-making (Adler, 1999a). Information is gathered and decisions are made primarily through the use of instinct, insider knowledge, and connections. Most useful information is collected through personal contacts developed through a trust-building approach (Info-Americas, 2001). Personal relationships appear to weigh heavily in the transformation process and are manifested in real terms when greater credibility is associated with research provided by individuals with higher education.[3]

It has been suggested that Mexican managers' practice of relying largely on intuition to make business decisions is changing because those same managers have less time to circulate in the social network and require faster decision turnaround time (Price, 2000). Instead, managers are relying on CI firms to provide the data required for an effective decision. However, the practice of engaging in primary research is limited to the larger companies as a result of the high cost associated with the gathering and analysis of data. The cost of research can be as high as three to six times the cost of obtaining the same level of information in more developed regions (InfoAmericas, 2001).

Outputs

Once the intelligence is ready for dissemination, the method of distribution in Mexico could take the form of a written report, presentation, or informal discussion. Given the high level of context in the Mexican approach to CI, reports are written in the context of the decision-maker. This is one particular area in which there is a strong correlation with the U.S. benchmark.

In Mexico, decision-making and information are typically controlled at the top of the organization. Moreover, there is little effort to disseminate information throughout the organization. However, anecdotal evidence suggests that centralization is evolving into a more decentralized approach.[4] This is attributed to managers having less time to be involved in all decisions, the increasing level of education among employees at some firms, and the action taken by the government to decentralize some elements of political decision-making.

There is little evidence regarding the extent to which decisions are reviewed or research implications are refined through a feedback process. However, given the emphasis on informal information-gathering techniques, one could propose that an ongoing refinement of information is inherent in this type of approach. As noted by one participant in the Mexican marketplace, the decision-making process and any feedback loop typically take time and depend heavily on the availability of money to implement a decision.[5]

CI PRACTICES IN THE UNITED STATES AS COMPARED TO MEXICO

The variations in CI practices between the United States and Mexico appear to correlate with the findings of the context in which the activities are performed. The external and internal CI environments in the United States support more advanced CI practices, and those practices appear to be developed. In Mexico, the lack of development of CI practices is consistent with the lack of support for CI in the external and internal environments.

Specific variations in practices are evident in every aspect of the CI process. The U.S. approach is based on a formal process driven by the need for timely and accurate information. The situation in Mexico appears to suggest a more relaxed approach, perhaps as a result of the relatively less competitive marketplace, but also because of the cultural tendencies in Mexico. For example, gathering useful information in Mexico requires a long-term approach to trust-building with important contacts. Making decisions may also take an extended period of time due to oft-limited financial resources.

The variation in practices is also evident when comparing analytical approaches. The general emphasis in the Mexican environment is on the analysis of the historical context of any information, in contrast to the U.S. desire to base most CI on objective data from a forward-looking framework.

Continuing the emphasis on context, the dissemination of intelligence in Mexico is delivered in a very descriptive way, beginning with the historical considerations and ending with implications. In contrast, U.S. reports tend to be written in a concise manner emphasizing action-oriented outcomes. In the United States, one of the benchmark activities is to ensure that reports are written in the context of the decision-maker. That is, a decision-maker in Germany would require different context for a given set of data than would a decision-maker in Mexico. Mexico is similar in this respect, and also pursues a contextual approach to report writing.

Decision-makers in the United States are more likely to accept CI as a critical part of the decision-making process. As a result, CI outputs are integrated into the organization and permeate all levels of employees. This is consistent with the U.S. approach to decision-making, which is largely pushed down the levels of the organization. Clearly, this approach contrasts with the Mexican tendency to maintain decision-making at the top of the organization. In Mexico little information is shared with the lower levels of the firm.

The process for looping back to the analysis and then refining the implications of CI work is an accepted part of the U.S. approach, whereas there is little evidence that a formal feedback loop exists in Mexican CI practice, making this a potential area for CI research.

As a result of the CI environment in the United States, CI practitioners in these countries have a wider scope of potential tools from which to draw to produce an effective output. The Mexican CI environment, in contrast, appears to support only a limited number of CI practices to produce equally effective outputs.

Overall, it appears that CI practices in both countries are aligned with the context of the CI environment in each respective region. It appears that CI in Mexico has not yet been used effectively to address business needs in the same way that CI practices have evolved in the United States.

Table 16.3 summarizes the key variations and similarities between CI practiced in the United States and CI practiced in Mexico. The CI practices in the United States refer to common practices as published in CI literature. Despite the current gaps in response to globalization and increased competition, CI practices in Mexico should begin to approach those in the United States within the next decade. The Mexican government will need to work with the business community to create an environment in which quality information is available to a broader set of managers on a timely basis.

IMPLICATIONS FOR MANAGERS

The following six implications for business managers flow from the comparative analysis of the external and internal CI environments of Mexico and the United States:

1. Be aware of the limitations of information in the Mexican marketplace. Moreover, given that the information gap is filled by a decision-making model based largely on intuition, it is critical to infuse significant local context into the decision-making process for the Mexican context. This approach may include a heavy reliance on qualitative data gathered from informal sources, rather than formally presented quantitative data.

2. Remember that CI skills required in Mexico tend to emphasize the historical and social perspectives. This is an important consideration when recruiting for any CI position for the Mexican context.

3. Develop relationships with key industry contacts in Mexico to build trust so that information may be gathered over the long term.

4. Establish ethical guidelines with CI practitioners in Mexico to minimize risk of future CI problems (Klein, 1998). There may be a

Table 16.3
Comparison of CI Practices in the United States and Mexico

CI Process	American Practices	Mexican Practices
Planning and direction	Treat time as a precious commodity; demand punctuality and time-saving practices; more formal	Typically a relaxed approach to doing business; less formal
Gathering data (sources of data, type, availability, usefulness)	Widely available; often free; in general data are reliable and valid; typically use the Internet for primary and secondary research; examples of valuable data are company financial statements, industry speeches, trade association benchmarks	Scarce; full of errors; not timely; personal contact is the primary source of data
Organizing facts	Tend to rely on technology to sort data for analysis	Tend not to rely on technology for organizing data
Analyzing information	Tend to rely on appraising the present and the near future as the basis for evaluating risk	Historical in thinking and tend to be more suspicious of "objective" data
Disseminating intelligence	Reports tend to be concise and action oriented; trust is developed based on work performance	Long explanations that go beyond simple facts to include high levels of context; trust is developed by getting to know others
Decision-making	Employees are expected to take charge of their field of responsibilities and make decisions accordingly; tend to be based on rational analysis of quantifiable data	Decisions tend to be made by "the boss"; tend to be based on intuition gathered from informal qualitative sources
Revisiting information and analysis	Accepted in most advanced CI activities, but not yet common	No specific evidence; however refinement may be inherent in the process of gathering information through personal contacts

Sources: Adler (1999b, 1999c, 2000a, 2000b); Fuld (1995); InfoAmericas (2001); Leidner, Carlsson, Elam, & Corrales (1999); Price (2000).

tendency for certain local CI practitioners (or more likely private investigators) to use practices that would not be considered ethical by U.S. standards.

5. Align CI practices with the external and internal CI environments. While there may be a limited number of tools that would provide appropriate outputs to resolve a particular issue in Mexico, the context in which the analysis is being performed will have a significant bearing on the effectiveness of the tools.

6. Rely on informal techniques for sharing information with key decision-makers in Mexico and remember that technology does not play a significant role in the process of organizing information

in Mexican firms. Moreover, informal sharing of information among top executives appears to be more prevalent than sharing with the entire organization, which is markedly different from the U.S. philosophy.

AREAS FOR FUTURE RESEARCH

Clearly there are significant gaps in the published research related to CI practices in Mexico. In particular, it would be important to investigate the following areas in more detail so that a close link could be made between the business environment and the CI practices that are deployed and operate most effectively.

First, a specific analysis of the typical internal CI environment in large, medium, and small firms in Mexico would allow for a more valuable comparison between practices at various companies. Second, further examination of specific CI practices for each step of the CI process would provide the basis for a more conclusive comparison between practices in Mexico and other countries. This would be particularly useful if the research covered not only current practices but also the historical trends that led to today's situation. Third, a segmentation of the analysis into regional differences, as well as variations by industry, would provide important insight into the different CI practices within Mexico. Fourth, and perhaps most important, the development of a comprehensive framework for comparing and contrasting CI practices in various contexts would be a very useful research subject.

CONCLUSION

A comparative analysis of CI practices in the United States and Mexico has demonstrated that the external and internal CI environments are a significant factor in determining the CI practices and general level of acceptance of CI in each country. The U.S. environment is, in general, supportive of CI practices. The Mexican environment, in contrast, is not generally supportive of CI but does offer some evidence that it may be supportive in the future.

Based on the analysis of CI practices in both countries, this chapter offered six implications for business managers regarding the practice of CI in Mexico. In addition, several key research issues regarding CI practice in Mexico were identified. Further progress in addressing these research issues would be a productive first step toward building more support for the future practice of CI in Mexico.

NOTES

1. Interview with Al Boluarte, Regional Sales Manager, George Kelk Corporation, on November 19, 2001. He has worked in Mexico since 1981, most recently as a sales representative to the Latin American region from Canada.

2. Ibid.

3. Ibid.

4. Ibid.

5. Ibid.

REFERENCES

Adler, I. (1999a). "In the Dark." *Business Mexico* 9(2): 18.

Adler, I. (1999b). "Pulling Together." *Business Mexico* 9(4): 18.

Adler, I. (1999c). "Risky Business." *Business Mexico* 9(10): 22.

Adler, I. (2000a). "Standard Procedure." *Business Mexico* 10(6): 26.

Adler, I. (2000b). "Between the Lines." *Business Mexico* 10(10): 24.

Adler, I. (2002). "Walking the Walk." *Business Mexico* 12(2): 17.

Baranauskas, T. (1998). "Insights into Brazilian Competitive Intelligence Practices." *Competitive Intelligence Magazine* 1(1): 41–43.

Blenkhorn, D.L. (2001). Presentation to a Wilfrid Laurier University MBA class on September 22, 2001, in Toronto, Ontario, Canada.

Clarke, D.E. (2001). "Competitive Intelligence in Service Industries," pp. 222–237 in C.S. Fleisher and D.L. Blenkhorn [eds.], *Managing Frontiers in Competitive Intelligence.* Westport, CT: Quorum Books.

Fleisher, C.S. (2001). "An Introduction to the Management and Practice of Competitive Intelligence," pp. 3–18 in C.S. Fleisher and D.L. Blenkhorn [eds.], *Managing Frontiers in Competitive Intelligence.* Westport, CT: Quorum Books.

Fuld, L.M. (1995). *The New Competitor Intelligence: The Complete Resource for Finding, Analyzing, and Using Information about Your Competitors.* New York: John Wiley and Sons.

Government of Province of Alberta, Canada. (2003). *Mexico Market Profile.* Alberta Economic Development. http://www.alberta-canada.com/markets/mexico.cfm.

Herring, J.P. (1998). "What Is Intelligence Analysis?" *Competitive Intelligence Magazine* 1(2): 13–16.

InfoAmericas. (2001). *Research Challenges in Latin America.* Coral Gables, FL: InfoAmericas.

Klein, C. (1998). "Cultural Differences in CI Techniques." *Competitive Intelligence Magazine* 1(2): 21–23.

Leidner, D.E., S. Carlsson, J. Elam, and M. Corrales. (1999). "Mexican and Swedish Managers' Perceptions of the Impact of EIS on Organizational Intelligence, Decision Making, and Structure." *Decision Sciences* 30(3): 633–658.

Lewandowski, R. (1999). "Secret Service." *CA Magazine* 132(8): 16–22.

Miller, S.H. (2001). *Competitive Intelligence: An Overview.* http://www.scip.org/Library/overview.pdf.

Parker, G. (2001). "Establishing Remuneration Practices across Culturally Diverse Environments." *Compensation & Benefits Management* 17(2): 23–27.

Prescott, J.E., J.P. Herring, and P. Panfely. (1998). "Leveraging Information for Action: A Look into the Competitive and Business Intelligence Consortium Benchmarking Study." *Competitive Intelligence Review* 9(1): 4–12.

Price, J. (2000). "Competitive Intelligence in Latin America: New Science Meets Old Practice." *Competitive Intelligence Magazine* 3(4): 16–18.

Robertson, M.F. (1998). "Seven Steps to Global CI." *Competitive Intelligence Magazine* 1(2): 29–33.

Werther, G.F.A. (1998). "Doing Business in the New World Disorder: The Problem with 'Precision.'" *Competitive Intelligence Magazine* 1(2): 24–26.

17

Competitive Intelligence in Brazil

Jeff Libis

Brazil is the ninth largest economy in the world and has a population exceeding 170 million citizens. This represents approximately half of South America's population (Central Intelligence Agency, 2001). Furthermore, Brazil boasts the largest land mass in South America and has the most primary urban centers; it also offers a diverse economic base composed of an equal mix of domestic and international industrial activity. These statistics are offered to provide a snapshot of Brazil and its relative importance to the global economy. In recent years, Brazil has become a preferred source for foreign investment. International firms looking to expand are increasingly turning to Brazil as their gateway into South America. The attractiveness of Brazil's domestic infrastructure, stabilizing economy, and emerging social frameworks sets the stage for increased competitiveness at all levels of business. Therefore, international companies looking to enter this region should undertake a detailed evaluation of Brazil's environment in order to better understand its underlying complexities and opportunities.

Such a detailed evaluation, however, is an analytical challenge. Consider the following advice from a local expert to companies looking to conduct business in Brazil: "Forget any stereotypes about particular countries—businesspeople need to engage in appropriate due diligence regarding legal, social, economic, and regulatory attitudes, especially in Brazil" (undisclosed source, 2002). According to Sheinin (1999), "Competitive intelligence on a global level is influenced by certain types of information relevant to all countries, but at different levels of intensity and perception." Therefore, a good understanding of sociological, educational, economic, political, and geographic criteria is critical to the evaluation of an international business environment. This chapter will apply Sheinin's (1999) global evaluation strategy to Brazil in order to develop a better understanding of its business environment while offering a framework within which considerations for competitive intelligence (CI) can be evaluated. The overall framework of this approach is displayed in Table 17.1 and is followed by an in-depth discussion of each analytical component of this global evaluation framework as applied to Brazil.

SOCIOLOGICAL STANDARDS

Sociological values in Brazil, as they relate to business, are representative of the historical background of the region. Until 1995, high-ranking politicians and military figures ruled Brazil and governed jointly through tight

Table 17.1
Global Evaluation Framework

Criteria	Key Considerations in Brazil
Sociological	• Class segregation and lack of middle-class demographic cause social problems • Suppressive social environment in the past has created an unstable social environment today • Until 1995, most citizens of Brazil worked in the public sector, e.g., government
Educational	• Eight years of mandatory education not yet enforced by government • Both private and public educational offerings • High differential in quality of education based on social and geographic location
Economic	• A volatile currency and economic recession has reduced foreign investment • The demise of Brazil's largest domestic trading partner, Argentina, has caused global concerns • Mexico's growth has put pressure on Brazil's performance expectations
Political	• Since 1995, President Cardoso has focused on the stabilization of the economy and the opening of markets in order to participate in the global marketplace • President Luiz Inácio da Silva (Lula), elected in 2002, has yet to prove his abilities but is predicted to use tight controls on spending and interest rates, which could slow economic development • Current social perception is that government still does not do enough for the people, yet is accomplishing productive economic goals
Geographic	• Largest country and domestic market in South America • Largest population and most primary urban centers in Latin America • Good location for distribution in South America • Limited infrastructure for transportation and resources

Source: Adapted from Sheinin (1999).

military rule. Citizens of the region became familiar with corrupt government activities and weak presidencies that, in turn, created a negative image for business among most Brazilian citizens (Department of Foreign Affairs and International Trade, 2001). These attributes have ingrained certain social characteristics that make common business activities and intelligence-gathering a difficult task.

Brazil has a divergent class structure. According to the U.S. Central Intelligence Agency (CIA) World Fact Book (2001), 50 million Brazilians are categorized as upper class while over 120 million are categorized as lower class. Most Brazilians in the lower-income segment have been suppressed for many years and have become resistant to authoritarian control. In addition, the population has been disheartened by prolonged and often unsuccessful progress in economic development. Barriers associated with this growth have created a negative viewpoint of "monetary-driven" inspirations. This presents a substantial challenge because a grass-roots work ethic does not exist in Brazil the way it does in North America. Even today, "the median income of the wealthiest 10% of the population is almost 30 times greater than that of the poorest 40%; and their disposable income is 80–100 times greater" (Price, 1999). As outlined previously, a skewed income distribution creates serious social pressure and mistrust throughout Brazil. The result of this environment is that "culture is not conducive to the creation or flow of information" (Price, 1999). It has created "a culture where information is closely guarded within both consumer and business circles" (Price, 1999), further creating barriers for researchers and companies looking to enter the Brazilian marketplace. According to a Brazilian CI expert, this attitude is changing as the Brazilian economy overcomes the ramifications of tight economic and social controls sanctioned in 1995 (undisclosed source, 2002). Furthermore, as citizens realize that business opportunities are viable in their current environment, Brazil seems to be adopting an entrepreneurial culture.

Brazilians are beginning to recognize that business opportunities and monetary success are accessible to the masses. As the Brazilian expert confirms, "Brazilians are starting to understand that considerable patience and resource investment is required to deliver on the goal of economic freedom and opportunity" (undisclosed source, 2002). The risk-equals-reward mentality is evolving, and materialistic goals are promoting further participation in both corporate and personal business. In 1995, Brazilians were forced to make serious concessions in order to reduce inflation and maintain the integrity of the country's future economy and position in the global marketplace. Furthermore, the financial collapse of Russia and several Asian countries, along with Argentina's debt problems, has slowed Brazilian progress considerably. Although faced with considerable obstacles, Brazil has continued to maintain a stable political and economic environment, setting the stage for an entrepreneurial revolution.

QUALITY AND ACCESSIBILITY OF EDUCATION

Approximately 85% of Brazil's population over the age of 15 is literate and has access to public and private educational institutions from first grade to graduate-level university education. (Central Intelligence Agency, 2001). This is due to eight years of mandatory education from grades 1 to 8. Participation is not required after the eighth grade, yet private and public educational outlets exist from high school (Grades 9–13), to university and college (one- to four-year programs), to postgraduate offerings. The Federal Council of Education in Brazil provides free education through public facilities in each state. According to the Brazilian expert, discrepancy does exist between the quality of education offered in private versus public institutions; this is closely tied to geographic location (undisclosed source, 2002). This is most likely due to the size of Brazil and the inherent obstacles associated with this attribute.

Problems with Brazil's education system stem from the government's focus on outward economic expansion rather than the development of fortified internal policies. According to a Brazilian expert, lack of attention in this area has resulted in limited enrollment and limited enforcement of educational participation from the lower class in Brazil (undisclosed source, 2002). Another issue stems from differences in educator compensation from private to public institutions. On average, salaries are below $1,000 per month for educators in public schools, whereas they are more than $1,500 in private institutions (BRAZILbrazil, 2001). This skews accessibility to quality education because above-average educators are motivated to transfer to private schools in large urban centers where wages and overall quality of life are better. In turn, quality education becomes inaccessible to a large portion of Brazil's population, which tends to be below the poverty line.

ECONOMIC CONDITIONS

Economic policies in Brazil have changed dramatically over the last eight years. Rapidly increasing inflation rates during the 1990s forced Brazil to implement reform policies designed to curb economic collapse. The first stage of this reform was "The Real Plan," a strategy that pegged Brazilian currency to the U.S. dollar. This action was undertaken as a preventative measure to control inflation and maintain currency value while setting a political-economic framework in motion that would accelerate

Brazil's growth into the future. Although there have been considerable setbacks along the way, Brazil has essentially delivered on these objectives (Price, 1999). An economic downturn in 1998 resulted in a 30% currency devaluation, which forced Brazil to "un-peg" its currency against the U.S. dollar. In spite of this setback, Brazil has remained relatively stable with regard to the global economy. Furthermore, the Brazilian economic environment has been somewhat reinforced by "a weaker currency [that] has provided an advantage in pricing exports," accented by "a relatively robust consumer spending rate and high demand for consumer and capital goods" (Tendencias, 2001a). This trend has bolstered confidence in foreign investors and enhanced the viability of a long-term economic strategy in Brazil. These reforms have been stimulating business activity to new levels while breaking down traditional social attitudes, thereby creating a greater acceptance of business and, in turn, a competitive business environment.

The second stage of this reform was the privatization of government-ruled industry. Through privatization, the government has reduced operational costs while creating a competitive and open environment for both consumers and business. Privatization has so far positively affected the telecommunications industry, and this policy is "slated for other sectors such as electricity and perhaps oil and gas" (Price, 1999). As competition increases in Brazil, prices will be forced down and overall quality will increase. The goal is to limit the gap between classes and stimulate the growth of a middle class, which should have a positive impact on business in Brazil.

Brazil is an attractive candidate for international companies looking to enter Latin America. Foreign policy in Brazil has "departed from traditional tendencies towards economic isolationism, strong adherence to national sovereignty, and projection of power through political-military means" (Price, 1999). With the largest domestic industry base in South America and a centralized location, Brazil can count on continued consideration from domestic and international investors. Furthermore, Brazil has established strong trade relations with other South American countries through the El Mercado Común del Sur (Mercosur) agreement (U.S. Commercial Service, 2001) and is seeking to solidify relations with the European Union. These agreements will fortify Brazil as a strong economic player in South America. As a local report suggests, the Mercosur trade agreement is "not only a mechanism for economic integration of the Southern Cone of South America, but an embryo of a quasi-political entity, eventually encompassing the whole of South America" (Department of Foreign Affairs and International Trade, 2001). The current environment in Brazil, which includes a trend toward increased privatization of public ventures, creates a highly competitive business setting. This will undoubtedly increase the need for competitive intelligence and market evaluation—functions that have historically never been a concern for local business leaders.

POLITICAL ENVIRONMENT

Brazil has a long history of political corruption, which changed in 1995 when the people elected President Cardoso. Cardoso single-handedly changed the political norm by implementing major economic and political reforms aimed at expanding the private business sector, increasing participation in business, stabilizing currency trends, increasing foreign trade, and empowering the average citizen through increased health care and education. Although President Cardoso was replaced in 2003, his political and economic policies continue to lay the foundation for the current environment in Brazil through strong public support.

President da Silva, who has been nicknamed Lula by the local Brazilian population, was elected in October 2002 and, in turn, brought along new political ideals and objectives designed to maintain and protect the state of the Brazilian economy. More specifically, Lula "aims to strike an unprecedented 'social pact' with all levels of society, which will enable Brazilians as a whole to take a leap into rich-world standards of prosperity, justice and equality, striving together to create 'the nation we have always dreamed of' " (*The Economist*, 2003). President da Silva's approach presents a significant shift in the political policies in Brazil. Because they could lead to slower economic development, his traditional leftist views have caused concern throughout the domestic marketplace and the international community (Ferreira, 2003). Recent indicators are showing a slowdown in economic growth, and some critics blame the recent economic reforms instated by the new government as the cause (Economic Intelligence Unit, 2002).

President da Silva initiated his regime with tight economic control over interest rates and spending. This approach is risky because it could slow economic growth and limit opportunities for business in domestic and international markets. Brazil has enjoyed abundant growth trends under the influence of ex-President Cardoso's economic expansion strategy and will continue to expect similar performance from its leaders. Experts agree that President da Silva will have to use his considerable political skills to convince his supporters to be patient while awaiting more substantial economic recovery (Economic Intelligence Unit, 2003).

Although it is premature to comment on the long-term impact of recent political and economic reforms, short-term indicators suggest that President da Silva has inherited a waning economy lacking international investment support (Ferreira, 2003). The Central Bank of Brazil reports that foreign investment has declined from US$30.5 billion in 2000 to US$24.7 billion in 2001. For the first time in seven years, these levels are forecasted to drop below US$20 billion in 2002 and 2003 (Central Bank of Brazil, 2002). This decline in foreign direct investment has created a highly competitive environment for companies vying for international investment and a tricky political arena for the newly elected government.

GEOGRAPHY & RESOURCES

Brazil offers limited infrastructure for business. Standards do not match North American expectations by any means. Only 10% of the roads are paved, and there is limited roadway access to neighboring countries (Tendencias, 2001b). Most exports to Argentina, Brazil's largest domestic trade partner, are shipped by sea. Railroad access is limited to Mercosur partners. Furthermore, Brazil has limited energy resources. This past year, a drought that reduced hydroelectric capabilities across the nation forced the country to implement an energy-rationing regime. This situation slowed business and reduced overall GDP in 2002 (Department of Foreign Affairs and International Trade, 2001). Analysts predict business in Brazil will accelerate as it plays a game of catch-up (Tendencias, 2001b). This should create a highly competitive environment as local businesses attempt to compensate for losses incurred earlier in the year.

Brazil is focused on the development of an internal infrastructure that will promote business expansion and bolster its economy. Continued development in this area is being used to position Brazil as an economic hub for South America. Furthermore, the quality of Brazil's infrastructure is important to trade partners such as the European Union, which sees Brazil as the gateway to South America.

SUMMARY OF GLOBAL EVALUATION OF BRAZIL

Although the economic and political environment does not presently seem favorable for business, there is hope for the future (Department of Foreign Affairs and International Trade, 2001). The issues and challenges that business must face in Brazil are similar to those in any developing country. The difference lies in Brazil's future potential. Although progress has been slow, Brazil seems to be making appropriate advancements toward economic and political success. This will continue to create a positive business environment that stimulates business growth and opportunity. In turn, competitive intelligence will increasingly find a role in this area of the world.

COMPETITIVE INTELLIGENCE IN BRAZIL

Competitive intelligence does exist in Brazil. Although immature and underdeveloped, it plays a key role in Brazilian business activities. A rapidly evolving business and political arena is forcing companies and organizations to monitor both domestic and international competition as never before. Brazil's challenging environment makes it difficult for decision-makers to identify new trends and keep track of the competition. According to Price (2000), "Latin business leaders used to base investment decisions on instinct, insider knowledge, and connections. Today's environment now requires research, intelligence, and strategy." Although competitive intelligence is an acknowledged discipline, there are several differences between Brazilian and North American practices. CI in Brazil and CI in North America are compared in Table 17.2. An analysis of this comparison follows.

Structured CI departments in Brazil are limited to large domestic firms such as telecommunications and international companies with head offices outside Latin America. This notion is supported by Cella and Pacheco (2001), who suggest that "when evaluating competitive intelligence around the world, one can mainly verify most competitive intelligence initiatives in larger companies, namely transnational corporations, motivated by international competition." This is a limiting factor for the growth and support of CI in the region. As Brazil's economy grows and the number of businesses increases, CI will increasingly become a commodity. Price (2000) of InfoAmericas reinforces this notion, stating that "long-term survival" in Latin America and Brazil will require CI.

LOCATION OF COMPETITIVE INTELLIGENCE

In Brazilian firms, the CI people are primarily located in the marketing department and are usually tactically oriented. In comparison, most North American companies extract CI from both a tactical focus and a strategic focus. A local expert on Brazilian CI comments that "most CI activities are tactical and focus on the creation of front-line, actionable intelligence and remain far away from senior employees" (undisclosed source, 2002). This is supported by Codogno's (2001) suggestion that "all too often CI departments are placed in a position where they can never reach their full potential." This seems to be the case in Brazil, for the CI function in Brazilian companies is outwardly focused and remains detached from the decision-maker. Furthermore, Codogno (1999) outlines a difference between the marketing and CI functions in North America and suggests that intelligence activities should be located in a more strategic position within the

Table 17.2
Competitive Intelligence: Brazil vs. North America

	Brazil	**North America**
Acceptance of CI	<ul><li>Limited, not widely accepted in business</li><li>Primarily used in international companies</li></ul>	<ul><li>Good. Most business understands that good CI is required, especially on the international stage</li></ul>
Location of CI	<ul><li>Primarily tactical (marketing) as decision-makers are not accepting</li><li>Strategic location in large companies only</li></ul>	<ul><li>A good mixture of tactical and strategic placement</li></ul>
Quality of Secondary Research	<ul><li>Limited. Lack of Internet content and online users</li><li>Government participation does not support secondary sources</li></ul>	<ul><li>Good. North America has the highest number of online users and content</li><li>High government participation and enforcement</li></ul>
Quality of Primary Research	<ul><li>Good, yet credibility and reliability are questionable</li><li>Often requires third-party introduction</li></ul>	<ul><li>Good. Most North Americans believe in the sharing of ideas as a way to promote economic growth</li></ul>
Capacity for Analysis	<ul><li>Limited due to lack of acceptance</li><li>Companies use easily digested models like SWOT, ratio analysis, etc., to win support</li></ul>	<ul><li>Good. Many analytical frameworks are used to present intelligence due to high acceptance from business and decision-makers</li></ul>
CI Education	<ul><li>Limited. Only two academic institutions in Brazil offer CI education</li></ul>	<ul><li>Good. North America has the largest number of CI academic offerings in the world</li></ul>
Ethics and Law	<ul><li>Limited. Ethical frameworks are not followed due to lack of support from government and lack of participation in industry associations</li></ul>	<ul><li>Good. Highly structured laws and industry association participation ensures adequate ethical practice</li></ul>

organization in order to maximize overall impact, effectiveness, and "buy-in" from decision-makers (Codogno, 1999).

According to a local expert, the CI function in Brazil struggles to create its own identity within the organization and does not directly reach the decision-maker (undisclosed source, 2002). Some larger private companies have developed tactical marketing departments to compliment their marketing functions; however, these CI units remain abstract by North America's definition. The only industries that have developed key CI departments are "public-gone-private" industries like telecommunications. Once controlled by government, these newly privatized sectors are now exposed to domestic and international competitors. This has forced a rapid implementation of CI departments with a direct line to the decision-maker, presenting unique challenges to most CI practitioners in Brazil. A healthy Brazilian infrastructure within which to network and stimulate growth for the discipline does not exist.

QUALITY OF SECONDARY RESOURCES

Compared to North America, Brazil offers limited secondary resources. Effective secondary research analysis attempts to answer questions about market trends and competitor motives. In North America, this information is derived from government sources, the public press, industry trade associations, and off-the-shelf studies. In Brazil, these sources are usually unreliable. A regional study of research practices in the area found that "in Latin America, rarely do sources provide reliable, substantive, or timely information" and relevant data "may not reach consumers for 12–36 months after being researched" (Price, 1999).

Secondary research deficiencies in Brazil can be attributed to an underdeveloped Internet infrastructure. North America enjoys a plethora of English-based Internet resources, with a tremendous variety of information sources and communication channels from which to collect data, generate insight, and develop actionable intelligence. In North America, Internet resources are driven by market demand from the fastest-growing population of online users in both business and consumer segments. Comparatively, Brazil offers limited Internet resources. Most of Brazil's 170 million citizens are too poor to buy a computer, and with only 9.3% of households earning over $12,000, there is limited motivation to promote the development of Internet resources (Tendencias, 2000). Along with this trend, an overall lack of online content exists in Brazil. This is partly due to slow growth in Brazil's online population. As a result of poor communication quality and a lack of online content published in Portuguese (Tendencias, 2000), most of the population refuses to go online.

The creation, dissemination, and maintenance of business information by government have been given limited attention in Brazil. Contrary to North American standards, public business reporting practices in Brazil are often questionable. According to Price (2000) of InfoAmericas, "Beyond corporate financials, even basic corporate profile data is hard to come by in Latin America." Furthermore, a continued focus on international economic stimulation policies rather than domestic issues has created business law loopholes that are commonly exploited in order to reduce taxes, increase profitability, and maintain competitiveness (Price, 1999). A heavily regulated, oppressive environment prior to 1995 created a setting where "business does not trust government" and "many companies undertake convoluted measures to avoid onerous tax levels" (Price, 1999). This environment continues to taint the quality and availability of secondary research on private and public companies and presents formidable challenges when conducting CI in Brazil.

QUALITY OF PRIMARY RESOURCES

Access to primary research in Brazil is abundant, yet the credibility of these resources is questionable. Due to the overall lack of secondary sources, primary research tends to be the main channel through which CI data are gathered, although primary sources are often not reliable or credible. As outlined previously, economic segregation in Brazilian society creates a negative environment that translates into a lack of interest in sharing information with strangers. A Brazilian source commented, "Information in Brazil is power and leads to promotion in most business circles." Information is therefore protected and hoarded in most business and social settings. In order to acquire information, a local expert suggested the use of a third-party referral, yet this does not guarantee access to the intended information (undisclosed source, 2002).

The oppressive environment in Brazil prior to 1995 has created large barriers to information-sharing among businesses and individuals. Most Brazilians are hard-pressed to share or divulge knowledge. This creates a challenging environment for the CI practitioner trying to access primary sources. A report published by InfoAmericas (Price, 1999) states that as "mistrust is well-founded given that competitors, rivals, and even tax authorities commonly practice unethical research," perception is a reality in Latin America. Logic suggests that when the environment cannot be trusted, information flow will become constricted, as is the case in Brazil.

Latin American culture is not conducive to the creation and flow of information. This perception is common among business professionals in Brazil. A local expert notes that "competitive intelligence practitioners are usually the persons with the largest amount of contacts since information is hard to come across" (undisclosed source, 2002). Most employees see this information as a commodity to be used as a vehicle toward personal promotion. It is common knowledge in Brazilian business that a third-party referral is required before any information-sharing will take place between parties (Price, 1999).

The quality of Brazilian primary research sources is well below the quality of North American sources. Significant barriers exist in Brazil, and the general business environment does not view information-sharing as a vehicle to success, which is contrary to the common North American viewpoint. A comment from Jan Smith Ramos of InfoAmericas confirms this notion. "Information is closely held amongst top-level executives. The American empowerment and knowledge-sharing practices do not exist in

Latin America, where revealing information at best dilutes your power and at worst can get you fired" (as quoted in Price, 2000).

CAPACITY FOR ANALYSIS

Current analytical frameworks for CI in Brazil are below North American standards. With limited primary and secondary resources, an underserved professional community, and no support from decision-makers, there is little need for complex systems in CI reporting. Present CI practitioners in Brazil are more concerned about generating support from decision-makers and acceptance from the business community. Therefore, according to local experts, practitioners in this field stick to basic frameworks, including strengths, weaknesses, opportunities, threats (SWOT), financial ratio, and historical analysis tools (undisclosed source, 2002).

Competitive intelligence professionals and businesspeople alike understand the value of information. Beyond this limited need for complex analysis, there is a strong respect for the creation and proliferation of information. According to a local expert, "Many years under a suppressive environment in Brazil has created high respect and acknowledgement for the current open marketplace, including access to new information sources" (undisclosed source, 2002). Although there is newfound respect for these sources, most practitioners in Brazil still utilize basic tools and analytical frameworks that effectively communicate intelligence analysis to decision-makers who do not have a lot of experience with CI. These processes will become more complex as acceptance of CI increases in the coming years.

EDUCATION AND PROFESSIONAL DEVELOPMENT

Education and training is an important building block in the development of CI as a functional discipline. As outlined in a recent Society of Competitive Intelligence Professionals (SCIP) report on education, "Academic theory drives consulting and industry practice," especially in competitive intelligence (Miller, 1999). North America has many schools that offer CI training at some level with several dedicated programs offered offline, online, and in seminar formats. These programs target a wide audience, from undergraduates to professionals.

Compared to North America, Brazil offers limited educational resources in CI. The first CI program in Brazil was launched in 1977. Today only two academic institutions offer a dedicated program in CI training and education. Both of these programs are run in partnership with Centre de Recherche Retrospective de Marseille (CRRM) in Marseilles, France, and are based on theoretical frameworks. According to a local expert, these theory-based programs are not useful in Brazil's rapidly expanding business markets because they create limitations to the "functional" practice of competitive intelligence (undisclosed source, 2002).

Networking takes on an important role in the development of competitive intelligence, especially in the absence of adequate academic and training resources. There are two professional agencies in Brazil: SCIP and the more recent Brazilian Association of Competitive Intelligence (ABRAIC). SCIP operates professional development seminars and conferences and actively promotes CI awareness programs. ABRAIC manages a library of CI resources for professional benchmarking and a local networking community. As a local expert comments, "Trade and academic organizations in Brazil have a long way to go in competitive intelligence. More participation and acknowledgement in this area is required to stimulate growth and support" (undisclosed source, 2002).

ETHICAL CONSIDERATIONS

CI is often regarded more as spying than as legitimate research in Brazil (Baranauskas, 1998). CI in Brazil finds its roots in the military. Military intelligence experts joined the ranks of CI practitioners in the private sector when industry began privatization in 1995. Their questionable and suspicious history prior to the development of an open and democratic market created mistrust and suspicion from the beginning. In addition, a lack of government support for formal ethical frameworks in business did not receive much attention. A local expert offering insight into the ethical environment in Brazil has this to say: "The Society of Competitive Intelligence Professionals has worked hard to promote ethical boundaries in Brazil. Yet many individuals who have responsibilities in this area [CI] do not follow a set standard" (undisclosed source, 2002). Brazilian practitioners operate under their own set of standards, which are governed by the morals and ideals of the individual CI practitioner. This creates a haphazard ethical environment that can generate a negative image for CI throughout the country.

Ethical considerations in CI are not governed the same in Brazil as in North America. Price notes, "A legal system [in Brazil] that is overburdened is often unable to be an effective enforcer of business law." Business law offers adequate deterrence through fines and other justice-based measures, which protect companies in North America. An example of this protection is the U.S. Economic Espionage Act, which has been designed and successfully utilized to protect trade secrets (U.S. Commercial Service, 2001). Due to the Brazilian government's focus on larger issues (such as economic recession and the potential bankruptcy of its largest domestic trading partner), these types of protective policies are not enforced. "The 'watch your back' mentality amongst business owners and managers is in many places exacerbated by a low-credibility legal system" (Price, 2000).

Overall, the ethical nature of North American CI is not reflected in the Brazilian business environment. The practitioners in this area must rely on their own standards to reflect the professional nature of the discipline. For ethical ideals to prevail, the Brazilian government will need to create a credible reputation that extends to the local business environment.

CONCLUSION

As this chapter outlines, the environment plays a large role in the acceptance and evolution of CI. Through an evaluation of Brazil's setting, it is easy to identify with the inherent obstacles and challenges that exist for the CI practitioner. These obstacles must be overcome if practitioners are to conduct effective CI. These challenges, if addressed properly, will lead to future business success in Brazil. As the environment continues to grow and stabilize, a significant need for CI will form.

There is a significant gap in CI practices between North America and Brazil; and the existing environment in Brazil, from economic uncertainties to sociological hardships, stems from historical influences that North America has long since addressed. It will be difficult to bridge these gaps; given that North America has, in the most part, found solutions to these issues some time ago. This does not reduce the importance of CI, however; it only modifies some of its characteristics as outlined in this chapter.

Although CI will follow a different evolutionary path in Brazil, its future will be fruitful. Increased foreign participation and escalating business activity will continue to generate a need for this service. Along with this demand will come a more diverse and accepting attitude for CI. In the very near future, CI will provide a foundation on which Brazilian business can decide its future.

REFERENCES

Baranauskas, T. (1998). "Insights into Brazilian Competitive Intelligence Practices." *Competitive Intelligence Magazine* 1(1): 41–43.

BRAZILbrazil. (2002). http://www.brazilbrazil.com.

Cella, C.R., and H. Pacheco. (2001). *The Silent Rose of Competitive Intelligence* Brazilian Association of Competitive Intelligence. http://www.abraic.org.br/noticias_eib.asp?txtcodautor=16.

Central Bank of Brazil. (2002). http://www.bcb.gov.br/mPag.asp?perfil=1&cod=217&codP=156&idioma=I.

Central Intelligence Agency. (2001). *The World Fact Book: Brazil Report.* http://www.odci.gov/cia/publications/factbook/geos/br.html.

Codogno, E. (2001). "Location! Location! Location! Positioning CI in Your Organization." *Competitive Intelligence Magazine* 4(5): 23–26.

Department of Foreign Affairs and International Trade. Canadian Federal Government. (2001). *Brazil Country Report: Profile* http://www.dfait-maeci.gc.ca/latinamerica/brazilprofile-e.asp.

Economic Intelligence Unit. (2003). "Mixed Signals on Growth," June 4. http://www.viewswire.com/index.asp?layout=display_article&doc_id=270681.

Economist, The. (2003). "Make or Break." *The Economist* February 20, 2003. http://207.68.164.250/cgi-bin/linkrd?_lang=EN&lah=fda4c286dcc0fa78c03 eaa3ccceb31cd&lat=1056683155&hm_action=displaystory%2ecfm%3fstory_id %3d1588135.

Ferreira, A. (2003). "Macro Measures on Right Track, but Economy Remains Sluggish." *InfoBrazil.* May 31–June 6. http://www.infobrazil.com/Conteudo/Front_Page/Analysis/Conteudo.asp?ID_Noticias=773&ID_Area=2&ID_G rupo=8.

Miller, S. (1999). *CI Academic Conference Focuses on Skill Sets: What CI Managers Look for in New Recruits.* Alexandria, VA: Society of Competitive Intelligence Professionals. http://www.scip.org/news/cimagazine_article.asp?id=46.

Price, J. (1999). "Mining for Opportunities in Latin America: After the Goldrush." *InfoAmericas.* http://tendencias.infoamericas.com/article_archive/1999/1299/Tendencias_9912.pdf.

Price, J. (2000). "Competitive Intelligence in Latin America: New Science Meets Old Practice." *Competitive Intelligence Magazine* 3(4): 16–18.

Sheinin, C.E. (1999). "Global CI: Assessing Global Competition." *Competitive Intelligence Magazine.* http://www.scip.org/news/cireview_article.asp?id=244.

Tendencias. (2000). *Industry Analysis: The Internet in Brazil. InfoAmericas Market Report.* http://tendencias.infoamericas.com/article_archive/2000/0100/0100_industry_analysis.html.

Tendencias. (2001a). *Clash of the Titans: Brazil vs. Mexico. InfoAmericas Market Report.* http://tendencias.infoamericas.com/article_archive/2001/1101/1101_regional_trends.html.

Tendencias. (2001b). *Economic Outlook for Brazil. InfoAmericas Market Report.* http://tendencias.infoamericas.com/article_archive/2001/0601/0601_economic_outlook.html.

U.S. Commercial Service. (2001). *Country Commercial Guide: Brazil.* http://www.usatrade.gov/website/ccg.nsf/ccgurl/ccg-brazil.2002-ch-1:-0069d575.

18

The Role of Competitive Intelligence in the Global Automotive Supply Chain

Keith Fishwick

In most industries, technology is intensifying competition on a global scale. Strategic management of technology will require competitive intelligence (CI) professionals to conduct industry analysis with an international scope. In this role, CI professionals will be called upon to determine how technological progress will impact the five competitive forces defining industry profitability: internal rivalry, threat of new entrants, threat of substitutes, bargaining power of suppliers, and bargaining power of buyers (Porter, 1980). Such analysis will allow CI professionals to develop rich insights into the future profitability and competitive strength of their firms, assess current and potential rivals from all continents, and strategically navigate the structure of evolving global industries. This chapter will provide an example of a global industry analysis that illuminates the probable impact of new technologies on one of the world's largest industries—automotive manufacturing.

The technology component in today's vehicles is growing nine times faster than the growth of the automotive industry itself (Shah, 2000), and new technologies will generate 80% of the growth in the automotive industry from 2000 to 2007 (Intex Management Services, 2002). Global technology consortiums, computer industry powerhouses, forward-looking entrepreneurs, and automotive suppliers are bringing innovations to the automotive industry. As new technologies are accepted by the general marketplace, the automotive manufacturers must provide complementary technology in order to remain competitive. Electronics represent 22% of the value of today's average vehicle, but by 2010 this is expected to reach 40% (ABOUT Publishing Group, 2002).

This chapter addresses the impact of future technology on the automotive industry, evaluates current manufacturing strategies, and reviews how these differ on a global perspective. The technology content in today's vehicles is increasing, which begs these questions: Who will hold the power in the automotive supply chain in the future, the automotive manufacturers or the technology suppliers? Will consumers be more concerned about automotive brands, or will they look to see whether the vehicle has "Intel Inside"? Will automotive manufacturers recognize this shift in market power, or will they continue to outsource proprietary information to their suppliers? The future power-holders in the automotive supply chain may turn out to be technology-based suppliers, rather than the original equipment manufacturers. CI can assist key decision-makers as they formulate answers to these questions.

FUTURE TECHNOLOGY GROWTH IN THE AUTOMOTIVE INDUSTRY

By 2010 one-third of the vehicles on the road in the United States will have Auto PC (personal computer) technology and navigation (Eisenstein, 1999). The navigation trend is already starting to appear in high-end European and Japanese vehicles. At the beginning of 2002, the world market for navigation systems was 9 million, but with an annual growth rate greater than 30%, the penetration of these systems will occur rapidly (ABOUT Publishing Group, 2002). As technology evolves, suppliers for the automotive manufacturers will change to reflect these trends in the industry, thereby driving changes for both the suppliers and the automotive manufacturers.

The areas of strongest compound annual growth in automotive electronics systems from 2000 to 2007 are predicted to be adaptive airbags (80%), adaptive cruise control (73%), and smart card entry (64%). Several of today's prominent technologies, however, are expected to experience negative growth over this time period. These include anti-lock braking systems (ABSs), ABS with traction control, conventional airbags, and passive cruise control (Intex Management Services, 2002).

As the price for technology drops, consumer acceptance of the technology will increase (Eisenstein, 1999). In 1999 Eisenstein suggested a number of new technologies that would be included in future vehicles. These included integrated display units, sophisticated sunroof and window controls, multiple antennae, and more sensors to detect various functions on a vehicle. These technologies are now appearing not only on high-end, segment-leading products but also on many of the vehicles within reach of today's consumers.

The electronic value portion in vehicles today represents an average of 22% of the total vehicle price. By 2010, this value will jump to 40% (Heidingsfelder, 2000). Dr. Franz Josef Paefgen, CEO of Audi AG, has noted that "Ninety percent of all future innovations for new vehicles will mainly be determined in their functionality and value to the consumer in new electronics components and systems" (Heidingsfelder, 2000). This vision is very similar to the overall vision of the automotive industry. Globally, North American and European companies will lead the automotive industry in technology (Heidingsfelder, 2000).

The rate of growth in the automotive components market is nearly 9% per year, compared to the overall growth in the global automotive market of only 1% per year (Shah, 2000). Growth in the automotive electronics components market is expected to continue to increase, even if the automotive manufacturers have to scale back production by 2% to 3% (Cataldo, 2003). With declining growth in the automotive market, manufacturers will have to change their marketing approach to maintain the dominant position in the automotive supply chain and will need to "insource" certain assemblies back into their manufacturing plants. These steps will be required in order to offset the growing power of their suppliers as more and more of the components are obtained from the supply chain. In the future, automotive manufacturers will rely more on the technologies developed by others as consumers demand more electronic components in future vehicles.

Automotive manufacturers are going to have to adapt to these new technologies in order to maintain their competitive positions in the marketplace. Consumers are demanding higher technology content in their future vehicles; and from a consumer perspective, switching costs are low when purchasing a new vehicle. To maintain brand loyalty, automotive manufacturers will have to keep pace with the technology and market their brands strongly to maintain market position.

FUTURE TECHNOLOGIES IN THE AUTOMOTIVE INDUSTRY

One of the best examples of future automotive technology is the OnStar system from General Motors. Acura, Audi, Isuzu, Lexus, and Subaru have all recognized the value of the OnStar system and are including it in their new models, even though it is technology from a competitor (OnStar Corporation, 2003a). The OnStar system provides consumers with many features, including airbag deployment notification, emergency services, stolen vehicle tracking, remote door unlock, remote diagnostics, personal calling, personal concierge service, roadside assistance, accident assist, information and convenience, virtual advisor, OnStar med-net, route support, ride assistance, and online concierge (OnStar Corporation, 2003b).

As comprehensive as these services seem, future systems will be even more expansive.

The underlying technology that allows all the OnStar services to be seamlessly presented to the consumer is telematics. "Telematics is an emerging market of automotive communications technology that combines wireless voice and data to provide location-specific security, information, productivity, and in-vehicle entertainment services to drivers and their passengers." (Motorola Corporation, 2002). Chip manufacturers are not only advancing their technology but at the same time are also reducing costs, which is pushing consumer acceptance of telematics to new levels (Cataldo, 2003). The market for telematics is expected to increase toward US$20 billion over the next four years (Murray, 2002a). Consequently, telematics will be key to exploiting future technology in the automotive industry and will be the backbone of interconnectivity in future vehicles, not only as the interface for consumer-supplied components and in-vehicle "infotainment" but also as a means of integrating electronic communications internal to the vehicle.

Managing all the communications between internal and external components in a vehicle is critical to ensure reliability and proper functionality. Currently, there is an average of 8,150 feet of wire in a vehicle, a vast increase from only 460 feet in 1960 (Allied Business Intelligence, 2003). As automotive manufacturers add features and increase the number of sensors, the current method of point-to-point wiring will become extremely difficult to manage, design, and install. Managing this data and information in the future will require a common high-speed bus in order to enhance operations and provide for further expansion. A common standard will allow automotive manufacturers to take advantage of the faster electronic product development cycle and add new features simply by plugging in a new device (Allied Business Intelligence, 2003).

In 2002, Texas Instruments announced that it had developed the industry's first automotive 1394B bus solution to support in-vehicle infotainment applications and telematics (Texas Instruments Corporation, 2002a). The addition of Bluetooth chipsets allows wireless connectivity for the vehicle, thereby supporting wireless communication links for games, personal computers (PCs), personal digital assistants (PDAs), and vehicle diagnostic tools (Texas Instruments Corporation, 2002a). Cost, as well as the ability to properly function in the automotive environment, had limited earlier introduction of this previously existing computer technology (Texas Instruments Corporation, 2002b). The capability to handle the wide range of temperature extremes and vibration experienced in the automotive environment was the important breakthrough that allowed this technology to enter the automotive industry.

Telematics will initially become a differentiator of vehicles and will eventually become standard, much like airbags and ABS brakes. According to the Fiat Research Centre, "Telematics systems have enormous potential and will play a fundamental role in establishing the competitiveness of vehicles in the future" (ABOUT Publishing Group, 2002). Market studies forecast that by 2005, 90% of luxury vehicles will have telematics technology. What is more surprising, however, is that the overall market saturation forecast for telematics one year later will be 50% (Beecham, 2002). Telematics will be for all consumers, not just for the wealthy.

Telematics technology eliminates costs in automotive manufacturing and adds increased versatility and functionality to vehicles. Most of this technology is being developed in a non-automotive environment; this is forcing automotive manufacturers to design products collaboratively with suppliers and ultimately to purchase their suppliers' technology through the supply chain. The Ford Motor Company tried to develop its own telematics through a company called Wingcast. However, after 20 months of supporting the program, Ford discontinued the funding (Murray, 2002b). This is just one indication that automotive manufacturers may not have a core competency and competitive edge in the development of this emerging technology. The astute utilization of a CI program can assist in predicting the future direction of telematics and who will be the key players.

An increasingly important component of CI, competitive technical intelligence (CTI), offers the global CI analyst an intelligence tool kit that is of great assistance for determining the strategic impact of technologies such as telematics. CTI allows firms to anticipate future technological trends with the *early* identification of modifications or changes in technology platforms due to developments and discoveries in the *underlying* applied and pure sciences. Some of the usefeul analytical techniques of CTI include these (Murphy, 2001):

- *Technology Prospecting*: monitoring new technological developments and "leapfrogging" into promising new technologies that have been developed by pioneers and are showing commercial promise
- *Technology Scouting*: identifying trends and business opportunities offered by various technologies with a focus on reducing analysis of a potentially overwhelming number of new technologies into a manageable number of relevant areas
- *Patent Analysis:* identifying trends and patterns in patent data in order to determine *who* is developing *what* types of technology *when* and *where*
- *Bibliometrics:* counting the number of times a certain technology is cited in various publications (e.g., academic journals, trade and practitioners' magazines) to identify whether a technology is reaching a critical mass

- *Technology Forecasting:* performing extrapolative analysis of current technologies, existing platforms, and near- to medium-term modifications of existing products and services
- *Scenario Analysis:* performing non-extrapolative analysis of future technologies, new platforms, medium- to long-term innovations based on new discoveries in the underlying applied and pure sciences
- *S Curve Analysis*: taking a rigorous approach to determining the limits of the current technology and the optimal time to "jump" to a new technology

It is critical that these analytical techniques of CTI be included as a core component in the CI program of global corporations operating in industries in which technology plays a significant role in defining the rules of competition. The value of CTI is that it does not analyze technology just for technology's sake but, rather, it frames technological trends and developments against the backdrop of industry structure analysis. This is important for two reasons:

1. CTI will help the global CI analyst determine which players will be able (or unable) to harness technological developments to increase (or decrease) their future bargaining power within an industry.
2. CTI will give global CI analysts and their firms a window of opportunity to proactively manage the anticipated impacts of strategic technologies (such as telematics) *before* they manifest into a deteriorating competitive position.

In technologically dynamic industries such as automotive manufacturing, the use of CTI will greatly increase the rigor of assertions made by global CI analysts regarding future changes in the bargaining power of industry participants. As a direct result, the predictive power of CI models such as global industry analysis should increase with the integration of CTI.

GLOBAL TECHNOLOGY CONSORTIUMS

Connecting all the components of future vehicles will require a common specification. This will allow automotive manufacturers to use noncore technology in their products while embracing the "plug and play" technology similar to that found in today's computer environment. This will allow consumers "to take anyone's hardware and move it to anyone's vehicle" (Eisenstein, 1999) and will allow wired and wireless connectivity to pagers, PDAs, phones, and games.

A cooperative agreement alliance signed by the Automotive Multimedia Interface Collaboration (AMI-C) of Germany and Media Oriented Systems Transport Cooperation (MOSTCO) of the United States shows that the automotive manufacturers are keenly interested in developing a common platform from which to build future interfaces for the automotive industry (Media Oriented Systems Transport Cooperation [MOSTCO], 2001). European, American, and Japanese automotive manufacturers are all founding partners in one or both of these consortiums. "MOSTCO and AMI-C are working to establish common specifications related to vehicle multimedia and telematics applications that will enable independently manufactured electronic devices to work across different vehicle platforms" (Media Oriented Systems Transport Cooperation [MOSTCO], 2001). Components that will become part of future vehicles include interconnected entertainment and navigation systems and internal and external computer systems (Automotive Multimedia Interface Collaboration [AMI-C], 2002a, 2002b, 2000c). Working together, these consortiums now represent over 80% of the automotive industry (Automotive Multimedia Interface Collaboration [AMI-C], 2002d).

These consortiums are a multi-linked community comprised of the key founding automotive manufacturers and suppliers, the automotive manufacturing industry, and the supporting supplier community (see Table 18.1). Members include well-known global companies and smaller lesser-known companies providing specific technologies. The automotive manufacturers have already announced future vehicles that will use the consortium technology. The 2002 BMW 7-Series incorporated these new technologies and introduced them to the world. Now other automotive manufacturers are quickly following suit, including the 2003 Saab, 2003 Volvo, Jaguar (already in use), 2003 Audi, 2002.5 DaimlerChrysler, 2003 Fiat, 2003 Porsche, 2003 PSA Peugeot Citroën, and 2003 Volkswagen (Automotive Multimedia Interface Collaboration [AMI-C], 2002d; Allied Business Intelligence, 2003).

The FlexRay Consortium is another group of automotive manufacturers and suppliers. It was formed in 2000 and includes BMW, DaimlerChrysler, General Motors, Bosch, Motorola, and Philips Semiconductors. Fiat, Ford, and Mazda also have interests in this consortium (Allied Business Intelligence, 2003). The mandate of this consortium is to develop a standard protocol for high-speed bus systems for internal distributed control applications. These systems will be required for future automotive control systems such as brake-by-wire and steer-by-wire (Intex Management Services, 2002).

Time-Triggered Protocol (TTP) is another protocol for high-speed bus systems for automotive control systems. If the TTP and FlexRay protocols were both accepted, development and production costs could become higher, making it more difficult to achieve penetration into the automotive

Table 18.1
Members of the AMI-C and MOSTCO Consortia

Automotive Manufacturers	Automotive Suppliers		

• Aston Martin
• Audi
• BMW
• DaimlerChrysler
• Fiat
• Ford
• General Motors
• Honda
• Jaguar
• Land Rover
• Nissan
• Opel
• Porsche
• PSA
• RenaultSaab
• Toyota
• Volvo
• VW
	• AAA
	• ACUNIA
	• ALK
	• Technologies
	• Alpine Electronics
	• AW Asin
	• B2I
	• Bosch
	• Bose
	• CAA
	• Clarion
	• Delco
	• Delphi
	• Denso Corporation
	• FCI
	• Fujikura
	• Fujitsu Ten
	• Furkawa AM3
	• GADV
	• Grundig
	• Harman/Becker
	• Harmonia Inc.
	• Hosiden
		• Hyundai Autonet
		• Infineon
		• Johnson Controls
		• Kenwood
		• Kostal
		  Kroschu-Kabelw
		• Kshema
		  Technologies
		• Lear
		• Magneti Marelli
		• Matsushita
		  Communication
		• Matsushita Electric
		• Mecel
		• Mindready
		• Mitsumi
		  Hamamatsu
		• Mitsubishi
		• Molex
		• Motorola
		• NavTech
		• Nokia
		• Oasis
			• Optitas
			• Parrot
			• Philips
			• Pioneer
			• Ruetz
			• Sensoria Corp.
			• Siemens VDO
			• Softing
			• Sumitomo Electric
			  Industries
			• Sun Microsystems
			• Telelogic
			  Hirschmann
			• Toray
			• Toshiba KN
			  Systems
			• Tyco Electronics
			• Vector
			• Visteon
			• Wipro Technologies
			• Xanavi
			• XM Satellite Radio
			• Yazaki

Source: Adapted from Automotive Multimedia Interface Collaboration [AMI-C (2002d, 2003)].

market (Allied Business Intelligence, 2003). In this scenario, suppliers would develop systems that would support both protocols, but the net result for the final consumer is a higher cost.

By joining together and utilizing a common technology, automotive manufacturers have regained some of the market power that they risked losing to their suppliers. The creation of these consortiums not only benefits the automotive manufacturers but affects consumers as well due to the interchangeability of consumer devices. Suppliers will have to adapt their technology to fit within the specification of the consortiums; they also must be able to adapt their products easily and quickly to meet any changes to these specifications.

The challenge to ensure that these new technologies remain safe and operational in the automotive industry may result in additional standards being developed. MOST, FlexRay, TTP, and others currently are part of a Class C Network. To ensure absolute safety, a new network standard may be implemented to meet the specific needs of the automotive industry (Allied Business Intelligence, 2003). Since development of electronic technology moves at a faster pace than development of automotive technology, full implementation of one standard may eventually prove to be impossible. As quickly as new specifications and standards are developed and created, they may just as quickly become obsolete with the addition of new requirements; this may cause shifts to new suppliers and allow some of the market power to return to the automotive manufacturers. This is yet another area where a comprehensive CI program is crucial to leading firms in the automotive industry.

INTEL AND MICROSOFT'S TECHNOLOGIES IN THE AUTOMOTIVE INDUSTRY

No stranger to securing market share and power with computer processors is the Intel Corporation. In the race to provide the fastest and newest technology to the automotive industry, Intel is developing new products specifically designed for the automotive telematics segment. The Intel PXA250 and PXA210 processors are designed to operate within the extremes of the automotive environment and to "bring high performance solutions and products that deliver wireless voice and data information to vehicles" (Intel Corporation, 2002). Intel's processors support hands-free cellular phones through Bluetooth technology and deliver multimedia content such as DVD video and MP3 audio through MOSTCO's network (Intel Corporation, 2002). Combined with high-speed wireless Internet technology, this will allow consumers to download entertainment from the Internet and download updated map and real-time navigation information (Heidingsfelder, 2000).

Microsoft is developing software to support the automotive telematics segment. Microsoft has created *Windows CE for Automotive* to merge the technologies provided by PDAs, e-mail, the Internet, and satellite broadcasts in an effort to create an all-encompassing automotive multimedia experience (Martin, 2000). "*Windows CE for Automotive* is an open platform that allows developers to quickly create powerful in-vehicle computing solutions. It offers flexibility and choice of computing platforms, hardware peripherals, and software components" (Telcontar Corporation, 2002). Microsoft has incorporated additional features including Bluetooth technology and speech recognition into its latest software (Murray, 2003). The flexibility and widespread adoption of Microsoft software in the computer industry now seems to be extending and integrating into the automotive industry. However, full penetration of the automotive industry by Microsoft may be limited by the AMI-C consortium. AMI-C's protocol specifications utilize Java rather than a Microsoft platform (Murray, 2002b). In addition, neither General Motors nor the Ford Motor Company uses Windows CE (Murray, 2002b).

Both Intel and Microsoft are industry leaders in the computing environment and wield strong marketing and consumer acceptance in the computer industry. In a world of many computer manufacturers, one thing is common to most of them: Intel Inside and Microsoft operating systems. In the computer supply chain, both of these companies have the highest brand equity and market power in their respective supply chains. As consumers demand these products in their vehicles of tomorrow, Intel and Microsoft are well poised to take advantage of their position and take away some of the market power that the automotive manufacturers enjoy. The automotive manufacturers will need to offset this shift of power by seeking expertise through mergers and alliances and through developing in-house electronics knowledge and expertise in their design and purchasing departments (Heidingsfelder, 2000). Again, a comprehensive CI program can assist management as they make key strategic decisions as to the future role of computing and the key players in the automotive industry.

GEOGRAPHIC DIFFERENCES IN THE AUTOMOTIVE INDUSTRY

Europe has traditionally led the automotive industry in technological advances (Autocentral, 2000). The AMI-C consortium had its beginnings in Europe and effectively brought together most of the European automotive manufacturers to develop a common telematics platform. The integrated technologies of navigation, hands-free cellular phones, drive-by-wire, and entertainment systems typically appeared first on the European vehicles manufactured by Audi, BMW, Jaguar, Mercedes, Saab, and Volvo. The small size of these companies allowed them to collaborate effectively on technology initiatives (EE Times, 2000). Interestingly, the Big Three automotive manufacturers (General Motors, Ford, and Daimler-Chrysler) now have stakes in some of these smaller automotive companies and have been able to access this market without giving away any corporate secrets.

Japanese and U.S. automotive manufacturers are beginning to take an interest in this technology, and through partnerships with AMI-C and MOSTCO are working toward a common worldwide standard (Automotive Multimedia Interface Collaboration [AMI-C], 2002b). The automotive manufacturers of the Asia-Pacific region, however, do not seem to be embracing this new technology (Autocentral, 2000). It is ironic that although there is a significant electronics industry in the Asia-Pacific region, the domestic infrastructure required to support many of these technologies has not been developed. As a result, a plan for incorporating these technologies into models for the domestic market is not being developed, and consequently there is limited availability on an international basis. In the future, the Asia-Pacific automotive manufacturers may be able to bring new technology to market quickly much to the chagrin of the European, U.S., and Japanese automotive manufacturers.

GLOBAL TRENDS IN AUTOMOTIVE OUTSOURCING

Automotive manufacturers are increasingly using outsourcing as a means of reducing costs and improving efficiency in their operations. The cost savings associated with outsourcing may be misleading, since the re-distribution of costs from the automotive manufacturers to their suppliers may not actually save money (Autobusiness Limited, 2003). Care must also be exercised to ensure that core technology is not given to suppliers. The automotive industry is mature, and the technology of yesterday's vehicles can be easily duplicated by others. The most powerful industry dynamic limiting the arrival of new automotive manufacturers, however, is the high barriers to entry that must be overcome to achieve economies of scale.

Magna International, a Canadian global automotive parts supplier, is entering into the automotive manufacturing industry in Europe. Magna is a large corporation able to leverage off the outsourcing mentality of the automotive manufacturers to a new extreme. It has already started European manufacturing for various players in the automotive industry (Canadian Press, 2002) and is currently manufacturing DaimlerChrysler Voyagers, Jeep Grand Cherokees, and several Mercedes Benz models. Magna has obtained future contracts to manufacture complete vehicles and large assemblies, including Saabs for General Motors, X3 SUVs for BMW, the complete box for Ford's Lincoln Blackwood, and entire interiors for General Motors full-size SUVs and pickup trucks. In the case of the BMW X3, Magna will not only be manufacturing this SUV but will also be co-developing it with BMW (Autobusiness Limited, 2003). The European manufacturers are turning to outsourcing to meet demand, and in the process they are allowing Magna's market power to increase.

In North America, outsourcing to the degree that is found in Europe will not likely materialize. Due to the highly entrenched unionized work-force in North America, these automotive manufacturers are outsourcing in a lower capacity. The North American automotive manufacturers are out-sourcing large modules or components, but one of the modules that has often been outsourced is the instrument panel. As the technology content of vehicles increases in the future, a significant portion of this technology will be housed in the instrument panels of tomorrow's vehicles. In order for the suppliers of these modules to be able to assemble, diagnose, and repair them, automotive manufacturers will need to release proprietary information to the suppliers. This will shift market power to the suppliers.

The Japanese automotive manufacturers use "insourcing" instead of outsourcing. Much like their European counterparts, union contracts (if any) are not as binding in Japan as they are in North America. This allows the Japanese automotive manufacturers to utilize contract labor within their assembly facilities, which not only eliminates the costs of an outside supplier's facility and the transportation costs of the modules but also maintains their technology in-house. The Japanese automotive manufacturers could, if needed, eliminate the contract workers in favor of company employees in order to protect proprietary information. The Japanese automotive manufacturers have been able to maintain market power while at the same time realizing the cost savings associated with outsourcing.

A FUTURE SCENARIO FOR TECHNOLOGY IN THE GLOBAL AUTOMOTIVE MANUFACTURING INDUSTRY

The impact of telematics technology on the structure of the global automobile manufacturing industry is summarized in Figure 18.1. The primary impacts have yet to play out, but dynamic industry structure analysis allows for reasonable speculation regarding one of two scenarios that are likely to materialize:

1. Suppliers will experience increased bargaining power as they develop superior core competencies in new technologies such as telematics.
2. Incumbent auto manufacturers will reverse their past decisions to outsource and will invest their superior resources in developing competencies in new technologies, thereby reversing the recent decline of their market power.

Technology in the automotive industry will continue to grow and develop. The development of common platforms and open architectures will allow consumers to "plug and play" various technologies. Analogous to the computer industry, the ability to interchange components and add new devices to any computing platform and the ability to use any software programs will extend to the automotive industry. Virtual mechanics may be able to fix problems with future vehicles by downloading software fixes, much like the computing industry does today. Automotive manufacturing is a mature industry, and future competitive advantage will be found by exploiting and bringing to market new technologies.

Automotive manufacturers will need to develop new competencies in order to take advantage of this technological growth in the industry. New suppliers will emerge, and many of the traditional suppliers of today will

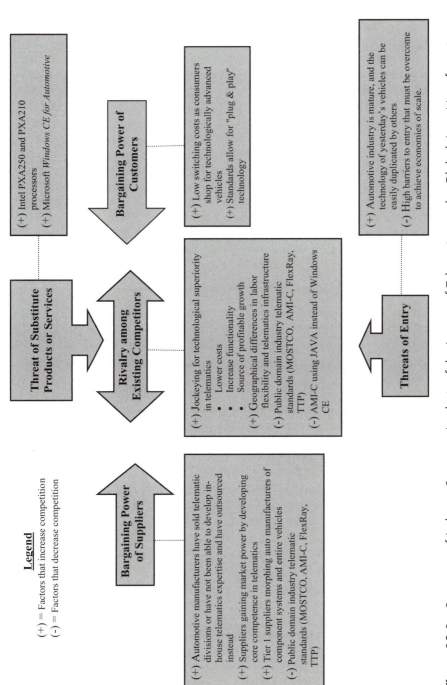

Figure 18.1 Summary of Industry Structure Analysis of the Impact of Telematics on the Global Auto Manufacturing Industry.

have to either adapt or close. As these new global technology suppliers emerge, market power may shift away from the traditional automotive manufacturers to technology suppliers. For example, in an effort to be "best in class," General Motors recently signed a contract with Bosch to supply braking components rather than developing them themselves (Autobusiness Limited, 2003). Another case in point is provided by General Motors' divestiture of its electronics and technology division, Delphi, which may ultimately build enough market power to turn the proverbial table on General Motors. In 2001, Delphi had the largest automotive supplier market share (Intex Management Services, 2002). Magna International, which is taking on complete manufacturing for some of the automotive manufacturers and, in the process, is learning more about proprietary information, is yet another example. This trend toward developing new competencies will probably continue in the future.

Automotive manufacturers have made many decisions in the past that will affect their future market power. They have divested and outsourced manufacturing to suppliers and have sought technology and knowledge from suppliers. This increasing dependence on suppliers in order to maintain cost-effective and efficient operations has forced the automotive manufacturers to lose some of their market power through these collaborative relationships. Most suppliers have already transitioned from suppliers of simple components to suppliers of modules and many are now integrating entire automotive systems for the automotive manufacturers (Autobusiness Limited, 2003).

A new approach will be required in the future if the automotive manufacturers want to maintain their market power, and once again Japanese automotive manufacturers seem to have the right chemistry for future success. European automotive manufacturers seem to have the highest current liability with their suppliers, but if they become acquired by one of the Big Three, their market power will instantly increase. As far as the Big Three automotive manufacturers are concerned, size will definitely make a difference in the future, provided they do not allow key suppliers to expand too rapidly.

The power in the automotive supply chain will evolve in the future as new players enter the market and attempt to gain market power. For the next decade, the power will likely remain with the automotive manufacturers if they continue to maintain their advantage of size and keep pace with technological advances.

CONCLUSION

Through giving an overview and specifics about the dynamic future of the global automotive industry—a future filled with the risk of making incorrect strategic decisions—the chapter has presented a solid justification for the utilization of a comprehensive competitive intelligence program. The more uncertainty and risk in an industry, the greater the value of CI in discerning industry winners from also-rans.

Perhaps the greatest risk factor in most global industries is the pervasive impact of technological discontinuity. As this chapter has shown, a useful case in point is the flux that telematics is inducing in the global auto-manufacturing industry. Telematics, like many other technologies, has the very real potential of redefining the rules of competition and redistributing bargaining power among industry participants. Indeed, many firms are currently rallying to harness telematics technology in an attempt to secure a greater share of industry profit.

Firms with well-developed CI capabilities, however, are armed with competitive foresight that allows them to proactively manage competition as opposed to reacting to competitive developments or, even worse, scrambling to recover from competitive blindsides. In this regard, industry analysis will continue to be a core component of the global CI analytical tool kit. However, as technological innovation and discontinuity can be expected to accelerate in many industries, the integration of CTI methodologies and techniques will greatly amplify the effectiveness of the time-honored analytical approach of industry analysis.

REFERENCES

ABOUT Publishing Group. (2002). *The Global Market for Mobile Multimedia: Forecasts to 2010*. Worcestershire, UK: Aroq Ltd.

Allied Business Intelligence Inc. (2003). *X-by-Wire*. Oyster Bay, NY: Allied Business Intelligence.

Autobusiness Limited. (2003). *OEM Sourcing Strategies*. Autobusiness Limited. http://www.just-auto.com/search_site.asp.

Autocentral. (2000). "Automakers Press for Low-Speed LIN Network." *Test and Measurement Online*. March 23. http://www.testandmeasurement.com.

Automotive Multimedia Interface Collaboration (AMI-C). (2002a). "In Car Computer: A Complete On-Board Telematics Demonstrator." Presentation given at the 2002 Society of Automotive Engineers (SAE International) Digital Car Conference. March 4–7, Detroit, Michigan. http://ami-c.org/presentation_b2i_files/slide0075.htm.

Automotive Multimedia Interface Collaboration (AMI-C). (2002b). "The B2i Telematic & Multimedia Product." Presentation given at the 2002 Society of Automotive Engineers (SAE International) Digital Car Conference. March 4–7, Detroit, Michigan. http://ami-c.org/presentation_b2i_files/slide0098.htm.

Automotive Multimedia Interface Collaboration (AMI-C). (2002c). Untitled presentation given at the 2002 Society of Automotive Engineers (SAE International) Digital Car Conference. March 4–7, Detroit, Michigan. http://ami-c.org/Presentation_B2i_files/frame.htm#slide0104.htm.

Automotive Multimedia Interface Collaboration (AMI-C). (2002d). "Shared Vision Points to Future Joint Projects between AMI-C and MOSTCO." http://ami-c .org/most-amic_rev8.asp.

Automotive Multimedia Interface Collaboration (AMI-C). (2003). "Supplier Overview." http://ami-c.org/overview_6-11-03_files/slide0113.htm.

Beecham, M. (2002). *The Global Market for Navigation Systems*. Worcestershire, UK: ABOUT Publishing Group/Aroq Ltd.

Canadian Press. (2002). "Magna Expands Assembly Capacity with Purchase of Chrysler Austrian Plant." http://www.autocentral.com/content/news.

Cataldo, A. (2003). "Recession-weary Chip Makers Turn to Auto Apps." *EE Times*. May 19. http://www.eetimes.com/story/OEG20030519S0042.

EE Times. (2000). "Europe Takes Lead in Search of 'One-Wire Car.'" *EE Times*. March. http://www.eetimes.com.

Eisenstein, P. (1999). "Surf the Net from Behind the Wheel." *Popular Mechanics*. September. http://popularmechanics.com/automotive/auto_technology/ 1999/9/in_dash_pcs/.

Heidingsfelder, M. (2000). "Electronics Growth Will Drive New Auto Industry." April 14. http://www.autocentral.com/content/news/article.asp?docid= {e31065c5-120b-11d4-8c36-009027de0829}.

Intel Corporation. (2002). "Intel Showcases New Telematics Products, Customers at Digital Car Conference; Intel XScale Technology Based Processors Power New In-Vehicle Systems." http://www.intel.com/pressroom/archive/ releases/20020304net.htm.

Intex Management Services. (2002). *The Worldwide Market for OEM Automotive Electronics*. Wellingborough, UK: Intex Management Services.

Martin, N. (2000). "Convergence 2000: The Promise of Technology." http:// www.autocentral.com/content/news.

Media Oriented Systems Transport Cooperation (MOSTCO). (2001). "AMI-C and MOSTCO Sign Cooperative Agreement Alliance to Speed Worldwide Spec-ifications." December 11. http://www.mostnet.de/news/Press+Releases/ 2001/1/17/files/011211MOU_MOST_AMIC_WebPressRelease.pdf.

Motorola Corporation. (2002). "Frequently Asked Questions: What Is Telematics." http://www.motorola.com/automotive/telematics/faq/.

Murphy, J. (2001). "Using Competitive Technical Intelligence Techniques to Complement Research and Development Processes," pp. 136–148 in C.S. Fleisher and D.L. Blenkhorn [eds.], *Managing Frontiers in Competitive Intel-ligence*. Westport, CT: Quorum Books.

Murray, C.J. (2002a). "Automotive Market Gets New Attention from Industry." *EE Times*. January 11. http://www.eetimes.com/story/OEG20020111S0037.

Murray, C.J. (2002b). "Microsoft Hopes to Rev Poky Telematics Market." *EE Times*. July 15. http://www.eetimes.com/story/OEG20020715S0057.

Murray, C.J. (2003). "Microsoft Rolls Out New Automotive Platform." *EE Times*. May 1. http://www.eetimes.com/story/OEG20030501S0048.

OnStar Corporation. (2003a). *Vehicles with OnStar*. http://www.onstar.com/us_ english/jsp/vehicles/vehicles.jsp?page=idont.

OnStar Corporation. (2003b). *What Is OnStar?* http://www.onstar.com/us_ english/jsp/whatisonstar/idont_whatisonstar.jsp.

Porter, M.E. (1980). *Competitive Strategy: Techniques for Analyzing Industries and Competitors.* New York: Free Press.

Shah, J.B. (2000). "Special Report: The Automotive Supply Chain: Racing for the Checkered Flag." *Electronic Buyers News.* February 14. http://www.ebnonline.com/supplychain/features/story/OEG20000214S0003.

Telcontar Corporation. (2002). *Telcontar Announces Microsoft Windows CE for Automotive 3.5 Features Company's Core Library and Tools.* http://www.telcontar.com/news/CEforAutomotive.htm.

Texas Instruments Corporation. (2002a). *Texas Instruments Introduces Industry's First Complete Multimedia IDB-1394 and Bluetooth™ Technologies for Automotive Market.* February 20. http://focus.ti.com/docs/pr/pressrelease.jhtml?prelId=sc02026?.

Texas Instruments Corporation. (2002b). *Automotive Q-Temp (−40°C to 125°C).* http://www.ti.com.

19

Management of Global Competitive Intelligence: The Way Ahead

Craig S. Fleisher and David L. Blenkhorn

This chapter illustrates the ways we believe the management of competitive intelligence (CI) will evolve on a global basis in the coming years. Our focus is primarily on the corporate practice, research, and teaching dimensions of the CI management field and the identification of trends that we believe will help define the field's future. We have little doubt that global and internationally focused CI will grow in importance as global commerce and trade gain increasing prominence, and we believe that consulting and corporate practitioners, researchers, and educators will have difficulty trying to keep up with the CI demands and needs created by globally competitive firms.

THE GROWING NEED FOR GLOBAL CI

Over the past several decades, we have witnessed the accelerating pace of change in the global business environment. This change has been manifest in the globalization of markets and production and driven heavily by declining trade barriers and dramatic improvements in communication, information, and transportation technologies (Hill, 2003). The growing integration of the global economy has given rise to increased needs for the management of intelligence by corporate decision-makers.

CI, as well as other forms of analyzed information, is needed to identify changes and trends in the business environment and feed them into the planning and decision-making processes used by multinational business organizations in an effort to perform more successfully (Blenkhorn & Fleisher, 2001). Effective global CI can bring a number of potential benefits to global competitors, including improving

1. a company's strategic planning process and plans (Jaworksi & Wee, 1993)
2. decision-making and decision quality (Hawkins & Tull, 1994)
3. the knowledge and understanding of key employees and decision-makers (McGonagle & Vella, 2002)
4. the risk profile of decisions by acting as a hedge against country-specific, industry, and operational risks (Gilad, 2001)
5. a company's competitive advantage, if it can develop its understanding in a way that allows it to outmaneuver its competitors (Fleisher & Bensoussan, 2003)

International competition has rapidly grown over the last few decades and has become a prominent feature of many organizations' environments, both market and non-market. There are no shortages of global business success and failure stories distributed in the popular media. Indeed, these stories often make up the focus of entire book-length treatments (Ricks, 1983), although the contributions or lack thereof made by CI practitioners and functions in these efforts rate nary a mention. The major international business and management textbooks used in educating students in most post-secondary institutions also often fail to mention CI. This is one indicator that the global management of CI has not yet hit the radar screen of most observers of the global business scene.

A lack of clarity about the management of global CI also exists because it overlaps in some ways with concepts and practices in international market information, international marketing, international environmental scanning, exporting and importing planning, and international strategy development. For the purposes of this chapter, we define global CI as *those processes by which organizations gather actionable information about global competitors and the environment in the host-country markets in which they compete and could potentially compete and, ideally, apply it to their decision-making and planning processes in order to improve their performance.* As the paucity of empirical research and scholarly writings in this area demonstrates (Dishman, Fleisher, & Knip, 2003), the global or international management of CI is a little-understood area of practice and scholarship that has shown recent signs of increased prominence in corporate and consulting practice.

CONTINUUMS FOR UNDERSTANDING CI IN GLOBAL AND INTERNATIONAL CONTEXTS

Based on the scattered published anecdotal evidence, as well as the frequency of its occurrence in the discussion of practitioners, researchers, and scholars as represented by peer-to-peer interchanges, conference proceedings, and the CI literature, we believe there are a limited number of critical dimensions that need to be studied if we are to make progress in understanding either the present or future status of CI management in global or international contexts. Table 19.1 shows ten continuums that are integral to understanding the differences between global or international CI in corporations and the predominant North American understanding of the field.

The following section expands upon these continua to provide a context that will subsequently allow us to illustrate future trends in the field. It also describes how we think the management of global and international CI will evolve over the next ten years along each continuum and offers testable propositions so that researchers may test the predictive accuracy of these views.

Continuum 1: Eastern versus Western Intelligence Conceptions

This dimension recognizes that there are key differences in the conception of CI, depending upon which geographic part of the world the corporation and its CI practitioners are located. These differences are primarily due to, among other things, culture and values (Hofstede, 1984), history, institutional contexts, and technological development. Eastern conceptions

Table 19.1
Key Continuums for Understanding Global versus North American Corporate CI

1   Eastern versus Western intelligence conceptions
2   Developing-country versus developed-country intelligence needs and processes
3   Integrated public and private sector intelligence versus independent private efforts
4   Relative dominance of human systems versus technological systems in CI
5   Importance of primary versus secondary sources
6   Implicit versus explicit recognition of CI's value
7   Transactional importance of the spoken versus the written word
8   Long-term versus short-term decision-making timeframes
9   R&D and technological versus marketing and strategy decision applications
10 Social codes versus legal definitions of allowable practice

of CI see the field more in terms of a natural part of market relationships and transactions, and CI is therefore considered a more 'natural' aspect of how groups do business; additionally, there is also more collaboration engendered among participants in these business systems that impacts the way CI is gathered and whether the task can or should be easily out-sourced (Fleisher, 2002). Compared to their Eastern counterparts, West-ern executives tend to view CI as part of the weaponry or "arsenal" of competitive firms, and tend to keep its existence quiet or secret because of their discomfort with the notion of CI and its frequent pairing by the public as being linked to industrial espionage or other unsavory practices (Hulnick, 2002).

Proposition 1: As Eastern-domiciled firms adopt Western practices and as Western-domiciled firms adopt Eastern conceptions, there will be convergence of these conceptions of CI between the present and 2015.

Continuum 2: Developing-Country versus Developed-Country Intelligence Needs and Processes

CI processes differ greatly between corporations that hail from devel-oped and less-developed countries. Participants who perform CI activities from companies domiciled primarily in less-developed or developing countries tend to rely far less on the information and communications technology (ICT) infrastructure (databases, intranets, digital networks, advanced telecommunication systems) that would be present, for exam-ple, in an established U.S. corporate CI practice. CI practitioners in devel-oping countries must rely far more heavily on their primary research skills and their ability to network among individuals who have the data they need to acquire. Also, CI in developing countries does not emphasize the counterintelligence side of CI nearly as much as would the typical developed-country company. This can be at least partly explained by the observation that developed countries tend to have higher-level mecha-nisms for protecting intellectual property relative to companies domiciled in less-developed countries (North, 1990); therefore, companies domiciled in countries that have subscribed, for example, to the Paris Convention for the Protection of Intellectual Property know that they can benefit from government enforcement if another company were to attempt to steal their patents, trademarks, or copyrights. They will therefore invest more time, money, and other resources in counterintelligence and security measures.

Proposition 2: Developing-country-domiciled corporations will increasingly accept and utilize CI between now and 2015. This can be measured by the number and percentage of practitioners who have designated, formal CI responsibilities.

Continuum 3: Integrated Public/Private Sector-Intelligence versus Independent Private Efforts

This dimension considers the nature and level of involvement of public-sector authorities in private-sector intelligence efforts (Calof & Skinner, 1999). In some countries, such as China, France, Israel, Japan, and South Korea, government support of private-sector intelligence activities carried out by firms headquartered within their borders is common and viewed as useful in assisting companies domiciled in those countries to compete on a global basis (Hulnick, 2002). As such, there is a far higher degree of integration of public- and private-sector intelligence efforts in particular countries. In North America, there have been frequent calls for government intelligence agencies to assist private corporations, but these have mainly been resisted and the private and public-sector practices of intelligence are purposefully kept separate (Quinn, 1994). A difficulty that arises in applying this continuum is the observation that modern private-sector organizations can often be viewed as being domiciled within multiple countries and are often not thought of as being the product of any particular nation-state. Another difficulty is the observation that even in nations such as the United States, where the government avoids assisting private-sector firms for offensive CI support, governments will generally assist industries as well as individual firms defensively by helping them detect unfair trade practices or foreign industrial espionage (Hulnick, 2002).

Proposition 3: By 2015, corporations domiciled in nation-states whose governments currently avoid supporting corporate intelligence efforts will benefit from increased government support through the active provision of CI resources.

Continuum 4: Relative Dominance of Human versus Technical Systems in CI

Most contemporary CI activities tend to rely upon both human and technological facets to support the process of gathering, analyzing, and disseminating intelligence. This dimension suggests that corporations can be arrayed along a continuum that is anchored by human and technological aspects. North American and European practitioners tend to rely upon and use technology in CI, especially ICT, more heavily than do corporations in most Eastern and Asian countries. In many Asian countries, a reliance upon primary research and collection methods is necessary because of a relative lack of digitized business transactions, transparency, and legal machinery, as well as because of the more common manner of reaching agreements through less formal means, such as handshakes (Fleisher, 2002).

Proposition 4: There will be more alignment of these system types between the present and 2015 as Eastern- and Asian-domiciled firms increase their relative use of technical systems while Western-domiciled firms will continue to show a predominance of technical systems usage.

Continuum 5: Importance of Primary versus Secondary Collection

CI practitioners ordinarily rely upon both primary and secondary sources of raw data for their data and information (Miller, 1994). This dimension refers to the proportion of the two collection methods they ordinarily use, more and less. A critical factor in placing organizations along this continuum is whether they are domiciled in collective-oriented or individual-oriented societies. "Collective-oriented" refers to ideologies whereby the needs of society and the common good are viewed as more important than the needs of the individual. Nation-states that are characterized by individualism, in contrast, emphasize the primacy of an individual's freedom, and this ideology is commonly translated into support for democratic ideals and free market economies (Spiegel, 1991). Primary collection methods are utilized more frequently by CI practitioners in collective-oriented countries (e.g., Asian nation-states such as China, Korea, and Malaysia), whereas secondary collection methods are utilized proportionately more in North American practice. We should also note that the freedom of expression and information in a nation-state will also influence where on this continuum CI practice will fall, with CI practice relying more on secondary sources in high freedom-of-information nation-states and greater relative reliance on primary methods in nation-states with lower degrees of freedom of expression and information.

Proposition 5: As practitioners in global corporations increase the relative proportion of their less-utilized collection techniques, there will be convergence along this continuum between now and 2015.

Continuum 6: Implicit versus Explicit Recognition of CI's Value

This dimension refers to the nature of accountability expected of corporate CI practitioners by decision-makers in corporations. CI is implicitly recognized as being a valuable function in many collective-oriented cultures, and it receives executive support in the form of resources without being required to regularly demonstrate its performance or worth. On the other end of the continuum, CI functions and practitioners in most North American companies must regularly prove themselves and make a formal case for requiring needed resources through the delivery of tangible accountability and control measures such as return-on-investment calculations or cost-benefit analysis (Fleisher & Blenkhorn, 2001). We should note that the counterintelligence and security aspects of CI tend to be evaluated and valued differently than proactive or offensive CI, since loss prevention is more easily measured, the costs are more tangible, and the concept has apparently been easier for managers to accept (McGonagle & Vella, 2002). Finally, that increasing numbers of managers in non-Western nation-states are being trained and receiving degrees in Western-style MBA programs (and mindsets) might suggest future movement away from the implicit recognition side of the continuum.

Proposition 6a: As determined through the application of surveys, senior executives in North American companies will increasingly recognize a greater implicit value of CI between now and 2015.

Proposition 6b: Managers in countries with increasing proportions of Western (versus non-Western or indigenous) MBA degree-holders between the present and 2015 will increasingly seek greater explicit demonstrations of CI value.

Continuum 7: Transactional Importance of the Spoken versus the Written Word

This dimension refers to the nature of transactions that CI practitioners must identify and understand to generate their insights. The spoken word, verbal transmission of information and testimonies, and oral traditions tend to take on greater relative importance in collective-oriented cultures and lesser-developed and low-literacy nation-states, whereas nearly anything in Western company business operations must be in writing to have any effect or force.

Proposition 7: More organizations will adopt and utilize written transactions and move away from relying upon the spoken word between the present and 2015.

Continuum 8: Long-Term versus Short-Term Decision-Making Time Frames

Global or international CI is used in a variety of applications, sometimes for immediate or short-term decision-making needs, other times for helping the firm address medium- to longer-term decisions. We have observed a difference in the typical timeframe being impacted by CI. Decisions affected by corporate CI tend to take on a longer-term perspective in Asian firms than they ordinarily would in North American firms' use of the discipline.

Proposition 8: By 2015, CI practitioners in Western companies will be asked to provide greater proportional support for long-term decisions than what they currently provide.

Continuum 9: Research and Development (R&D) and Technological versus Marketing/Strategy Decision Applications

This continuum examines the predominant functional orientations of organizational decisions that CI supports. This dimension would require the researcher to understand the dominant business function in organizations within particular nation-states. Non-Western, and particularly Asian, versions of CI tend to focus more on technology and R&D-related CI aspects than would ordinarily be found in Western firms. Indeed, much of China's and Japan's initial and current CI efforts are focused primarily on the technological aspects of CI, as opposed to the more common strategic business- and marketing-oriented focused efforts pursued by the majority of North American firms (Fleisher, 2002).

> **Proposition 9:** *Between the present and 2015, Western firms will increase the proportion of their CI time devoted to R&D and technological applications.*

Continuum 10: Social Codes versus Legal Definitions of Allowable Practice

This dimension refers to the nature of principles that corporate and consultancy-based CI practitioners rely upon to guide the conduct of their work and to avoid breaching ethical or legal guidelines. Social, less formal, and often unwritten codes tend to predominate and guide behavior in non-Western CI practice, whereas written codes and regulations in the form of policies and laws tend to guide North American practice.

> **Proposition 10:** *More global organizations will adopt codes of ethical conduct for their CI and move away from the use of unwritten codes between the present and 2015.*

These continuums are very helpful in arraying the corporate management practice of global and international CI both in the present and in the future. Like most schema, however, we recognize that the ten continua discussed have some deficiencies. Limitations in using this scheme for empirical research include the following

- Not all countries or regions of the globe cleanly fit into categories of Eastern or Western, developed or less developed, or even into categories like Asian, European, or North American. Countries may be transitioning between development stages or may contain companies that have multiple influences beside the dominant one in the country or region in which they are domiciled.

- CI usage by practitioners domiciled in some nations-states, like those from Latin America or Africa, may not be cleanly captured by the proposed continua. Again, we recognize that there will be path-based differences in national CI practice based on variables such as culture, geographic proximity to other nations, history, institutional development (e.g., legal and political bases and policies, university diffusion, and progress), media, social mores, and technology development and utilization.

- Accurately pinpointing practices along the continua will require more elaborate definitions of the anchoring constructs. For the time being, we see the continua as providing perspective and anchoring more than precision placements.

- Sample design problems in identifying those persons or units specifically responsible for CI, as well as clearly distinguishing CI from other forms of marketing, strategy, or policy insights and recommendations, will remain difficult for researchers of global corporations.

Because there has been a dearth of research performed in this field, it can be difficult to project the future of global or international CI. In other words, the field has very few baselines developed by which to track its progress—and this is true across a wide variety of CI management dimensions. There are undoubtedly a myriad of opportunities for interested researchers to purse these questions empirically and systematically—and we are encouraged that there are a number of rising scholars from around the globe who have an interest in CI.

RESEARCH CHALLENGES

While there is nearly an unlimited opportunity to perform research on evolving CI phenomena in a global context, it is important to recognize that this research is not likely to see explosive growth over the next decade. This is because of the increased complexity associated with planning and conducting the research, as well as for the following prominent reasons:

- *Very little research has been performed to date on global or international CI.* The literature needs significant expansion before the field reaches a critical mass of understanding that usually underlies fields that move toward established and professional status (Dishman, Fleisher, & Knip, 2003).

- *Few persons are steeped in the literature of the field.* There are less than a handful of doctoral-level CI programs available around the globe, and few international business students have demonstrated an interest in studying CI phenomena. Until or unless this changes, the critical impetus for new research in the field will not be gained.

- *Global CI research is more expensive and resource-intense than domestic CI research.* Because of difficulties in interpretation (e.g., translation, understanding, and being sensitive to foreign cultures) and the costs of international communication (whether through postal or face-to-face survey methods), most researchers prefer to study CI phenomena in their domestic contexts. The difficulties inherent in assuring the comparability of the instruments used to gather data as well as assuring the responses in the research are well known by companies that do international market and marketing research and are expected to be just as complex to address in studying CI phenomena. This at least partly explains the presence of nation-state-specific studies conducted in Australia, Canada, Korea, and the United States but the lack of cross-national comparisons.

- *Sampling challenges and design.* Attempting to properly identify persons with knowledge in CI is difficult enough in U.S. firms, but doing so can be even more troublesome in international firms that lack personnel with titles in the CI area or in nation-states where CI is not as clearly a recognizable concept as it would be in the United States. A related challenge is in dealing with non-response, specifically in determining if those surveyed chose not to respond because they do not want to identify or publicize their CI efforts.

- *Challenges of theory and construct definition.* There are some concepts that are difficult to interpret from one language or culture to another, which means that achieving conceptual equivalence can be a great challenge for global CI researchers. For example, the concepts of intellectual property, ethical codes, legality, or competition can mean different things to people in the United States than they do to people from selected Asian countries.

- *Addressing lingual inconsistencies.* Some words and ideas do not have an accurate translation in another language. Even the term "competitive intelligence" has different meanings in China (where the term itself was borrowed from a Japanese definition) and Australia, not to mention how it differs again from the way that it is used in a variety of European countries.

- *Variations in order of development.* Across countries, as well as sometimes between regions within countries, the researcher is likely to uncover differences in the relative level of development of CI practices.

Effectively addressing these challenges nearly always requires researchers doing cross-national research to work with and utilize collaborators from the other countries in which their research is focused. The formation of multicultural research teams can help alleviate several of these problems, as can the effective employment of translators familiar with the CI subject matter domain.

We encourage researchers interested in CI to study their phenomena of interest in international and global contexts. The propositions we provided in the previous sections were intended to serve as a guideline for researchers who are intent on studying these phenomena.

TEACHING AND INSTRUCTIONAL CHALLENGES IN GLOBAL MANAGEMENT OF CI

CI education has been growing in recent years, but it remains mainly a secondary or ancillary course of studies relative to its older and more established cousins in business, management, marketing, and policy studies. There are still relatively very few CI programs in established global institutions of higher (post-secondary) education. There are a handful of Ph.D programs in intelligence, and a lesser number in the specific field of CI. According to the research on educational opportunities in CI published by Burkhardt (2002), there are a dozen MBA and undergraduate programs around the globe with specializations or concentrations in CI. Further, approximately two dozen specialized certificate programs in the area have also been developed. In particular, there has been recent growth in the number of private-sector, for-profit programs in CI from such entities as the Academy of Competitive Intelligence (U.S.), Competitive Business Intelligence Analysis (South Africa), Competia (Canada), Frost & Sullivan (U.S.), Helicon Group (U.S.), Marcus Evans (global), and the Mindshifts Group (Australia), among others.

Despite the moderate growth in for-profit programs that are typically delivered by experienced practitioners, we don't expect too much improvement or a rapid expansion of post-secondary instruction in the global or international CI area. We base our observation on the following indications:

- *Shortage of qualified instructors.* Few practitioners are trained in educational techniques, and most seldom go beyond giving occasional guest lectures in post-secondary courses. We suggest that there is a significant difference between teaching a one- or two-day program and a 40-hour university course in terms of content, depth, and the cumulative benefits generated by doing classwork, groupwork, and independent projects. Few academicians have been trained in or have developed expertise in global CI (Fleisher, 2001).

- *Lack of accepted educational standards.* The scholarship in CI is still relatively embryonic in terms of its development (Dishman, Fleisher, & Knip, 2003). As such, there is no agreement or consensus in the field as to what should constitute the critical subjects that might make up a global or international CI degree, the critical concepts that might underlie those subjects, or the manner and qualifications of those who would be entrusted with teaching future generations of practitioners.

- *Inter- and multidisciplinary nature of the area.* Despite much talk in the last two decades about the interdisciplinarity of business organizations and business schools, most university-based business schools are still organized along functional (e.g., accounting, finance, human resources, and marketing) specializations. This does not favor courses or subjects like CI, where the subject matter and behavioral phenomena associated with the field crosses functional and disciplinary boundaries.

- *Connection to governmental and national intelligence context.* Many potential practitioners of global CI will never be interested in pursuing the field because of its association with public-sector intelligence practices, many of which would be unethical or illegal in a CI context (Fleisher, 2002). This observation often depends heavily on the national context in which the prospective practitioner is located. Future practitioners in some nation-states (e.g., South Africa, Colombia, and Indonesia) will need to overcome this negative association from their histories before CI can be a popular and attractive career route.

- *Need for on-the-job and applied practice.* Most corporations require their global CI practitioners to have gained practical experience in their industry or product and service market contexts before they will be hired. This creates problems for entry-level university graduates who need to have industry experience in order to gain these positions but who do not have access to programs or co-op positions in the field.

- *Finding balance between intelligence process competencies, particularly collection and analysis.* Many university schools of information or library sciences primarily focus on the collection aspects of CI—if they have any focus on CI at all. Schools of business, management, or policy sciences would be the ones most likely to help students develop analysis skills to be used in CI. Unfortunately, there are few examples of collaboration among these types of schools, which means that students are likely to be specialized in one or the other, but not both, CI process tasks.

- *Difficulty in modifying CI curricula so that they are culturally responsive.* We define culture responsiveness as being aware of differences among diverse racial, ethnic, and minority groups, respecting those differences, and taking steps to apply knowledge of those cultural differences to the practice of CI education and training. Most university-based CI teaching efforts to date have been nation-state and culture-specific to the instructors' places of origin and guided toward the practice of CI in the particular places where the educational-granting institution is domiciled. There is a clear need to increase the cultural responsiveness of CI curricula and to recognize cultural differences if CI education is to grow in global contexts.

CONCLUSION

Because the future of globalized business is bright, most people expect the future of global CI practice to be optimistic. Although there are some trends underlying developments in the organizational practice of CI, there are also a number of missing developments in the institutional context of global CI that will likely retard some degree of optimism. In this chapter we have portrayed a number of these important trends and developments in an attempt to illustrate how the field will evolve in the future.

REFERENCES

Blenkhorn, D.L., and C.S. Fleisher. (2001). "The Future of Competitive Intelligence," pp. 284–295 in C.S. Fleisher and D.L. Blenkhorn [eds.], *Managing Frontiers in Competitive Intelligence*. Westport, CT: Quorum Books.

Burkhardt, K. (2002). List of universities offering undergraduate and graduate courses in competitive intelligence available at http://www.scip.org/education/degrees.asp.

Calof, J., and B. Skinner. (1999). "Government's Role in Competitive Intelligence: What's Happening in Canada?" *Competitive Intelligence Magazine* 2(2): 20–23.

Dishman, P., C.S. Fleisher, and V. Knip. (2003). "A Chronological and Categorized Bibliography of Key Competitive Intelligence Scholarship." *Journal of Competitive Intelligence and Management* 2003: 1(1–3).

Fleisher, C.S. (2001). "An Introduction to the Management and Practice of Competitive Intelligence," pp. 3–18 in C.S. Fleisher and D.L. Blenkhorn. [eds.] (2002), *Managing Frontiers in Competitive Intelligence*. Westport, CT: Quorum Books.

Fleisher, C.S. (2002). "Competitive Intelligence in Asia: Comparisons with Western Practice." *Canadian Association for Studies in Intelligence and Security (CASIS), 2002 Annual Conference*. Ottawa, ON, Canada.

Fleisher, C.S., and B. Bensoussan. (2003). *Strategic and Competitive Analysis: Methods and Techniques for Analyzing Business Competition*. Upper Saddle River, NJ: Prentice Hall.

Fleisher, C.S., and D.L. Blenkhorn. [eds.] (2001). *Managing Frontiers in Competitive Intelligence*. Westport, CT: Quorum.

Gilad, B. (2001). "Industry Risk Management: CI's Next Step." *Competitive Intelligence Magazine* 4(3): 21–27.

Hawkins, D.L., and D.S. Tull. (1994). *Essentials of Marketing Research*. New York: Macmillan Publishing Company.

Hill, C.W.L. (2003). *International Business: Competing in the Global Marketplace*. 4th ed. New York: McGraw-Hill.

Hofstede, G.H. (1984). *Culture's Consequences: International Differences in Work-Related Values*. Newbury Park, CA: Sage Publications.

Hulnick, A.S. (2002). "Risky Business: Private Sector Intelligence in the United States." *Harvard International Review* 24(3): 68–72.

Jaworski, B., and L.C. Wee. (1993). *Competitive Intelligence: Creating Value for the Organization*. Final Report on Society of Competitive Intelligence Professionals (SCIP) Sponsored Research. Vienna, VA: Society of Competitive Intelligence Professionals.

McGonagle, J.J., Jr., and C.M. Vella. (2002). *Bottom-Line Competitive Intelligence*. Westport, CT: Quorum Books.

Miller, J.P. (1994). "The Relationship between Organizational Culture and Environmental Scanning: A Case Study." *Library Trends* 43(2): 170–205.

North, D.C. (1990). *Institutions, Institutional Change, and Economic Performance*. Cambridge, UK: Cambridge University Press.

Quinn, J.F. (1994). "Commercial Intelligence Gathering: JETRO and the Japanese Experience." Prepared comments from a speech delivered to the Fifth National Operations Security (OPSEC) Conference on Managing Risk in the Information Age, May 2–5, Maclean, VA.

Ricks, D.A. (1983). *Big Business Blunders: Mistakes in Multinational Marketing*. Homewood, IL: Dow Jones Irwin.

Spiegel, H.W. (1991). *The Growth of Economic Thought*. Englewood Cliffs, NJ: Prentice Hall.

Index

About the Editors and Contributors

TRACY ANNETT has most recently worked as a project manager responsible for environmental remediation services for clients located throughout North America. After completing her MBA at Wilfrid Laurier University, Waterloo, Ontario, Canada, she plans to pursue a career in project management with a focus on environmental management and sustainable business development.

BABETTE BENSOUSSAN is a director of The MindShifts Group, Sydney, Australia, a company specializing in competitive intelligence, strategic planning, and strategic marketing projects in the Australasian region. A founder of the Society of Competitive Intelligence Professionals in Australia (SCIPAust), she was awarded a Fellow of SCIP in the USA in 1996. She is an adjunct lecturer at the Sydney Graduate School of Management, University of Western Sydney, in international business and competitive intelligence. She has had published numerous articles on strategic planning, competitive intelligence, and strategic marketing and is an invited speaker and guest lecturer both domestically and internationally. She is the coauthor (with C. Fleisher) of *Strategic and Competitive Analysis*.

DAVID L. BLENKHORN is professor of marketing at the School of Business and Economics, Wilfrid Laurier University, Waterloo, Ontario, Canada. He teaches, researches, and consults in the areas of competitive intelligence, business-to-business marketing, customer relationship management, and supply chain management. His other books are *Controversies in*

Competitive Intelligence: The Enduring Issues (with C. Fleisher), *Managing Frontiers in Competitive Intelligence* (with C. Fleisher), and *Reverse Marketing: The New Buyer-Supplier Relationship* (with M. Leenders).

KEITH FISHWICK is an employee relations representative at CAMI Automotive Inc., a joint venture between General Motors and Suzuki located in Ingersoll, Ontario, Canada. As an employee relations representative, he is involved with all hourly employees, with a focus on skilled trades, and in contract negotiations.

CRAIG S. FLEISHER is the Odette Research Chair and Professor of Business (Strategy and Entrepreneurship), Odette School of Business, University of Windsor, Ontario, Canada. A member of the Canadian Who's Who, he has held faculty positions at the University of Pittsburgh (United States), Sydney (Australia), Calgary, New Brunswick, and Wilfrid Laurier universities (Canada). Canada's first fellow and a current board member of the Society of Competitive Intelligence Professionals (SCIP), he is an active author and researcher who has written six books and over 120 articles, has facilitated workshops or guest lectured on CI around the globe, and is executive Coeditor of the *Journal of Competitive Intelligence and Management*.

RAHIM KASSAM is a market intelligence analyst with VISA Canada Association, Toronto, Ontario, Canada, where he performs marketing and competitive intelligence activities to support corporate and business unit strategic planning processes.

ROSS KERR is a senior project leader with The Canada Life Assurance Company, Toronto, Ontario, Canada, where he is accountable for improving the efficiency and effectiveness of Group Wealth Management operations.

VICTOR KNIP is a solutions manager for Novintel. With offices in Helsinki, Finland, Toronto, and Toronto, Canada, Novintel is an integral partner of the Global Intelligence Alliance. He is also the managing editor of the *Journal of Competitive Intelligence and Management* and has been published in several books and journals relating to competitive intelligence.

SANDY KOKKINIS is an accounting manager with Nobel Biocare Canada Inc., Toronto, the Canadian subsidiary of an innovative medical devices and esthetic dental solutions company based in Switzerland. Her responsibilities include accounting, financial reporting, and internal control for the business operations of the Canadian subsidiary.

SCOTT A. LAPSTRA is the national marketing manager for Grant Thornton LLP, an international accounting and consulting firm based in Toronto, Ontario, Canada. He is responsible for leading marketing strategy, including brand management and new service development.

ATTILA L. LENDVAI is a consultant and proprietor of Sunspeare Strategic Communications, Stratford, Ontario, Canada. Sunspeare Strategic Communications is a business strategy, marketing, and communications (StratCom) consulting firm dedicated to providing companies and organizations strategic business, management, and marketing communications solutions.

JEFF LIBIS is an account manager with General Electric (GE) Medical Systems in Toronto, Ontario, Canada, where he executes comprehensive sales strategies that cultivate GE's leadership position in medical imaging equipment and information technology infrastructure sectors of the global health care industry.

JEFF MACDONALD is a regional manager for MDS Laboratory Services, a division of MDS Inc., a health and life sciences company providing pharmaceutical and biotechnology companies and health care providers with products, services, and information for the prevention, diagnosis, and treatment of disease. At MDS, he is accountable for Laboratory Operations for Central Ontario, Canada.

KELLY MAH is a certified managing consultant with IBM Business Consulting Services at the IBM Canada Corporate Offices in Markham, Ontario, Canada, where he provides strategic business consulting to IBM clients who are seeking advice and thought leadership in the areas of business processes, project management, and organizational transformation. He is responsible for leading consulting teams through client engagements by providing strategic direction, mentoring, and industry expertise.

MEERA MODY is the founding president of Mody Biotech Insights Inc. (MBI), a consulting firm specializing in providing strategies for the commercialization of new inventions, business development, and new venture creation in biotechnology and high-tech industries. She has coauthored 22 scientific publications in peer-reviewed medical journals.

MICHELLE MURRAY is a quality assurance/product engineering associate with 3M Canada, Health Care Markets Division in London, Ontario, Canada. At 3M, she works with global teams to develop quality systems and products that meet regulatory and customer requirements in the original equipment manufacturer (OEM) and institutional health care markets for wound care, animal care, microbiology, dental care, and infection prevention products and services.

KIRSTEN ROWATT is with Manulife Financial in the Canadian Group Benefits Division as a training and development consultant. Manulife Financial is a leading Canadian-based financial services company that operates worldwide and provides a diverse range of financial protection products and wealth management services. The Group Benefits business unit specializes in providing comprehensive benefits packages to businesses of all sizes. In the role of training and development consultant, she provides both strategic and tactical training support to all levels of the business unit's salesforce.

MICHELLE SANDILANDS is a production engineer for Petro-Canada, Oakville Refinery, Oakville, Ontario, Canada. At Petro-Canada, one of the largest integrated oil and gas companies in Canada, her role is to ensure the optimal operation of the process units by solving operational problems, monitoring performance and providing technical recommendations, budgeting and tracking catalyst and chemical usage, initiating yield investigations and providing input, and making economic recommendations for capital projects.

MICHELLE S. STEVER is a trust accounts examiner with the Kitchener, Ontario, Canada, branch of the Canada Customs and Revenue Agency, where she completes payroll and GST examinations on non-compliant and compliant accounts, deals with employee complaints, meets with clients and their representatives to review source documents, prepares leads to related departments in the agency for additional follow up, and completes employment status rulings.

BETTY TOCZYDLOWSKI is Corporate Projects Coordinator at Nacan Products Limited, Brampton, Ontario, Canada, a subsidiary of National Starch and Chemical Company. She is responsible for management of ISO 9001:2000 registration, Responsible Care®, and is also involved in the company's regulatory affairs.